A fish cannot disregard the water in which it lives; neither can man disregard the atmosphere he breathes and in which he has his present existence. God is the ineffable, but real element, in which our life is immersed. He is its beginning, its norm and its term.

Let the listener exult: God is love, an ocean of love![1]

The man of today listens to witnesses more willingly than to teachers; or if he listens to teachers, it is because they are witnesses.[2]

[1] Pope Paul at a General Audience, Sept. 17, 1975 (OR, Sept. 19, 1975; ORe, Sept. 25, 1975).

[2] Pope Paul to a Congress on the Lay Apostolate, Oct. 2, 1974. Repeated in an audience for participants in the World Meeting on the Lay Apostolate, Oct. 11, 1975 (ORe, Oct. 23, 1975).

# Edward D. O'Connor, C.S.C.

# POPE PAUL AND THE SPIRIT

Charisms and Church Renewal in the Teaching of Paul VI

**Ave Maria Press**
Notre Dame, Indiana 46556

To Tom Bonaiuto
whose remarkable gifts were indispensable
in the preparation of this work
and whose friendly helpfulness made it a joy to call on him

*Nihil Obstat:*

Charles J. Corcoran, C.S.C.
Censor Deputatus

*Imprimatur:*

William E. McManus, D.D.
Bishop of Fort Wayne-South Bend

Library of Congress Catalog Card Number: 78-55013

International Standard Book Number: 0-87793-157-7 (cloth)
0-87793-151-8 (paperback)

Cover photo: NC News Service
Cover design: Cae Esworthy

Printed and bound in the United States of America.

# CONTENTS

## Appendices

# Foreword

Father O'Connor's book gives us an exhaustive survey of what Pope Paul has said about the Holy Spirit during his pontificate. At the same time, it gives us a glimpse into the soul of the Sovereign Pontiff, who has a great personal openness to the Holy Spirit.

It is Paul VI who said that the Second Vatican Council needs to be followed up by emphasis on the role of the Holy Spirit: "The Christology and particularly the Ecclesiology of the Council must be followed by a new study of and devotion to the Holy Spirit; this precisely is the indispensable complement of the Council's teaching" (June 6, 1973).

The theme of the Holy Spirit recurs again and again as a leit-motif in the Pope's letters and allocutions. One can sense that he regards the "spiritual" life as nothing other than the life of the Holy Spirit at work in Christian existence in order to make us live in communion with the Trinity.

On the theological as well as the pastoral level, therefore, a valuable and fruitful ensemble is presented to us here.

\* \* \*

But Father O'Connor is not only a man of painstaking erudition; he is also one of those who first drew attention to the Charismatic Renewal, which Pope Paul called "that good fortune for the renewal of the Church" (Monday after Pentecost, 1975). In this regard, the present book renders a valuable service to the Renewal itself by gathering together and analyzing the texts which are of special interest—either directly or indirectly—to those involved in the Renewal. The danger inherent in revivals always is that one aspect of the rediscovered truth may be emphasized to the neglect of others needed to counterbalance it, thus producing a onesided vision. Hence those involved in the Charismatic Renewal will profit particularly from the texts in which Pope Paul, following St. Paul, carries on with the authority of his office, the function of "discernment of spirits." They will benefit likewise from the important passages in which he insists on the necessary connection between charism and hierarchy, charism and sacramental life, charism and devotion to Mary. In the closing session of the International Charismatic Conference at South Bend in 1974, I pointed out that the future of the Charismatic Renewal as well as its fruitfulness would depend, so far as Catholics are concerned, on the latter being deeply rooted in the Church. Concretely, this means their acceptance of the *magisterium* of Peter and of the spiritual motherhood of Mary. Christ was born of Mary and the Holy Spirit, and this indissoluble association remains a vital one.

In offering us this rich collection of texts, Father O'Connor is making a contribution to the indispensable osmosis between Institution and Charism, and to the healthy balance of complementary factors which call for one another within that apostolic Church which is their supreme guarantee.

L. J. Cardinal Suenens,
Archbishop of Malines-Brussels
Malines, February 8, 1978

# INTRODUCTION

There is an irony in the life of Pope Paul.

His pontificate comes in an age which clamors for religious leaders who will be spiritual men, not mere administrators. Paul VI fulfills that requirement splendidly, but this is rarely acknowledged. His public reputation has been determined mainly by his stand on contraception, by the changes (too fast for some, too slow for others) that have occurred under his direction in the liturgy and government of the Church, by the voyages he has made to all the continents of the world and his appearance at the United Nations, or by his unwillingness to use his full power in repressing dissidents of either the right or the left.

No doubt, these acts and non-acts carry weight for the evaluation of his pontificate. But they are public acts which often do not tell us much about the heart of the man. Many of them were positions which he was compelled to take, sometimes with great reluctance and anguished regret, by the circumstances of his time. But if you want to know what is deepest and most personal in Paul VI; if you want to grasp the principal and persistent aim of his pontificate as he himself visualizes it; you must see him before all else as a deeply spiritual man working for the spiritual renewal of the Church.

Although his activity in this regard has not been greatly publicized, it has not been fruitless. Pope Paul knows well the ways of the Holy Spirit, and has articulated an impressive corpus of spiritual wisdom for all who are ready to learn it. "The Great Guru of the Catholic Church," I am tempted to call him; yet he is not just a teacher for Catholics or for Christians. Anyone seeking to lead a deep spiritual life will profit by a study of the instructions given in Part II, which is the chief part of this book. Let me say simply that he is a faithful pastor of the people called to be a living temple of the Holy Spirit.

There is another irony in the fact that the Charismatic Renewal erupted in the Catholic Church during his pontificate. For this, charismatics should be grateful to Providence and shout *Alleluia*! God has given them a spiritual leader who is himself a real man of the Spirit. It is hard to think of any other Pope as congenial to the deepest aspirations of this movement as Paul VI. Conversely, among all the movements of the Spirit in our time (and they are many) it would be hard to find another which fulfills the express wishes of the Holy Father to the letter so well as the Charismatic Renewal. And yet charismatics by and large are very little acquainted with the Pope's teaching, and the Pope in his turn (despite the great breakthroughs of 1973 and 1975) has been somewhat reserved in his appraisal of them. His addresses to the Renewal have been rather heavily laden with cautions and warnings. This is not, in itself, a great loss; for his admonitions have been salutary and pertinent. But for charismatics to be unaware of his teaching is a great loss; and it is to redress this that the present work is partly intended. Not that the Charismatic Renewal is the main concern here; the Pope's teaching is addressed to all who are open to the Spirit of Jesus. But the Charismatic Renewal, as a big fact in the spiritual history of our time, is inevitably one of the major focal points for an appreciation of this teaching.

Paul's doctrine focuses on the mystery of the Church; and it is precisely on this topic that he can give the most needed direction to the Charismatic Renewal. For the moment in which this movement has arisen, with the aim of renewing the Church, is also a moment of supreme confusion about the nature of the Church. The 20th century is indeed the "Age of the Church." This means, among other things, that an unprecedented profusion of diverse and contradictory ecclesiologies has appeared in the Vatican II era, like mushrooms on a dank spring morning. Some of them bring the beauty of fresh theological reflection to our appreciation of the People that God has taken for his bride; but others are derived more from the arrogance of free spirits than from the obedience of minds to Christ. Whether the prodigious energies of the Charismatic Renewal will be spent building up or tearing down the Church of God depends largely on the vision that guides it. Obliged to select among many competing voices, it can hardly do better than to listen with attentive and faithful ear to the Vicar of the Good Shepherd.

On two points especially this is crucial: ecumenism and lay ministry. The loving, prayerful fellowship that is occurring in the Charismatic Renewal is the most hopeful instance on today's horizon of an effective, grass-roots ecumenism. But it is sometimes articulated in, and then directed by, a naive, amorphous theology that aims, in effect, at uniting mankind around Jesus, without regard for the structure of which Jesus himself is the architect and builder. Such a project can have no enduring results. "Unless the Lord builds the house, they labor in vain who build it.'' And such a blunder ought not to occur to people who are heirs of the wise and accurate principles of ecumenism given us by Vatican II. Paul VI, one of the greatest ecumenical figures of our times, is also the most faithful custodian and authentic interpreter of the Council teaching for the postconciliar period.

Secondly, the Charismatic Renewal has been marked by a great flowering of nonordained ministries, the fruit largely of such gifts as prophecy, healing, counsel and leadership. This development is right in step with the historical movement of the Church; for the present era is also the ''age of the laity.'' This can mean, and in the Providence of God is surely meant to mean, the full deployment of the authentic energies of the lay Christian, in harmonious complementarity with the ordained pastors who perpetuate the apostolic ministry. Or it can mean, as it has in times past, a resentful depreciation of that secret, sacred and most efficacious charism imparted by Jesus to those he has associated with himself in the office of priesthood.

Paul VI's great gift is that of balance and equilibrium. He has always been an eloquent promoter of the lay apostolate—not out of expediency, but out of a natural generosity illumined by faith. But he also maintains firmly that traditional understanding of Sacred Orders which in the course of centuries has been distilled out of Sacred Scripture in the prayerful reflection and experience of the Church under the gentle warmth of the Holy Spirit—which precious liqueur academics now want to replace with a soda pop ministry manufactured by the ''new hermeneutics.'' It is Paul's vision that can teach the Church today how the ''grace given to each of us according to the diverse measure of Christ's gift'' is meant to ''equip the saints for the work of ministry, for building up the Body of Christ . . . from whom the whole body, joined and knit together by every joint with which it is supplied when each part is working properly, makes bodily growth and upbuilds itself in love'' (Eph 4:7–16).

Edward O'Connor, C.S.C.
Octave of Prayer for Church Unity
Jan. 18–25, 1978

# PART 1
# An Overview of the Pope's Teaching

# CHAPTER ONE

# The Pope of the Holy Spirit

An indication of how much the Holy Spirit meant to him was given by Pope Paul at the very outset of his pontificate. He added the ejaculation, "Blessed be the Holy Spirit, the Paraclete," to the Divine Praises.[1]

In itself, this was a minor, almost trivial, act. But that very fact heightens its significance, given the circumstances in which it occurred. Paul had become Pope on June 21, 1963, halfway between the first and second sessions of the Second Vatican Council. Along with the heavy office of the papacy itself, he had to take over top responsibility for the planning of the Council. The experience of the first session had made evident the need of a revised schedule and new methods of operation for the second. It was Paul who had to make the decision to allow press reports on the Council meetings, to admit lay auditors, etc.[2] The second session dealt with the weightiest of all the topics treated by the Council, the revised Constitution on the Church, *Lumen Gentium.* It was followed by the precedent-shattering pilgrimage to Jerusalem and meeting with Patriarch Athenagoras (Jan. 4–6, 1964), and then the intense planning for the third session. All through this period, the Pope must have been at work on his first encyclical, *Ecclesiam Suam,* which was to appear in the summer of 1964.

In the midst of all this pressing business (and of how much more, we can only conjecture), Paul took the time and trouble to add an act of homage to the Holy Spirit in a prayer that had no connection whatsoever with the Council or its work. This can only mean that it was very close to his heart, and probably had been in his mind for a long time already. The official proclamation[3] was issued April 25, 1964, just a few weeks before the first Pentecost which he celebrated as Pope.

3

The impact of this action was not great, since the Divine Praises have since then fallen largely into disuse.[4] But the gesture was an accurate index to the Pope's intense personal devotion to the Holy Spirit, and a portent of his concern to deepen this devotion in the Church.

His first encyclical letter, *Ecclesiam Suam*,[5] was concerned with the Church, the main topic of the Vatican Council. Nevertheless, it makes an impressive number of references to the Holy Spirit dwelling in each of the faithful to give them grace, joy, and illumination (39) as well as ineffable inspirations (36) and other gifts (51). It speaks also of the Spirit as giving life to the Church as a whole (22), guiding (26), energizing and developing it (10), enlightening its prophetic consciousness (22) and appointing its bishops (9). Paul is confident that the Spirit will help the Council in its forthcoming session (26, 32). He urges the Council Fathers to be docile to the inspirations of the Spirit (32), who is still ready to fulfill the promise of Christ, that he would send a Paraclete to teach his disciples all truth (26). He prays that the Holy Spirit "will breathe upon 'the ecumenical movement'" (112).

The spiritual teaching of this encyclical is summed up in a single line:

> The interior life still remains the great source of the Church's spirituality, her own proper way of receiving the illuminations of the Spirit of Christ. . . . (30)

## RENEWAL OF THE CHURCH

The subsequent years of Paul's pontificate have not belied these first indications. His chief goal has remained the spiritual and interior renewal of the Church, which he sees as the mandate of Vatican II.[6]

*Aggiornamento,* the term of Pope John which promptly became the popular designation for the purpose of the Council, has generally been taken to refer to an updating of the structures, procedures and idiom of the Church. Paul's characteristic touch, however, has been to insist that interior reform and renewal are far more important than any exterior changes that can be wrought. When the Constitution on the Sacred Liturgy emerged as the first document published by the Council, he pointed to this as a sign that the Council's chief message was a summons to pray well.[7] Later he declared more pointedly:

> Many people have directed interest in renewal toward an external and impersonal transformation of Church structure . . . rather than toward that primary and principal renewal sought by the Council: one that is moral, personal and

interior. This is a renewal which will rejuvenate in the Church an awareness of its own mystery, of its adherence to Christ, of its being animated by the Holy Spirit, of its structure at once fraternal and hierarchical, of its mission in the world and its purpose that transcends the world, as a result of which it pursues its journey through time as a poor pilgrim.[8]

Years later, he told another group:

There is no true ecclesial reform without interior renewal, without obedience, without the cross. Only holiness produces fruits of renewal.[9]

This stand disappointed, perplexed and ultimately alienated many intellectuals and radicals in the Church, who were preoccupied above all with a reform of structures. In their view, the energy of the Council was being allowed to dissipate ineffectually. Paul has not by any means neglected structural and stylistic changes,[10] as witness the reform of the curia and of Canon Law, the implementation of the Bishops' Synods, the erection of secretariats for non-Christian religions and for nonbelievers, of the Council for the Laity and the Justice and Peace Commission, the encouragement of responsible lay participation in Church councils at various levels, the unprecedented reform of the liturgy of the Mass, the sacraments and the Divine Office, etc. Moreover, he:

abolished the papal aristocracy, the noble guards; trimmed papal functions to a severe simplicity; and inaugurated a series of journies to all five continents. . . . While authorizing a series of discussions between Catholic theologians and representatives of other Christian churches and communities aimed at exploring areas of common belief, he engaged in prayer sessions with both Christians and non-Christians, welcoming into the Vatican leaders of other religions and chiefs of atheistic governments.[11]

In fact, Paul's pontificate has been responsible for the most extensive and expeditious *aggiornamento* in the history of the Church. But its characteristic stance, adopted in the first encyclical and maintained in the face of unrelenting pressure ever since, has been to insist that spiritual renewal take precedence over all of these necessary but more superficial changes.

The "Year of Faith" (June 29, 1967–June 29, 1968[12]) was a basic factor in the Pope's program for spiritual renewal. But it was the Holy Year of 1975 that was his supreme effort in that regard. The celebration of a Jubilee every 25 years is an old tradition in the Church;

but it was Pope Paul who assigned interior renewal as the principal aim of the 1975 celebration:

> In view of the variety of purposes, it is necessary to stress what is the essential concept of the Holy Year. It is the interior renewal of man: of thinking man, who in his thought has lost the certainty of truth; of working man, who in his work has come to realize that he is so extroverted that he no longer has full communication with himself; of the man who enjoys life, and who so amuses himself, and has so many exciting ways to experience pleasure, that he soon feels bored and disillusioned. Man must be renewed from within. This is what the Gospel calls conversion, repentance and a change of heart.
>
> . . .
>
> In other words, man needs an interior renewal such as that hoped for by the Council. Now the Holy Year is oriented precisely to this personal and interior renewal, which under certain aspects is also exterior.[13]

Paul did not regard the Holy Year simply as one of those acts in the life of the Church over which he had to preside in the routine of his office. As it was about to begin, he urged people to "consider it as the opening of a new period of religious and spiritual life in the world . . . as a principle, a genetic fact, a sequel to the Council, destined to mark an interior and moral renewal in the conscience of men" (May 23, 1973). His weekly audiences, a sure index to his deepest concerns,[14] were nearly all devoted to this topic, not only throughout the two and a half years which the Jubilee lasted, but also in the weeks that preceded and followed it. He said in one of them that the spectacular masses of pilgrims which this celebration attracted to Rome were not its primary aim, but presupposed another more important one: "the conversion of hearts, the interior renewal of spirits, the personal adherence of consciences."[15]

## NEED OF THE HOLY SPIRIT

Such a renewal, however, cannot be brought about through human efforts alone. Man's endeavors to lead an interior life are only a preparation, a way of making himself sensitive and responsive to the action of the Spirit.[16] Consequently, Paul insists over and over on our need of the Holy Spirit. In an early allocution he declared:

> If we really love the Church, the main thing we must do is to foster in it an outpouring of the Divine Paraclete (Oct. 12, 1966).

He went on to add that "the Church's first need is always to live Pentecost," and that the Council's guideline for fostering the Church's vitality and renewal as well as orienting our own personal Christian lives, leads "toward the Holy Spirit."

In answer to the question, "What is the greatest need of the Church today?" he replied, as he said, "almost trembling and praying":

> The Spirit, the Holy Spirit, who animates and sanctifies the Church, who is her divine breath, the wind in her sails, the principle of her unity, the inner source of her light and strength, her support and consoler, the source of her charisms and songs, her peace and joy, the pledge and prelude of her blessed and eternal life (Nov. 29, 1972).[17]

Pope Paul may well have done more to promote devotion to the Holy Spirit than perhaps any other Pope in history. While he has not composed any single document surveying the whole theology of the Spirit, as Leo XIII did,[18] he has spoken insistently and eloquently on this subject throughout the whole course of his pontificate. Joyously he proclaims the fact that the Spirit has been poured out on us by the Risen Christ; in rich detail and from various points of view he describes the workings and gifts of the Spirit; he constantly exhorts his hearers to seek and prepare for them. Again and again he recommends devotion to the Holy Spirit as the greatest of all devotions (April 26, 1964), the first devotion (May 18, 1967) and the summit of devotion (May 26, 1971). "The work of the Holy Spirit," he says, "is decisive for the Christian religion" (May 17, 1972).

In this too, he is prolonging the action of Vatican II. This council had been a kind of rediscovery of the importance of the doctrine of the Spirit by the bishops who took part in it,[19] and a personal experience of his action.[20] After a slow start,[21] the Council went on to mention the Holy Spirit 258 times in its official documents, as the Pope himself points out (May 23, 1973). But Paul did much more than carry on routinely the impetus given by the Council; he added an insistence of his own. After declaring that the Council was occupied mainly with the topic of the Church, he added:

> The Christology and particularly the ecclesiology of the Council must be followed by a new study of and devotion to the Holy Spirit (June 6, 1973).

His long emphatic and often eloquent passages on the Holy Spirit or on Pentecost suggest the urgency he attributes to this subject. He strains to drive his points home, and seeks to give pungency to familiar doctrine by unusual twists of language, as when he speaks of the "symbiosis" of the Holy Spirit and the human soul (April 26, 1964), the metamorphosis of the disciples at Pentecost[22] or refers to all invocation of the Spirit as an *"epiklesis"* (May 21, 1972).

## EXPERIENCE OF THE SPIRIT

Pope Paul teaches explicitly that the action of the Holy Spirit can be a matter of experience, and implies that this is to be expected. This action may also remain entirely hidden, he points out (May 18, 1967); nevertheless, it is normal, he says, for the soul filled with grace to experience the joy and peace that are fruits of the Holy Spirit (May 25, 1969). In explaining how the original Pentecost is relived by the Church of today, he says:

> It is as if our customary invocation, "Come, Holy Spirit," were met by the reality of his response and his presence, infusing into us some slight yet living experience of his beatifying coming (May 17, 1970; cf. Sept. 9, 1970).

In fact, he affirms:

> Of all the experiences afforded by human life, the finest, the most joyful, the richest in promise and consolation is that of possessing the Spirit of God (May 26, 1968).

On the abiding presence of Jesus with his disciples on earth, he cites the text of Formari:

> Although Jesus Christ made himself invisible to our eyes after his resurrection, we nevertheless feel that he is still living with us, because we are aware of his breath. By his breath I mean the breathing and outpouring of the Holy Spirit (May 25, 1969).

On Pentecost of 1975 (at the Mass attended by the participants in the International Charismatic Charismatic Conference), he laid particular stress on the experiential aspect of the Spirit's action:

> ... we today would like, not only to possess the Holy Spirit at once, but to experience the tangible and wonderful effects of his marvelous presence within us; for we know that the Spirit is light, strength, charism, infusion of spiritual vitality, the capacity of going beyond the limits of our natural activity... (May 18, 1975).

Experience of the Holy Spirit is not just a theoretical possibility for Pope Paul. Many of the things he says give every indication of having arisen out of his own personal experience. In a homily on Pentecost, for example, he mentioned "the enthusiasm and inebriation of peace and joy of those whose lot it is to believe in the Holy Spirit, and to live in the spirit which he now gives us" (May 25, 1969). Paul's usual style of speech tends to be stiff, formal and intellectual. But whenever he speaks about the Holy Spirit, there is a remarkable change, as if a light turned on within him. An unusual warmth and liveliness well up in his language. Thus, on the 50th anniversary of his ordination, he prayed:

> Thanks be to you, enlivening Spirit, who have been our inspirer and comforter in the weighty yet sweet ministry of fifty years, and who still comes to our aid so that we may not betray, but rather portray our Master Jesus, and may always seek to be holy through you, and to communicate holiness in you (May 17, 1970).[23]

Sometimes it is an unexpected touch of color in his language that suggests its experiential basis. "Christ," he says, "lets us taste the intoxicating outpouring of his Holy Paraclete."[24] He mentions "those sweet, impetuous preludes of God's life in us" (April 25, 1970). The traditional appellation, "Spirit of love," becomes for him "Spirit of living love" (May 17, 1972) or "God-Love" (passim). He speaks of the "surprises of joy given by the Spirit" (April 25, 1970), who is "the one from whom we receive the blessed possibility of uttering the name of Jesus, as well as the mystic source of the most deeply touched orison" (May 18, 1967). On the other hand, Paul's term of predilection for the Holy Spirit seems to be the traditional appellation, *dulcis hospes animae*, literally, "sweet guest of the soul."[25]

The most eloquent statement Paul ever made about the Holy Spirit came in a routine public audience on Nov. 29, 1972. There he listed the effects of the Spirit in terms that cannot but evoke the sense of personal experience. Besides the classical works of animating, energizing and sanctifying the Church, the following particular effects are singled out: light, strength, consolation, charisms, songs, peace, joy, pledge and prelude of beatitude, fire in the heart, words on the lips, prophecy in the glance; the eagerness, taste and certainty of the truth, the teaching voice (of the Church), the wave of love flowing through hearts, the pressure and urge to action, and the voice of prayer that rises out of the Church's inner depths. On several occasions Paul expresses a lively interest in the "psychological and ontological realities" corresponding to this inner action of the Spirit, and recommended a study of them.[26]

## PENTECOST

After the preceding texts, it will not come as a surprise that Pentecost was a favorite theme of Pope Paul's preaching.[27] He spoke of it, not only on the feast itself, but often also during the weeks that preceded and followed it, and sometimes even at other seasons of the year. It seems to have been the most meaningful of all the liturgical seasons for him. He sometimes chose Pentecost as the date for important acts, for example, the launching of the Holy Year. He declared expressly that this was deliberate:

> Why does the Holy Year start with Pentecost? Not only because this beautiful feast, which can be defined as the historical birth of the Church, offers a propitious and inspiring occasion, but above all because we hope and pray that the Holy Spirit, whose mysterious visible mission we celebrate at Pentecost, will be the principal source of the fruits desired from the Holy Year (June 6, 1973).

He associated the establishment of the Secretariat for non-Christians with the feast of Pentecost.[28]

The Pope's Christmas sermons are filled with a remarkable tenderness, and those on Easter are often electrified with a thrill of lively joy, but on Pentecost his homilies turn into rhapsodies as he dwells meditatively on the great, vivid signs that made the event so remarkable: the wind, the fire, and the speaking in tongues, all of which seem to be laden with profound symbolism.[29] Several times he declares that a gift of poetry would be needed to express all the meaning of this day,[30] which he calls the greatest, fullest and most beautiful of all feast days (June 6, 1965), the source and "metropolis" (i.e., parent) of all others (June 6, 1965; May 18, 1966). Pentecost is "the pivotal point of the whole religious and theological system" (May 18, 1975); for not only did the Church receive the first impulse of its life on the original Pentecost, but Pentecost represents a permanent reality (June 12, 1974), ongoing miracle (May 18, 1967), the perennial animation of the Church by the divine source of its life:

> ... it is God's Spirit of Love who instils a new awareness, an insuperable energy and a lively joy into each and every one of the 120 people gathered in the Cenacle. The Church is born in that moment of wind and fire. Life is breathed into the mystical Body of Christ, and his promise of perennial consolation is fulfilled. What a stupendous truth, what a stupendous event! Man becomes a temple of the Holy Spirit.

> But from the depths of man's heart comes the searching question: Did this event take place only then? Is it over and done with, like all the other events of human history? No! ... in every sacramental act, in every humble prayer, the "good Spirit" is present and operative (May 21, 1972, I).[31]

## A CHARISMATIC POPE?

In a day when so much is said about the charismatic, the texts we have examined make it inevitable that we pose the question, is Pope Paul a charismatic? There is a sense, of course, in which every true Christian is charismatic; and a more special sense in which the priesthood, the episcopate and the papacy all involve special charisms.[32] If the question is asked in those terms, it is platitudinous. But there is also a sense in which not all Christians and not all clergy can be said to be charismatic. It is hard to define this sense, or rather medley of senses. The word is often used, for example, to designate people who have an uncanny power to influence others. Pope John was called charismatic because of his remarkable gift for statements and actions that won a prompt and cordial response from millions of people, including many non-Catholics. Paul is not charismatic in this way. Neither does he seem to have the gift of tongues, healing, or any other of those somewhat sensational gifts that have given the Charismatic Renewal its name and its fame. But if by *charismatic* is meant one whose personality, sentiments and style of action bear the impress of a deep, personal experience of the Holy Spirit, the texts of Pope Paul are convincing evidence that he is charismatic indeed.

Kathryn Kuhlman once had an audience with him, and came away saying that he knew more about the Holy Spirit than any other spiritual leader of her acquaintance.[33] It would be hard to imagine two people more unlike one another than this flamboyant evangelist who preached Jesus from her heart without concern for theologies or denominations, who affected gorgeous dresses and dramatic manners, and the reserved, reflective, proper head of the Roman Catholic hierarchy. But across the gulf of temperament, culture, doctrine and ministry that separated them, there must have leapt a spark by which one Spirit-filled person recognized another.

In any case, there are aspects of his thought and style that would make charismatics sense a deep kinship with him. The address with which he opened the Third Session of the Vatican Council was not unlike that of a leader addressing a charismatic prayer meeting. To this grave assembly of the world's bishops, solemnly vested in their pastoral robes, and lined up in orderly rows on either side of the basilica like two huge banks of carefully arranged flowers, 2,300 venerable men of great age, wisdom and experience, hardly prone to be swayed by gusts of enthusiasm, the Pope declared:

> The Spirit is here, and we invoke him, we wait for him, we follow him.

The discourse proceeded to explain that the Spirit is present:

... chiefly for this reason: that once again we may appreciate fully and completely our communion with the living Christ. For it is the Spirit who unites us to him (Sept. 14, 1964).[34]

Paul is the first Pope to use the term *charismatic* as a usual part of his vocabulary.[35] He also speaks much more freely than his predecessors of the "prophetic" aspect of the Church. Up to Vatican II, Catholic doctrine had reserved this term almost exclusively for the official teaching office in the Church; but Pope Paul likes to use it in a broader and livelier sense, as when he seeks to arouse in his hearers "the prophetic spark of witnessing," and reminds them that on Pentecost, "the Apostles are filled with prophetic breath to proclaim the amazing, innovative event: Christ has risen from the dead."[36]

There are many other little traits in the Pope's style of teaching which, without being specifically charismatic, harmonize well with the usual manner of charismatic groups. He frequently summons Christians to a living, personal faith in Jesus, and calls on them to be joyous[37] and enthusiastic in their faith. He has a great predilection for the term *alleluia,* which he even made the subject of a sermon reminding his hearers that it means, "Praise the Lord" (April 25, 1970). He insists that scripture is a living word, by which God speaks to us here and now. He urges us to take our questions to the God present within us (June 23, 1971), because the Holy Spirit speaks to those who know how to listen to him (May 25, 1969). He stresses the importance of bearing witness to Christ, but adds that, in order to be able to do this effectively, we must first have the inner witness of the Holy Spirit in our own hearts (May 24, 1972). And even though Paul is no glossalalic, a finer representation of the sense of the gift of tongues could hardly be found than following:

> We must pray, and pray earnestly. This, we think, should be a consequence of the Holy Year, which has done so much . . . to unseal the silent, closed lips of modern man and to restore to his capacity of expression the babble, the conversation, the invocation, the song of his renewed relationship with God.[38]

### IN THIS OUR DAY ...

But Pope Paul does not speak of the role of the Holy Spirit in our lives merely as a timeless truth that needs to be repeated in every age. He is convinced that our age has a particular need of the Spirit. When the Second Synod of Bishops met in Rome in October 1969, he said:

This is one of those moments when we realize that human
reason . . . is not sufficient. . . . Divine help is needed. . . .
We have to ask for a transcendent intervention, an outpouring of the Holy Spirit (Oct. 15, 1969).[39]

Pope John had envisioned Vatican II as a kind of new Pentecost, and in his last message to the assembled bishops had predicted
that after the Council "will dawn that new Pentecost which is the
object of our yearning."[40] Pope Paul took up this theme, and at the end
of the Council urged Christians to pray for a new Pentecost that would
renew both the Church and the world.[41] Looking back years later, he
declared:

One must . . . recognize a prophetic intuition on the part of
our predecessor, John XXIII, who envisioned a kind of new
Pentecost as a fruit of the Council. We have wished to place
ourself in the same perspective, and in the same attitude of
expectation. Not that Pentecost has ever ceased to be an
actuality throughout the entire history of the Church; but the
needs and dangers of the present age are so great, the horizons of mankind are so vast, as it finds itself drawn toward
global coexistence, but powerless to achieve it, that there is
no salvation for it except in a new outpouring of the gift of
God. May the Creator Spirit come, therefore, to renew the
face of the earth![42]

Likewise, the Holy Year was intended, according to Pope Paul,
"above all to obtain from God a new infusion of the Holy Spirit."[43]
The force and definiteness of such statements suggest that they were
expressing, not merely a vague wish, but a serious expectation. That
this was in fact the case is confirmed by other texts which express the
conviction that the longed-for renewal is indeed going to take place,
and in fact has already begun. As early as October 26, 1967, Paul
alluded to the "movement of renewal that (the Holy Spirit) is bringing
about everywhere in the Church!" The date is striking, for it was in
February of that very year that there had occurred at Duquesne University the Pentecostal outburst that touched off the Charismatic Renewal.
However, it is unlikely that this small and distant event had already
been drawn to the attention of the Holy Father.[44] Moreover, it was
apparently not until much later that he came to regard the Renewal
somewhat favorably, as will be shown in chapters 3 and 4.

In making this remark, addressed to Patriarch Athenagoras of
Constantinople, Paul did not specify the renewal he had in mind.
Elsewhere in the same speech, however, he spoke of the intentions and
decisions that had led to this historic meeting between himself and the
leader of the Greek Orthodox Church as "a marvelous sign of the Holy

Spirit's action." Likewise, he interpreted the remarkable similarity between the programs of the Pan-Orthodox Conference at Rhodes (1961–1964) and the Second Vatican Council (1962–1965) as a sign that the Holy Spirit "demands with greater insistence than ever that we be one that the world may believe" (*ibid.*).

Pope John had brought instant fame to the expression, "signs of the times." Pope Paul has been a constant observer and interpreter of such signs. Besides those which he mentioned to Patriarch Athenagoras, he has subsequently cited may other "signs of the Holy Spirit's action": the liturgical movement (May 18, 1967 and passim), the ecumenical movement (April 28, 1967; . . . ), the Bishops' synods (Oct. 26, 1967), the flowering of small communities dedicated to a more intense living of the Christian life,[45] the renewal of prayer life among large numbers of the faithful,[46] and even certain aspects of the feminist movement.[47] He cited the remarkable conversion of André Frossard as an example of the "strange and consoling symptoms of man meeting God" in spite of adverse circumstances (Feb. 21, 1973), and even averred that "the strange forms of collective mysticism" among today's youth are not always cases of mystification, but seem to represent a sincere thirst for God.[48]

In addressing a consistory at which 20 new cardinals were created, the Pope gave a long list of signs that "the Holy Spirit is truly at work in all spheres." In addition to some of those mentioned above, he cited as happening in many countries: witnessing to the faith, the rediscovery and enjoyment of prayer, spiritual joy, developing love of the brethren and solidarity with the poor, the carrying out of the Council guidelines, the flowering of missionary undertakings, the generous response of youth to the Christian ideal, and the revival of priestly and religious vocations (after a period of decline).[49]

Because of such signs, Pope Paul makes a basically positive appraisal of our times. He is of course keenly aware of the "formidable problems which the world of today poses for the Church," as he pointed out at the opening of the Bishops' Synod of 1974.[50] He acknowledges that, as measured by the statistics of the sociologists, Christianity could seem to be failing (Feb. 21, 1973; Sept. 26, 1973). He is greatly concerned about problems of faith in the contemporary world, and again and again he expresses his grief over the spirit of rancor, division and contention in the Church today. Nevertheless, his view of the present situation is dominated by a vision of "the immense possibilities . . . which today's world offers along the paths of those who 'bring the Good News' (Rom 10:15) in the name of Christ." "To renounce these favorable opportunities," he went on to say at the aforementioned synod, "to restrict ourselves to corrosive criticism, would mean failing to keep the appointment with the hour of God. . . ."

In one survey of the state of the Church, he described it as: "afflicted interiorly by ever new anxieties, as well as animated by the impulses and consoled by the signs of the life-giving Spirit" (Dec. 21, 1973). To the College of Cardinals, he said: "A current of intense spirituality pervades the world and one would have to be blind not to recognize it" (June 23, 1975). The Apostolic Exhortation on Evangelization affirms:

> We are living in a privileged moment of the Spirit in the Church. People everywhere are trying to know him better, as he is revealed in scripture. They are happy to place themselves under his inspiration. They gather themselves around him; they want to let themselves be led by him (Dec. 8, 1975).

On September 26, 1973, he said that the apparent setbacks of religion in our time may well be a prelude to a distinctively "Christian manifestation of the Holy Spirit." As to what form this might take, he suggested two possibilities: it could take place in the form either of martyrdom, or of marvelous works of the Lord. Martyrdom is a fact in many countries of the world today. Marvels are the manifestation of the Spirit that mark the Charismatic Renewal. Whether or not Paul was consciously alluding to this movement here, he was defining its place in the movement of history.

---

We can sum up this chapter by saying that a profound and thoroughgoing renovation of the Church by a new outpouring of the Holy Spirit has been one of the chief goals of the pontificate of Paul VI. This spiritual renewal he conceives as involving a personal experience of the action of the Spirit manifested in joy, love, zeal and enthusiasm for the faith. From the very start of his pontificate, the Pope has called for such a renewal, prayed for it, and exhorted people to prepare for it by interior life. Finally, he confidently expected it to happen, and perceived signs that it was already beginning to take place.

## NOTES

1. The Pope declared later that he did this in order to fill a gap in popular piety, namely, forgetfulness of the Holy Spirit, "the supreme gift of God's love." (May 20, 1964. "On the Divine Praises," see note 2 to that allocution.)
2. Cf. Xavier Rynne, *The Second Session,* New York, Farrar, Straus & Co. [1964], pp. 54, 56, etc.

3. *De nova pia invocatione in laudem Spiritus Sancti Paracliti (AAS* 56, 1964, p. 338).

4. This was not in any sense the result of Pope Paul's action, but was the incidental by-product of the decline of Benediction of the Blessed Sacrament, and of the abolition of the traditional prayers after low Mass, where these praises had mostly been used.

5. *AAS* 56 (1964), pp. 609–659. In this official text, the paragraphs are not numbered. I have cited it according to the sections as numbered in English translation, *Paths of the Church,* published by the National Catholic Welfare Conference, Washington, D.C.

6. See, for example, the statement of May 23, 1973.

7. Dec. 11, 1963 (*OR,* Dec. 12, 1963). Cf. *OR,* Nov. 8–9, 1965, where he speaks of the "religious and moral renewal which the Council decrees had intended to produce."

8. General Audience of Jan. 15, 1969 (*OR,* Jan. 16, 1969; *ORe* Jan. 23, 1969).

9. At the canonization of two Spanish saints, May 25, 1975 (*ORe* June 5, 1975).

10. An exposition of his understanding of *aggiornamento* as an adaption of the Church's heritage to the socio-cultural needs of modern times is found in the Pope's address to a group of Italian bishops taking part in a theological *aggiornamento* program, Nov. 14, 1975 (*ORe* Nov. 27, 1975).

11. Xavier Rynne (F. X. Murphy), *New York Times Magazine,* Oct. 12, 1975, p. 60.

12. These dates were selected because June 29 is the feast of Sts. Peter and Paul, the two greatest teachers and witnesses of the faith in the Church.

13. General Audience of May 9, 1973 (*OR,* May 10, 1973; *OR,* May 17, 1973).

14. Cf. Jean Guitton, *OR,* March 20, 1975.

15. General Audience of June 20, 1973 (*OR,* June 21, 1973; *OR,* June 28, 1973).

16. This point will be developed in chapter 6.

17. Even more frequently, Pope Paul has declared that the greatest need of the Church today is faith. (See note 1 to the text of Nov. 29, 1972.) However, these are not conflicting answers; faith, which is man's fundamental response to the Holy Spirit, is itself the work of the Holy Spirit. Thus, after indicating some of the factors in modern culture that create obstacles for a religious outlook, and after insisting that, in order to confront them, we need to have the powers of reason restored, both at the level of common sense and at the level of philosophical thought, the Pope adds: "There exists another source of knowledge in addition to the purely rational one (which is too weak and vulnerable to solve all the problems of human existence); another . . . this is the Holy Spirit, it is "faith working through love" (Gal 5:6). He goes on: "We need this interior illumination . . . this gift from the seven rays of the Holy Spirit. . . ."

18. *Divinum illud munus,* May 9, 1897 (*ASS* 29, 1896–1897, 644–658). English translation: "The Holy Spirit," in *Great Encyclical Letters of Pope Leo XIII,* New York, Benziger, 1903.

19. It was especially prodding by the bishops of the Eastern rites that led their Western brethren to rectify their relative neglect of the Holy Spirit in the early documents.

20. Cf. "The Hidden Roots of the Charismatic Renewal in the Catholic Church," in *Aspects of the Pentecostal-Charismatic Origins,* edited by Vinson Synan, Plainfield, Logos, 1975, pp. 183 ff.

21. The Holy Spirit is mentioned only three times in the Constitution on the Liturgy, and not at all in the Decree on the Instruments of Social Communication. These were the first two documents issued.

22. May 24, 1972 (*OR,* May 25, 1972; *ORe,* June 1, 1972).

23. This passage does not appear in the excerpt cited in Part II.

24. To Italian Episcopal Conference, June 8, 1974 (*ORe*, June 20, 1974). Cf. May 17, 1964.
25. E.g., May 18, 1967; May 17, 1972. This expression comes from the sequence of the Mass of Pentecost.
26. Oct. 12, 1966; May 24, 1972; *etc.*
27. This largely accounts for the heavy predominance of material from the months of May and June in the present collection.
28. In his homily for Pentecost of 1964 (May 17), he declared: "Look at the efforts the Church is making . . . to approach those who belong to other religions. In this regard, we will give you some news, so that it may take on the force and tone of Pentecost. It is this: as we announced some time ago, we are going to establish a Secretariat for non-Christians here at Rome during the next few days" (*OR*, May 18–19, 1964. *TPS* 10 (1964–65), p. 81).
29. E.g., May 17, 1972; June 26, 1974.
30. E.g., May 17, 1964 (but not in the excerpt reproduced in Part II).
31. See also May 14, 1964; June 6, 1965.
32. Cf. the third usage of the term discussed in Appendix I.
33. This statement was made in a service she conducted at the University of Notre Dame Sept. 20, 1975. I cite it from memory; it has not been printed and I have been unable to find a tape recording of her talk.
34. Cp. the address of May 17, 1964.
35. For more on this, see chapter 2, and Appendix I.
36. April 12, 1972 (*OR*, April 13, 1972; *ORe*, April 20, 1972). Cp. the allocution of May 17, 1972, below.
37. Repeatedly; but see above all the great encyclical, *Christian Joy* of May 9, 1975, from which an excerpt is given in Part II.
38. March 17, 1976 (*ORe*, March 25, 1976).
39. General Audience of Oct. 15, 1969 (*OR*, Oct. 16, 1969).
40. Dec. 8, 1962 (*OR*, Dec. 10–11; *TPS* 8 (1962–63), pp. 401–2).
41. Letter to the Bishops of the Church, Nov. 4, 1965 (*OR*, Nov. 7, 1965).
42. Apostolic Exhortation, *Gaudete in Domino* #VII, May 9, 1975 (*OR*, May 17, 1975; *ORe*, May 29, 1975).
43. General Audience, Aug. 6, 1975 (*ORe*, Aug. 14, 1975).
44. We cannot wholly discount the possibility that he was at least aware of it already, for example, through the article, *"Ceux qui le peuvent parlent en langues,"* which had appeared in *Informations catholiques internationales* 298 (15 octobre, 1967) just ten days before his address.
45. Cited in chapter 8 at note 14.
46. Remarks addressed to the participants in the meeting of the International Union of Superiors General of Women Religious, at the end of the second General Audience of Nov. 12, 1975 (*OR*, Nov. 13, 1975; *ORe*, Nov. 27, 1975).
47. "In the contemporary effort to promote the advancement of women in society, the Church has already recognized a 'sign of the times,' and has seen in it a call of the Spirit. . . ." Address of Nov. 6, 1974, to Mrs. Helvi Sipila, Assistant Secretary General of the United Nations for Social Development and Humanitarian Affairs, and Secretary General of the International Women's Year (*ORe*, Nov. 14, 1974).
48. General Audience, Aug. 22, 1973 (*OR*, Aug. 23, 1973; *ORe*, Aug. 30, 1973). In this connection, the Pope recalled the death of Simone Weil on Aug. 24, 1943, just 20 years previous to this address.
49. May 24, 1976 (*OR*, May 24–25, 1976; *ORe*, June 3, 1976).
50. Sept. 2, 1974 (*OR*, Sept. 2–3, 1974; *ORe*, Oct. 10, 1974).

# CHAPTER TWO

# Misgivings About the Charismatic

Early in 1967, stories about newly formed "Catholic Pentecostal prayer meetings" began to appear in the American newspapers.[1] Even before the novelty of the thing had worn off, the "Catholic Pentecostal Movement" was firmly entrenched and rapidly spreading. Within five years it was the most talked-of movement in the Church, and long before its tenth birthday, it was worldwide. As it developed, it began to be spoken of more and more as the "Charismatic Renewal" because of the spectacular reappearance of the gifts of tongues, prophecy, interpretation, healing, etc.—New Testament charisms which, for many centuries, had been little heard of outside of the lives of the saints or the ambience of great shrines such as Lourdes. The central inspiration of this movement, however, was simply a renewed awareness of the sanctifying action of the Holy Spirit in the believer— the very theme which has been central to the ministry of Pope Paul.

This movement was not conceived as a deliberate response to the appeal of the Pope, nor to the call of Vatican II for renewal. Although the atmosphere was undoubtedly prepared for it by the Council, as well as other developments of modern Catholicism,[2] and although it was powerfully influenced also by the Pentecostal movement in the Protestant world,[3] the Charismatic Renewal originated quite spontaneously, and not as the result of any deliberate plan. Only after the Renewal had already begun did its leaders begin to advert to the great texts of Vatican II which could be regarded as its Magna Carta.[4] And when, from time to time, a text of Pope Paul on the Holy Spirit was noted, this was welcomed as a confirmation of what was already going on in the movement, but not as its initiating idea.

Nevertheless, the Charismatic Renewal corresponds to the teaching and appeals of Pope Paul so precisely, and on so many points, that the latter could easily be taken as a blueprint for it. Even before he became Pope, and therefore long before the first stirrings of this movement, Cardinal Montini had formulated an astonishingly prophetic description of it. He once described Catholic Action as:

> ... the Christian people rising to its feet as if driven by a charismatic grace reawakened out of the dawn of Christianity and transforming itself into apostles.[5]

Although written about a movement that flourished during the decades before and after World War II, these lines make an even better description of the Charismatic Renewal.

The term *charismatic* as used here does not, of course, imply that the future Pope expected that the gift of tongues and the like were about to reappear. In fact, even after the Charismatic Renewal was very much in the news, Pope Paul continued to speak of the gift of tongues in the primitive Church mainly as a symbol of the Church's unity amid diversity. He once pointed out that Pentecost still goes on in the Church "even if not accompanied by such perceptible signs."[6] However, the fact that he did not anticipate an outpouring of charisms in the narrow sense does not mean that the Charismatic Renewal is incompatible with his hopes, but rather that it surpasses them.

One might, therefore, have expected Pope Paul to welcome the Renewal enthusiastically as the answer to his prayers.[7] Instead, however, he reacted to it with considerable diffidence, as we shall see in the following chapter. The aim of the present chapter is to determine the reason for this reaction.

In the Pope's first encyclical, *Ecclesiam Suam* (dealt with in the previous chapter), the term *charismatic* occurs just once, and with a negative connotation:

> And let us not be fascinated by the desire to renew the structure of the Church charismatically, as if that were the new and true form of the Church which sprang from the ideas of particular groups or individuals,[8] who are no doubt fervent, and are sometimes persuaded that they are divinely inspired, but whose ideas introduce[9] an arbitrary dream of artificial renewal into the basic plan of the Church.[10]

This letter was issued in the summer of 1964, two and a half years before the Charismatic Renewal made its first appearance in the Catholic Church. Already then at the very beginning of his pontificate, the Pope was concerned about an unacceptable concept of Church renewal which he associated with the term *charismatic*.

If we had only this contorted sentence of the encyclical to go by, it would be impossible to delineate exactly the position so vehemently denounced. But three years later the Pope made a statement that was much more clear and specific. He cautioned gently against looking upon the visible aspects of the Church, namely, its "hierarchical, dogmatic, sacramental and canonical" aspects, as "alien, superfluous, contrary, and almost abusive in comparison with the intimate and 'charismatic' relationship of the soul with the Holy Spirit" (May 18, 1967).[11]

Beginning in 1969, and especially from 1971 onwards, the Pope refers more often and more sharply to those who appeal abusively to the charismatic aspect of Christianity. The following text is typical of a whole series of others:

> Why have many become apostles of contention, laicization and secularization, as if thinking (thus) to give freer course to the expressions of the Spirit? Or sometimes trusting more in the spirit of the world than in that of Christ? Again: why, have some people slackened, and even denounced as troublesome chains, the bonds of ecclesial obedience and of jealous adherence to communion with the Church's ministry? Under pretext of living according to the Spirit, they free themselves from the forms and norms characteristic of canonical institutions of which the visible body of the pilgrim Church, historical and human even though mystical, must be made up? Is recourse to the Holy Spirit and his charisms a pretext, perhaps not too sincere, for living, or thinking that one lives, the Christian religion authentically, whereas those who use this pretext are actually living according to their own spirit, and their own arbitrary and often ephemeral interpretation? (Nov. 29, 1972).

Neither here nor in any other text does the Pope identify any contemporary representatives of the attitude he describes. But a comparison of the above text with numerous similar ones permits us to determine the chief features of the falsely charismatic concept of the Church that exercises him. Basically, it is one that postulates an opposition between the charismatic and institutional. (This point is brought out most explicitly in the allocution of August 29, 1973, which expressly denies "the substantial distinction between the institutional Church and the presumed purely charismatic Church.")[12] In this context, *charismatic* means guided and animated by the personal inspirations of the Spirit; but the concept opposed by Pope Paul is not belief in the charismatic, so understood. As we have seen, one of his main objects is to make people more aware of and obedient to the Spirit's inner action. What is condemned is the supposition that structures in the Church are a hindrance to openness to the Spirit, or an inferior substitute for it (Nov. 24, 1971).

This view leads directly and obviously to the rejection of obedience to authority (Nov. 29, 1972). Disobedience, not only in the case of the laity neglecting the laws of the Church, but also in the case of priests who refuse to implement these laws, has been a major problem for Pope Paul. He points out sharply that those who act thus are not only rejecting authority but also disrupting the harmonious communion that ought to be a mark of the Church and the tone of its ministry (June 23, 1971; June 6, 1973). But besides disobedience, a more subtle and hence more widespread and corrosive consequence of this ideal of a "charismatic Church" is the spirit of contention, criticism and complaint, which is probably one of the most painful and stubborn obstacles with which the present Pope has had to contend.

Along with disobedience in the practical order, this pseudocharismatic outlook is marked by a refusal to accept the doctrinal authority of the Magisterium (June 23, 1971). Paul recognizes the possibility of a legitimate pluralism in the Church; but among the "negative consequences of the shallow preference many today are wont to give to a so-called charismatic church as compared with the traditional, institutional Church," there are mainly two: "disobedience and a pluralism that exceeds its legitimate limits."[13]

The main theme of Pope Paul's criticism of such views and attitudes is that they contradict the very nature of the Church as we have it from Christ, which is to be a balance of both external structure and interior inspiration. Besides this basic doctrinal position which will be dealt with at length below, Paul points out the terrible harm done to the unity and harmony of the Church, in its apostolic activity as well as in its communal life, by such discordant tendencies.

> ... habitual dissent has become fashionable nowadays, even among those who profess to be Christians. Often harmful, and sometimes unbridled, it diverts from the path of charity, and sometimes from that of truth, much valuable energy that could serve the apostolate constructively.[14]

As the persons envisaged are often zealous ecumenists, Paul stresses the irony of their destroying unity within the Church by their way of seeking unity with those outside.

He points out what he believes to be the real motives of those who make specious appeals to the inspirations and charisms of the Holy Spirit. They live according to their own spirit, and their own arbitrary and often ephemeral interpretations (of Christianity) he says on one occasion (Nov. 29, 1972). Elsewhere: they are giving autonomy to the spiritual caprices of their own instincts (March 17, 1972). Habitual dissent (May 24, 1972) and "a bitter taste for contradiction" (June 2, 1974) are the motives assigned in other texts.

After noting that "internal contention and selfish restlessness" have prevailed (at least in publicity) in the Church since Vatican II, under the guise of legitimate pluralism, the Pope observes severely that "an alleged charismatic sufficiency will not succeed in preserving an authentic animation of the Holy Spirit in these spiritualistic movements in which it is often only too easy to discern the infiltration of dissident or secular mentalities."[15]

This suffices to outline the abusively charismatic conception of Christianity about which Pope Paul is so deeply concerned. Now it remains for us to determine how this concern arose, and in particular its relevance to the Charismatic Renewal.

Since the Pope was speaking of this matter even before the Renewal began to affect Catholics, it is clear that this is not what originally provoked his concern. Accordingly, our first task is to determine what did. But since this concern seems to have intensified greatly from 1969 and especially from 1971 onwards, our second task will be to investigate the reason for that.

The first of these tasks is by far the easier. The idea of an inherent opposition between "charismatic" or inspired leadership in the Church, and fixed institutional structures, has been in the air for at least 250 years. It dates back as far as Gottfried Arnold, the German Lutheran whose key works appeared around 1700.[16] It is expressed or implied in many historical and philosophical studies of primitive Christianity. At first it was promoted mainly in Germanic Europe by such figures as Neander, Harnack and Sohm, and is perpetuated today notably by Von Campenhausen and Edouard Schweizer. During the present century, the discussion has spilled over into other language groups, and the body of literature dealing with the problem has become enormous.[17] Meanwhile, a secularized version of the notion of "charismatic personality" has been introduced into social thought by Max Weber, and thereafter popularized. The connotations and ideologies that have thus become attached to the term *charismatic,* and have influenced even exegetes, impede every effort to recover the primitive sense in which it was used by St. Paul.

One of the most radical declarations of the inherent opposition between charism and institution is that of Auguste Sabatier in *The Religions of Authority and the Religion of the Spirit,* the French original of which appeared in 1903. By the time Giovanni Battista Montini, the future Pope Paul, was pursuing his seminary studies in theology (1916–1920) this work was notorious as one of the more prominent contemporary attacks on the Catholic understanding of Church. It is the one work occasionally cited by the Pope as typifying the view he is denouncing.[18]

Catholic theology in the past made little use of the notion of charism, preferring to treat the action of the Holy Spirit in terms of grace, gifts and fruits. During the present century, however, the term *charism* has come into more and more use, but with a variety of meanings and in the context of various theories, many of them quite orthodox.[19] Whether or not the term is used, and regardless of its sense, it is traditionally and characteristically Catholic to hold that there is no necessary conflict between, for example, the institutional offices of bishop or priest, and the free, personal initiatives of men and women inspired by the Holy Spirit, but outside the framework of an office.

In the past three or four decades, however, a growing current of reaction among Catholic thinkers against what they regard as excessive institutionalization and authoritarianism in the Church has expressed itself in emphasis on the "charismatic" values of Christianity. Before Vatican II, Karl Rahner's relatively moderate essay, "The Charismatic Element in the Church,"[20] was the foremost representative of this tendency, which affected many authors in varying degrees and with diverse nuances. In not a few, there could be sensed a pervasive, amorphous and not always frank tendency to belittle institutional authority.

As early as 1943, Pius XII dealt with this problem in a famous passage of the Encyclical *Mystici Corporis*. He contrasted two opposite misconceptions of the Church's structure. One restricts it to the hierarchy, whereas the other makes it consist "exclusively of charismatics."[21]

Farther on, the encyclical reproved the related error of conjuring up an imaginary "Church of Charity," and opposing it contemptuously to the "juridical Church."[22]

Although the stands taken by Pius XII were reiterated by Vatican II,[23] the condemned views have not only persisted but have gained in influence, if not in the precise forms cited, at least in their general attitude. In the period immediately after the Council, Hans Küng became the best-known proponent of a "charismatic" concept of the Church. Although his *Structures of the Church*,[24] written while Vatican II was in preparation, frankly and vigorously maintained (in opposition especially to Ernst Käsemann) the "Catholic" concept of Church office, according to which a charism is conferred by ordination,[25] his later book, *The Church* (1967),[26] reversed this earlier position. It adopted a concept of Church leadership approximating that which had developed in the line from Gottfried Arnold to Edouard Schweizer. This does not appear so much in the chapter on the "continuing charismatic structure of the Church,"[27] as in the conclusions

drawn in section E, "Offices in the Church." Insisting on the priesthood of all believers, and on the "charism of the Spirit" (p. 401) given
to all, Küng presents the development of ordained priesthood in the
Church as an imitation of "pagan and Judaic patterns," "contrary to
the New Testament message" (p. 383). It results in human mediators
(p. 373) "standing between God and men and barring the direct access
to God which the whole priestly people should enjoy" (p. 383).

The radical tendency of Küng's views was confirmed in subsequent writings, especially *Infallible?*,[28] which appeared in 1970.
*Why Priests?*[29] (1971) and *On Being a Christian* (1976)[30] confirm
implications that were more obscurely implied in earlier writings, and
make it clear that Küng's conception of charismatic leadership involves a categorical denial of Holy Orders as a sacrament in the Triden-
tine sense. Küng rejects the doctrine of a "sacramental character,"
i.e., a sacred and indelible spiritual seal that entitatively distinguishes
the ordained minister from the layman, in particular by the power to
consecrate the Eucharist.[31] Küng's work is a complex amalgam. The
theological issues therein which call for discussion are seldom proposed directly as theses.[32] More often they are implied in a mass of
historical material, or assumed in the exposition of positions that may
be otherwise unexceptionable. It would be impossible to undertake
here the painstaking analysis and nuanced assessment which so complex a figure requires. However, all that has to be noted for our present
discussion is that in the course of the late 1960's and early 1970's, his
views, which were clearly irreconcilable with the traditional[33] and
official doctrine of the Catholic Church, came to be looked upon as the
foremost exposition of a "charismatic conception" of the Church, and
were the object of very intense concern at the Vatican.

The Sacred Congregation for the Doctrine of the Faith made an
examination of the books, *The Church* and *Infallible?*, and sent Küng
two letters (May 6 and July 12, 1971) about the unorthodox views they
contained. On June 24, 1973, the document, *Mysterium Ecclesiae*,[34]
was issued by the Congregation, condemning Küng's interpretation of
infallibility, but without mention of his name. Shortly thereafter (July
4, 1973), he was summoned to appear before the Congregation, but in
a widely publicized press conference refused to go. Finally, in a statement of Feb. 15, 1975, in which Küng was cited by name, the Congregation declared three of his positions to be contradictory to Church
doctrine, while reserving judgment on others. The points condemned
were: 1) the interpretation of infallibility as merely an overall indefectibility; 2) the rejection of the teaching authority of bishops; and 3) the
thesis that, at least in cases of necessity, laymen can consecrate the
Eucharist.[35]

Küng has been singled out here, not as though Pope Paul necessarily had him in mind in the texts presented above, but simply because
he was by far the most notorious proponent of the kind of charismatic
ecclesiology the Pope was denouncing. Besides Küng, a great panoply
of other theologians, not always less radically, but in any case with less
publicity, were reconsidering, challenging and remodelling traditional
ecclesiology. Not only infallibility, apostolic succession and the
charism of Holy Orders were questioned, but even the very necessity
of the Church for salvation, and the rationale for proclaiming the
Gospel to adherents of non-Christian religions. This critical reflection,
which was often but not always associated with a charismatic theory of
the Church, arose from many sources. In part it was a by-product of a
new appreciation for such things as the pilgrim character and historical
dimension of the Church, the properly ecclesial value of the local
community, the activity and responsibility of the laity, etc. In part, the
ferment of reflection was due to the stimulus of Vatican II. In certain
areas it was intensified by local conditions, such as the stirrings of
liberation theology in Latin America, or of process theology in the
English-speaking countries. But its most widespread and powerful
cause was probably the disenchantment that fell upon a large part of the
Church in the postconciliar years.

The most diverse expectations of "reform" had been awakened
by the Council. Although many of them were incompatible with one
another, and with the very texts of the Council documents, and although some even involved the abandonment of fundamental Christian
postulates, such considerations hardly blunted the insistence with
which they were demanded, or an angry reaction when they were not
forthcoming. In a gesture of protest, a number of priests abandoned the
priesthood, such as Charles Davis (1966) and James Kavanaugh
(1967). The reaction to *Humanae Vitae* in the summer of 1968 brought
the storm to its paroxysm.

Thus the theoretical "charismatic" anti-institutionalism which
the Pope had briefly warned against in his first encyclical had, within
four years, turned into an ominous rumble of discontent, criticism and
accusation so serious that *Time* Magazine, for example, devoted its
cover story of November 22, 1968, to this topic. The portrait of Paul
VI was set against a background mosaic of the papal tiara and the Keys
of Peter crumbling into bits.[36]

*Contestazione,* i.e., contention or contentiousness, is the term
by which Pope Paul usually designates this negative attitude, which
embraces complaint, criticism, disobedience and rebellion. Reflecting
on the "sad phenomenon of Catholics who are intent on afflicting the
Church of God today," he observed that "it is as if they adopted as

their motto the prophetic and bitter words of our Lord, 'A man's enemies will be those of his own household' (Mt 10:36)'' (June 26, 1974).

This *contestazione* seems to be the chief object of the Pope's concern in the texts from 1969 onwards that were examined earlier in this chapter. To dismiss them as merely the defense reaction of an embattled establishment would be to misconstrue the sense of the papal office. The Pope bears chief responsibility for preserving authentic Christian tradition amid the temporal pressures that would distort it, for maintaining the apostolic authority conferred by Christ on himself and all the bishops, and for defending the Church's unity. As pastor of all the faithful, he is concerned for members of his flock whose faith is liable to be wounded, alarmed and confused by irresponsible speculation and criticism. ''I will strike the shepherd, and the sheep will all be scattered'' (Mt 26:31). In distinction from legitimate, measured criticism, contentiousness is corrosive of the unity of the body; and to suppose that, in denouncing it, the Pope is merely clinging to power, would not be ''honest realism,'' but mischievous glibness.

In any case, there seem to be two chief provocations of the texts we are considering. One is the theoretical view that charismatic Christianity is irreconcilably opposed to the institutional Church. This has been in the air for two or three hundred years, and has made progressive inroads into Catholic theology during the past few decades. The other is the actual contentiousness that has erupted within the Church since Vatican II, and especially since the publication of *Humanae Vitae* in 1968.

If we seek for the link that joins these two together as objects of Pope Paul's concern, the most obvious possibility is the work of Hans Küng. This does not imply that the texts on charismatic contentiousness were aimed uniquely at him. Those analyzed above do not seem to depict any single theologian or movement. They portray a composite of trends, attitudes and notions that were and still are widespread and virulent, cohere logically with one another, but are perhaps not fully and purely incarnate in any one instance. But given this qualification, the positions taken by Küng are indeed representative of those denounced by the Pope.

By an ironic coincidence, Küng's book, *The Church,* appeared in the same year as the Catholic Charismatic Renewal, 1967. This casts an ambiguity on any statements about the charismatic issuing from the Vatican thereafter. They could be aimed either at Küng or at the Renewal or both. As a matter of fact, a number of newspapers, *The Wanderer,* in particular, often presented Pope Paul's statements as condemnations of the Renewal. Obviously, this cannot be taken for granted, especially in the early years, when the charismatic movement was not nearly so well known as the Tübingen theologian. What can, however, be safely conjectured is that Küng's theology may well have had the effect of casting a cloud of suspicion over any view associated with the term, *charismatic*.

Is there any positive evidence that Pope Paul's statements were aimed at the Renewal? We have already noted that the earliest ones preceded the beginning of the Renewal, and therefore could not have been concerned with it. As for the more frequent and urgent statements from 1969 onwards, we cannot be so sure. In 1969 the American Bishops made their first official statement on the Renewal, and this could well have drawn the Pontiff's attention to the subject. However, the Bishops' report was, on balance, favorable. Although cautioning against emotionalism and abuse, it does not even allude to the danger of anti-institutionalism, which is central to Pope Paul's concerns.[37]

Furthermore, neither an anti-institutional ideology, nor a contentious spirit, have been prominent traits of the Renewal. On the contrary, both objective observers and those involved have repeatedly testified that one of the most striking fruits of the Renewal has been a more wholesome appreciation of the sacraments, the hierarchy and scripture, the three chief institutions of which the Church consists.[38]

But if anti-institutionalism has not dominated or characterized the Charismatic Renewal, it is a real danger to which this and all charismatic movements are naturally exposed. The Catholic movement has understandably been much less affected by it than the Pentecostal and Protestant counterparts; but even among Catholics, the notion that inspirations of the Holy Spirit make a person independent of the institutional Church crops up often enough that it needs to be dealt with in earnest. From this point of view, Pope Paul's admonitions have a pastoral timeliness that is providential.

But as for the Pope's personal judgment on the Charismatic Renewal—this must now be sought for in a broader selection of texts.

## NOTES

1. I have given a list of the earliest reports in *The Pentecostal Movement in the Catholic Church* (Notre Dame, Ave Maria Press, 1971), p. 297.
2. I have written about some of them in "The Hidden Roots of the Charismatic Renewal in the Catholic Church," in *Aspects of Pentecostal-Charismatic Origins*, edited by Vinson Synan, (Logos, Plainfield 1975), pp. 169 ff.
3. Cf. *The Pentecostals*, by W. Hollenweger, Augsburg, Minneapolis, 1972.
4. See especially the Constitution on the Church, #4, 12, 15, 21 and 34; Decree on Ecumenism, #3; Decree on the Apostolate of the Laity, #3; Decree on the Church's Missionary Activity, #4; Constitution on the Church in the Modern World, #11, 15, 26, 38.

5. "The Mission of the Church," address given in October, 1957. Cf. Cardinal Montini, *The Church* (Baltimore and Dublin, Helicon, 1964), p. 28.

6. General Audience of June 5, 1974 (*OR*, June 6, 1974; *ORe*, June 13, 1974). Cf. chapter 4 at notes 5–9.

7. The Charismatic Renewal has often been related to the famous prayer for the Council, in which Pope John asked the Lord to renew his wonders "in this, our day, as by a new Pentecost" (*AAS* 51, 1959, p. 832. *Documents of Vatican II*, Abbott, p. 793). Pope Paul, however, has continued this prayer with a much more prolonged persistence. Cf. the preceding chapter, at note 41.

8. The Italian "translation" (presumably the original on which the official Latin text is based) here reads: *"da idee particolari,"* literally: "from particular ideas." *AAS* 56 (1964), p. 630.

9. Italian: *"introducendo cosi,"* literally: "thus introducing." *Ibid.*

10. Cf. the NCWC translation of this encyclical, *Paths of the Church,* #47. I have, however, made my own translation of this obscure paragraph.

11. It is a striking coincidence that this statement comes just a month after the first newspaper reports on "Catholic Pentecostal Prayer Meetings," (*National Catholic Reporter,* April 19 and 26). It is utterly impossible that the Pope was aware of these reports.

12. Address at a General Audience (*OR*, Aug. 30, 1973; *ORe*, Sept. 5, 1973). Cp. the opposition between the hierarchical and charismatic Church in the allocution of Feb. 13, 1972.

13. General Audience of Aug. 29, 1973 (*OR*, Aug. 30, 1973; *ORe*, Sept. 5, 1973). In the same address, he announced his intention to treat these two points "fully and frankly" on a future occasion, but I have not found any later statements that seem to carry out this intention.

14. General Audience of May 24, 1972 (*OR*, May 25, 1972; *ORe*, June 1, 1972).

15. General Audience, Oct. 25, 1972 (*OR*, Oct. 26, 1972; *ORe*, Nov. 5, 1972).

16. *Unpartheyische Kirchen-und Ketzerhistorie . . .*, Frankfurt, 1699; Fortsetzung, *ibid.* 1700; *Historia et descriptio theologiae mysticae . . .*, Frankfurt, 1702.

17. A lengthy bibliography of studies on ministry and office in the early Church is given in one of the more recent works on this subject, *Les ministères aux origines de l'Eglise,* by Andre Lemaire, Paris, Cerf, 1971 (*Lectio Divina* 68). A recent study with more specific attention to the question of the role of the Canon of Scripture is by James L. Ash, Jr. "The Decline of Prophecy in the Early Church," *Theological Studies* 37/2 (1976) 227–252. I have dealt with this topic theologically in "Charism and Institution," *American Ecclesiastical Review* 168/8 (Oct. 1974), 507–525.

18. In 1960, while still Archbishop of Milan, Cardinal Montini gave an address on "The Papacy and Unity in the Church," in which he said:

> "If . . . those who still turn to Christ as the world's salvation were to view with a serene eye the papacy's real essence and real activity rather than dwell on the often reiterated separation between spiritual and corporeal Christianity (Luther), between the visible and the invisible Church (Calvin), between the religion of authority and the religion of the Spirit (Sabatier), between the Church of law and the Church of love, the Church as an institution and the Church as event, the hierarchical Church and the charismatic Church, they would realize how wrong and unjust it is to turn these distinctions into real antinomies and apply them, especially today, to the Roman pontificate." Cardinal Montini, *The Church,* Baltimore and Dublin, Helicon, 1964, p. 100. Sabatier is also cited in the address of May 17, 1972, at note 9.

19. Thus, for example, Humbert Clérissac, *Le mystère de l'Eglise,* 1918. I have surveyed this development of Catholic theology in "The New Theology of

Charisms in the Church," *American Ecclesiastical Review,* 161/3 (Sept. 1969), 145–159.

20. The original essay appeared in *Stimmen der Zeit* 160 (1967). It was later included in the volume, *The Dynamic Element in the Church,* published in German by Herder, Freiburg, in 1958, and in English translation by Herder and Herder, New York, in 1964.

21. *"Minime autem reputandum est hanc ordine digestam, seu 'organicam,' ut aiunt, Ecclesiae Corporis structuram solis hierarchiae gradibus absolvi ac definiri; vel, ut opposita sententia tenet, unice ex charismaticis constare; qui quidem donis prodigialibus instructi, humquam sunt in Ecclesia defuturi."* Mystici Corporis, AAS, 35, (1943), p. 200. NCWC translation, 1943, #17. Note that the Pope goes on to define charismatics as "endowed with prodigious gifts," and to affirm that they will never be wanting in the Church.

    I have been unable to find any indication of particular theologians that Pius XII may have had in mind here. Sebastian Tromp, S.J., who is generally acknowledged to have been the theologian most involved in drafting the encyclical, gives no hint of their identity in his commentary, *Documenta varia quae prodesse possunt ad explicandas litteras encyclicas* "Corporis Mystici Christi," in Pius Papa XII *De Mystico Iesu Christi Corpore,* ed. S. Tromp, Romae, Gregoriana, 1943 (note 17a).

    In his *Corpus Christi quod est Ecclesia* (Roma, 1937–1960), Tromp simply observes that "in modern times... the opposition between charismatics and authority is emphasized more than in previous ages; wrongly, however, since Church authority has its own charism, which is indeed a very great one, the Sevenfold Spirit himself" (tome III, p. 132).

22. *AAS* 34, 224; NCWC ed. #64. This passage is cited by Pope Paul in his allocution of March 26, 1969.

23. Vatican II, *The Church,* #8.

24. New York, Sheed and Ward, 1961; this is also the date of the German original.

25. Pp. 131 ff. of the English translation.

26. The English translation of this work, *The Church* (New York, Sheed and Ward) appeared in the same year as the original German, 1967.

27. This relatively moderate and orthodox essay (C, II, 3) had already appeared in *Concilium* 4/1 (April, 1965) without attracting much attention.

28. *Unfehlbar: Eine Anfrage.* Benziger Verlag. English translation: *Infallible?,* New York, Doubleday, 1971.

29. *Wozu Priester? Eine Hilfe.* Benziger Verlag. English translation: *Why Priests? A Proposal for a New Church ministry.* New York, Doubleday, 1972.

30. *Christ Sein,* Munich, Piper, 1974; English translation: *On Being a Christian,* New York, Doubleday, 1976.

31. See especially, pp. 60–69 and 73–95 of *Why Priests?*

32. The main thesis of his work, *Infallible?* is an obvious exception to what is said here; but the rest of the book is not.

33. I say *traditional,* not in the sense of something that has always been held in this present form, but in the sense of a living tradition in the Church which never ceases to progress in drawing out and defining the implications of the Christian message. It implies authentic continuity with Christian origins, but not a dead conformity.

34. *AAS* 65 (1973), pp. 396–408.

35. *Ibid.* 67 (1975), pp. 203–204. The German Bishops Conference issued a statement two days later, declaring that "if Prof. Küng does not want to keep in mind as the premises of his theological work the norms of faith of the Church set forth in these principles, there cannot but be conflicts with the Magisterium of the Church." In November, 1977, in a statement concerned with *On being a Christian,* they said that the theological method of the latter disregards the faith-

tradition of the Church and uses scriptural passages arbitrarily, with the consequence that the content of the faith is impoverished. An English translation of the latter statement appears in *ORe* February 16, 1978. Küng replied with the book, *Um Nichts als die Wahrheit,* Munich, Piper, 1978, which I have not yet seen. A report on the whole matter appeared in *Time Magazine* for February 27, 1978, as I was correcting the proofs of the present work.

36. *Look* Magazine published an article in a similar vein entitled, "The Power and the Glory Are Passing," Oct. 19, 1971.

37. Cf. "Report of the American Bishops," published as an appendix to the work cited in the following note.

38. I have discussed this point in *The Pentecostal Movement in the Catholic Church,* Notre Dame, Ave Maria Press, 1971, pp. 153 ff., 166 ff.

# CHAPTER THREE

# Pope Paul and the Charismatic Renewal

There is no way to determine when or how Pope Paul first began to take notice of the Charismatic Renewal. He studiously avoids calling it by name, even when speaking directly to its participants, much more so when addressing general audiences. The reason for this avoidance, is partly, no doubt, the disquieting connotation which the term carries for him, from the lines of thought we have just examined.

Nevertheless, the Pope has been speaking about "charisms" or "charismatic" aspects of the Christian life during the period in which the Charismatic Renewal was developing. It is certain that he was aware of the Renewal by the beginning of 1973, and some of his addresses thereafter had obvious reference to it. Before 1973, he makes many statements which could possibly have been formulated with the Renewal in mind, but about which it is impossible to be certain. On Nov. 14, 1969, the Committee on Doctrine of the American Bishops presented a report on the movement, on which they had been working for several months.[1] It is plausible that this drew the Holy Father's attention to the subject.

At any rate, it was about this time that he began to speak more frequently about the charismatic aspect of the Church.[2] Chapter 2 examined what he had to say about abusive appeals to this aspect; but we also find him speaking of the charism of charity (March 26, 1969), the charism of grace (May 25, 1969), the charism of joy (April 25, 1970), the charism of sacrifice (Oct. 27, 1971),[3] the charism of the religious life,[4] the charisms peculiar to each religious institute,[5] etc. On Nov. 12, 1969, he mentioned that the Church is "an organic society with different charisms, different functions and different responsibilities."[6] A year later he spoke of grace as a "charism infusing into the heart an unmistakeable pull toward the God who is real, living

31

and present" (Sept. 9, 1970). This list, which could be prolonged endlessly, suggests a deliberate determination to show that the notion of charismatic is fully at home in the Church, and represents a normal element of its life and a familiar pattern in its thought. We can also detect perhaps a growing flexibility in the way the term is used for all forms of the Holy Spirit's interior action.

Whether or not this increased attention to the charismatic has any relationship to the rise of the Charismatic Renewal, the Pope's doctrine is of interest in its own right. The present chapter will review all of his major statements on this subject from 1969 through 1976. This period of time is punctuated by three major dates: On Feb. 21, 1973, Cardinal Suenens spoke with the Pope about the Charismatic Renewal. On Oct. 10 of that same year, the Pope met with some leaders of the Renewal. Finally, on May 18, 1975, he addressed the International Conference on the Charismatic Renewal in the Catholic Church.

### 1969–1972

This period opens with a statement of March 26, 1969, in which the Pope declares that it would be necessary to "rectify certain opinions which some people form about (the Holy Spirit's) charismatic action." The opinions he cites are precisely those which we have examined in the preceding chapter, and need not be gone into any further here.

Two months later, in his homily for Pentecost, he recommended cultivation of that interior silence which knows how to hear what the Spirit says. He added:

> This is the mark of anyone who wishes to be led by the
> Spirit (as we hear so often these days) and to benefit from
> charismatic inspiration (May 25, 1969).

To whom does the parenthetical remark refer? It is certainly tempting to see an allusion to the Charismatic Renewal in the wish to be "led by the Spirit" and to "benefit from charismatic inspiration," but still we cannot be certain. Appeals to the leading of the Spirit were at this time a common theme in spiritual writing, and perhaps even more in ecclesiological discussions. In any case, it is to be noted that this text, instead of reproving misconceptions, is pointing out the right way to be a charismatic. These two themes continue to alternate throughout the following years. Pope Paul's dearest work is that of encouraging people to seek the guidance of the Spirit; but he finds himself constrained again and again to denounce the misconceptions that threaten to turn this aspiration from its right path.

In 1971 (Jan. 28), in an address to the judges and officials of the Sacred Roman Rota, which is a court of appeals for cases of ecclesiastical law, the Pope spoke at some length on the subject of charisms. He was concerned with the error of those who ignore the sacred power given by Christ to his pastors, and replace it with a "charismatic" power proper to the Christian community as distinguished from its pastors. He reminds them that St. Paul, the very patron invoked by those who hold this view, spoke forcefully about his pastoral power over charisms and charismatics, which power he did not hesitate to exercise when there was need. The Pope acknowledges that the Spirit acts with freedom, and that his action should not be quenched. "But it is also true," he adds:

> ... that charisms are for the benefit of the community, and all do not possess the same charisms. Moreover, as a result of human frailty, charisms may be confused at times with one's own disordered ideas and inclinations. Hence, it is necessary to judge and discern charisms in order to check their authenticity, and to correlate them with criteria derived from the teachings of Christ, and with the order which should be observed in the ecclesial community. Such an office pertains to the sacred hierarchy, which is itself established by a singular charism (Jan. 28, 1971).[7]

Both themes appear in the address of June 23, 1971. This came shortly after several talks on the action of the Holy Spirit, occasioned by the feast of Pentecost, which fell on May 30 of that year. It also came just three days after the International Conference on the Charismatic Renewal in the Catholic Church, which had been held at the University of Notre Dame June 18–20.[8] It seems quite plausible that the Pope's remarks were directed partly at them. Those who seek authenticity in their Christian life, he said, assert that "we must live according to the Spirit." This principle is true and great, he agreed, but must be "integrated into the context of full Christian reality," which includes communion with one's fellows in the Church, and obedience to its pastors. The true sense of living by the Spirit, he affirmed, is to live in grace and in love. It is to live out of the mysterious presence of the God who is present and active within us, speaking to us both by his inner presence and through his word in scripture.

Then he asked:

> Are we perhaps to align ourselves with those charismatic contemporaries of ours who claim to draw the inspiration of their activity from some inner religious experience of theirs?

> (St.) Paul's answer to this question was, typically, not yes or no, but: Prudence! Here opens one of the most difficult

and complex chapters of the spiritual life, that of the "discernment of spirits." Misunderstandings are very easy in this field; illusion no less so.

The Pope recalled that this subject has been treated by many authors, such as St. Ignatius and Cardinal Bona, besides innumerable others cited in an article of the *Dictionnaire de Théologie Catholique*. Finally he recommended a brief text in the *Imitation of Christ* (Book III, ch. 54), from which we can learn "humbly to discern the language of grace speaking within us." This stress on the need for discernment would remain the chief theme of Paul's messages to the Charismatic Renewal.

On November 24 of that same year (1971), the Pope again spoke of those who oppose the Spirit to the structures of the Church. In this talk there is nothing that would seem to refer particularly to the Charismatic Renewal, except possibly an allusion to "collective excitement" as one of the dangers of separating spirituality from the organic community of believers which is the Church.

At the ordination of 19 bishops, Feb. 13, 1972, Paul again spoke of "some who have recently ventured to place the charismatic and hierarchical Church in opposition." In reply, he stressed that a charismatic gift is intimately connected with hierarchical office. He added:

> The particular charisms of the faithful are not denied—quite the contrary. The same passage from the first letter to the Corinthians presupposes and recognizes these charisms, for the Church is a living body animated by the very life of God—a life which is mysterious and manifold, ever moving, never predictable, a life which sanctifies and transforms. But as (St.) Paul also emphasizes, the charisms granted to the faithful are subject to discipline, which is ensured only by the charism of pastoral power, in charity.

In a meditation preparatory for the feast of Pentecost, May 17, 1972, he warned of the danger of confusing the mysterious work of the Holy Spirit with "equivocal forms of spiritualism and spirituality." It is always necessary to "test the spirits." Then he returned to a favorite theme of his, that, while we cannot draw up any absolute norms for the intervention of the Spirit, who acts freely and unexpectedly, nevertheless an interior life is ordinarily required of "anyone who wishes to pick up the supernatural waves of the Holy Spirit." The man of today is so captivated by the exterior world, he declared, that he finds himself unable to pray.

> We claim perhaps to have special "charisms" in order to demand blind autonomy for the spiritual caprices of our

instincts, instead of trying to bring our feelings and thoughts
back to the authentic phase of divine inspiration.

The true way to prepare ourselves for the work of the Spirit within us,
he asserted, is to give interior life a primary place in the program of our
busy existence.

The following autumn brought the warmest, richest, most
eloquent and, one is tempted to say, the most charismatic statement
Paul ever made on the Church's need of the Holy Spirit. (The text can
be found in Part II, at Nov. 29, 1972). It does not seem to have been
provoked by any special occasion other than a series of allocutions
which he had been devoting to the question, What does the Church
need? Previous talks had answered, for example, that the Church needs
faith or interior life. In this one, the answer is that the first and last
need of the Church is the Holy Spirit. If Paul composed this talk with
the Charismatic Renewal in mind, as seems quite probable, it may
have been his purpose, not so much to rouse the apathetic, as to
demonstrate to the fervent, the "official" Church's high esteem for the
Divine Spirit.

In any case, the close of the talk turns once again to Paul's
inveterate target, those who use "living by the Spirit" as a cover for
disobedience, contentiousness, laicization and secularization.[9] Thus,
even at this late date, the Pope sees as the main counterfeiters of the
spiritual renewal so dear to his heart, not those who claim that the
primitive charisms have reappeared, but those who, under pretext of
personal inspiration, are really following only their own self-will.


## 1973: A CRUCIAL YEAR

The year 1973 was crucial, although probably not decisive, in
the evolution of Pope Paul's attitude toward the Charismatic Renewal.
It began with a visit from Cardinal Suenens, and ended, so far as we
are concerned, with a meeting with several leaders of the Renewal.
The two events were obviously closely related.

Léon-Jozef Cardinal Suenens, Archbishop of Malines and
Brussels, had, while still a seminarian, acquired a deep devotion to the
Holy Spirit under the influence of his bishop and predecessor, Cardinal
Mercier.[10] At his episcopal ordination in 1945, the device he chose for
his coat of arms was *In Spiritu Sancto*—"In the Holy Spirit."[11] During the Second Vatican Council, he spoke up vigorously and successfully in defense of a paragraph on the charisms given to all the faithful,
which Cardinal Ruffini and others wanted to delete from the Constitution on the Church.[12]

On learning about the development of the Charismatic Renewal in the United States, the Cardinal sent one of his aides to investigate it along with the Marriage Encounter movement, both of which interested him greatly. Then, on Feb. 21, 1973, the Cardinal discussed the Renewal with Pope Paul in a private audience, of which he said later:

> I had a long audience with the Holy Father and I spoke to him for over a half hour of that time about the Charismatic Renewal. I shared with him my discoveries in that field. I know he appreciated what I shared with him and listened very sympathetically.[13]

Whether the topic was taken up at the initiative of the Pope or of the Cardinal was not announced, and details of the conversation have never been published.

Two days later, in a public audience, the Pope pointed out that, despite all the signs which seem to indicate a decline of modern man's religious sense, there are "strange and also consoling symptoms" of men discovering God under the most adverse circumstances of the modern world. He cited the case of the miraculous conversion of André Frossard in France, and indicated that there are innumerable others less notorious. Then he added:

> This is the charismatic sphere, about which so much is said today. "The Spirit blows where he wills." We will certainly not suppress (his breath), remembering the words of St. Paul, "Do not quench the Spirit" (I Thes 5:19). However, we must at the same time recall the following words of the same Apostle, "but test everything; hold fast what is good" (ib. 21) (Feb. 21, 1973).

The Pope went on to pose the question which must have been a crucial one for him, as the supreme pastor of the institutional Church:

> Does the Spirit breathe only outside the usual framework of canonical structures? Has the "Church of the Spirit" left the institutional Church? Is it only in spontaneous groups, as they are called, that we will find the charisms of the real, original, Pentecostal Christian spirituality?

This is obviously a reflection on the topic discussed with the Cardinal two days previously. Its implications are not as negative as they might seem at first. The Pope went on to answer his own question by insisting that "the ordinary and institutional structure of the Church is always the great highway by which the Spirit comes to us"; but nothing in this brief closing paragraph negates the main point of the allocation, which is that man's encounter with God may take place in ways that defy all human calculation.

A week later, in the course of a very similar address pointing out that man's essential relationship with God does not reside in anything that can be computed in terms of sociological data, but simply in grace, the Pope interjected:

> ... we must point out something new in contemporary spirituality, not just within our own fold, but also among those who are near to us, and sometimes even among those who are far off. It is esteem for the charismatic elements of religion over the so-called institutional ones ... (Feb. 28, 1973).

No doubt the Pope is still thinking of what Cardinal Suenens had said to him about the Charismatic Renewal. However, he views it in the perspective of a broad tendency in spirituality today that affects not only the Catholic Church. Those who are "near to us" without being "within our fold" are presumably Christians outside the Roman Catholic communion; "those who are far off" must refer to non-Christians.

The Pope goes on to give a brief appraisal of this tendency, in the balanced style that is characteristic of him. On the one hand, he warns against the danger of autosuggestion or the influence of "imponderable psychic causes" which can lead to spiritual error. On the other hand, he says, it can also lead to that supernatural contact with God which we call grace. In other words, he neither blesses nor condemns the movement as such, but rather tries to discriminate between that which is good in it and that which is at least dangerous.

On May 9, Pope Paul announced the Holy Year, devoted to the "personal, interior renewal" of modern man, and to reconciliation, which was to begin on the feast of Pentecost, June 10. Two weeks later, he declared:

> The fact that the Holy Year unfurls its sails in the individual local churches precisely on the blessed day of Pentecost is not without significance. It is in order that believing mankind may be carried in a single direction, and with harmonious emulation, toward the new goal of Christian history, its eschatological "port," by a new current or movement that will be truly "pneumatic," that is, charismatic (May 23, 1973).

The addition of this last term is striking. It would be more in keeping with Paul's usual style, if he used so 'dangerous' a term as charismatic, to explain it by another. Instead, here he gratuitously adds it on to the term *pneumatic*,[14] by which he had already indicated the centrality of the Holy Spirit to the intentions of the Holy Year.

The explanation may lie in the fact that an international conference on the Charismatic Renewal in the Catholic Church was due to be held at the University of Notre Dame the following week (June 1–3), at which Cardinal Suenens was to give the principal address.[15] If Paul chose his language with the intention of winning the hearts of the charismatics, his timing could not have been better. It was reprinted in leaflet form and distributed to the people who attended the Conference. Its effect was electrifying, as a tangible sign, beyond any that might have been hoped for, of the profound accord between the movement and some of the most urgent intentions of the Holy Father.[16]

In spite of this benevolent allusion, Pope Paul did not relax his warnings against abusive appeals to the charismatic. On June 6 he asked:

> What Spirit could be encountered through a selfish communion—that is, one which arises out of a flight from the true communion of ecclesial charity? What experiences or what charisms could make up for the lack of unity and of the supreme encounter with God?

On Aug. 29,[17] he declared that making a real distinction between the charismatic and the institutional Church leads to disobedience and exaggerated pluralism.

During that same summer, in a talk on prayer, the Pope made an observation about strange forms of modern mysticism:

> ... the need for God is connatural to the human heart. But so often the heart is hurt, or falls into illogical skepticism, because of the repression of that voice within it which, for a thousand reasons, would call to heaven, not as to an empty, terrible and mysterious universe, but as to the Prime Being, the absolute, the Creator, the living God. In fact, for what they are worth, at least as psychosocial phenomena, one finds strange forms of collective mysticism among today's youth. These are not always cases of mystification. Instead, they seem to represent a thirst for God, which is perhaps still unaware of the true spring at which it may be quenched, but is sincere in its wordless acknowledgment of what it is: a thirst, a deep thirst.[18]

In honesty, we must at least wonder whether the Pope may not have considered the Charismatic Renewal to be one of these "strange forms of collective mysticism."

On the other hand, just a month later, he asserted that traces of a manifestation of the Spirit seem to be glimpsed in the chronicles of our own day (Sept. 26, 1973). He did not specify what these traces were; he may well have been thinking, for example, of the heroism of

Christians behind the Iron Curtain. But it is quite plausible that he had in mind likewise the reports on the Charismatic Renewal, leaders of which were due to meet in Rome two weeks later.

## THE GROTTAFERRATA CONFERENCE (OCT. 10, 1973)

The "International Leaders' Conference of the Catholic Charismatic Renewal," met in Rome,[19] Oct. 9–13, attended by about 120 persons from 34 countries. At the request of Cardinal Suenens, 13 representatives from among them were given a brief audience. The Pope's allocution (Oct. 10, 1973) was extremely reserved. It avoided the term, *Charismatic Renewal,* altogether, addressing the leaders simply as "members of the Grottaferrata Conference."[20]

The Pope spoke of his joy at the renewal of spiritual life in the Church today, manifested in different forms, in all of which he recognized "the mysterious and discreet work of the Spirit." The "common notes" of these various forms of spiritual renewal read like a catalog description of the Charismatic Renewal itself:

> ... the taste for deep prayer, whether personal or in groups, a return to contemplation, emphasis on the praise of God, the desire to devote oneself completely to Christ, great availability for the calls of the Spirit, a more assiduous reading of scripture, generous brotherly devotedness, and the will to contribute to the service of the Church.

Then, in the abrupt manner characteristic of his talks, the Pope turned to the role of bishops in regard to renewal movements. He addressed them as pastors, responsible for the spiritual life of their flock. Above all it is their task to maintain intact the faith on which this life is based. Furthermore, they are responsible for the discernment necessary to weed out the bad elements which may be found even in the best movements of renewal.

This carefully balanced statement adheres closely to the notes struck in the Pope's initial reaction to the conversation with Cardinal Suenens on Feb. 21. It refrains from any overall evaluation of the Charismatic Renewal in its concrete existence, neither blessing nor condemning it. In fact, the existence of the Renewal as a distinct movement is not even acknowledged. However, this cautious allocution is by no means a diplomatic formality, constructed out of banalities that succeed in saying nothing without being rude. The "common notes" of the spiritual renewal which the Pope cites have obviously been assembled by someone well informed about the Renewal. Likewise, the admonition on the responsibility of bishops is remarkably apposite, for not many bishops had been exercising this responsibility with any vigor in regard to the Charismatic Renewal. Moreover, the statement of the role of bishops is not merely a warning against dangers; it is a reminder of the positive role of pastoral authority in the Church, as the indispensable means by which charismatic energy can be governed and made ecclesially fruitful.

Thus, laconic as it is, this statement contains a truly significant teaching for the Charismatics. And although the Pope was obviously farther removed from actual contact with the Renewal than any of the local bishops, very few bishops had, up to this time, made any statements about it as pertinent as this one.[21]

More important, however, than this prepared speech was the direct encounter of the Holy Father with the leading personalities of the Renewal. Several of them said it seemed to have been a very moving experience, not only for them, but also for Pope Paul. The French Dominican, Albert de Monleon, described it as a "deep and reciprocal communion with Peter in love," which marked a new phase in the Renewal by authenticating its Catholicity. That the Pope, too, was favorably impressed would seem to be indicated by the statements he made in the course of the following year.

This was not, however, apparent in some remarks made a month later. He was pointing out, at a General Audience, that if the spirituality of the Holy Year were to attain its full development, bringing people to listen to the voice of Christ and be taught by the Holy Spirit, the effects would be felt even in the realm of culture. Modern thought would "emerge from the speculative darkness in which it is now plunged" and "overcome the state of metaphysical uncertainty in which it suffers and is dissipated today," recovering confidence in its capacity for knowledge and joy in its activities of analysis and synthesis. This statement, so characteristic of the Pauline combination of spirituality and intellectuality, was followed by the question:

> All the effort that is being made in various countries to impose a teaching that radically denies God—will it not come to an end, either through the intelligent reflection of those who promote it, or through an irrepressible explosion of instinctual and irrational "new faiths," which many of the present generation of youth are creating for themselves?

The direct allusion may be to countries in which a communist regime systematically undertakes to suppress religion; but the experience which the Pope seems to have in mind is that of the whole Western world, in which the dismissal of God by academics and intellectuals has been followed by an astounding florescence of anti-intellectual cults employing anything from mescaline to yoga to attain mystical experiences or preternatural powers. The Death of God has led to the rise of the occult. Nothing indicates positively that the Charismatic Renewal is classified by the Pope among the "instinctual and irrational new faiths" created by modern youth; but the tenor of his other remarks makes it plausible that he considered this possibility. Moreover, the same address goes on to observe that religious knowledge "cannot be content with subjective spiritual phenomena generated by a sentimental, auto-charismatic, idealistic religion," which remains blind to the transcendent Reality.[22]

A month later, addressing the Cardinals at the close of a Consistorial Assembly, the Pope made a kind of general report on the state of the Church. While the latter is "afflicted interiorly by ever new anxieties," he said, it is at the same time "animated by the impulses and consoled by the signs of the life-giving Spirit." He went on to be more concrete:

> ... the breath-giving influence of the Spirit has come to awaken latent forces within the Church, to stir up forgotten charisms, and to infuse that sense of vitality and joy which in every epoch of history marks the Church itself as youthful and up-to-date, ready and happy again to proclaim its eternal message to the modern age (Dec. 21, 1973).

While it would certainly be exaggerated for the Charismatic Renewal to claim a monopoly on the impulses and signs of the Spirit today, this reference to "the stirring up of forgotten charisms" can hardly be understood as anything other than a favorable and specific allusion to it.

The following June, again speaking to the College of Cardinals, the Pope made another apparent reference to the Renewal:

> There are signs everywhere today of a great need for prayer, which makes itself known also in particular ways of listening to the voice of the Spirit.[23]

On July 3, he reminded his audience of some of the New Testament warnings about testing but not quenching the charisms:

> St. Paul warns us (especially with regard to charismatics): "Do not quench the Spirit, do not despise prophesying, but test everything; hold fast what is good, abstain from every form of evil" (I Thes 5: 19–22). "Try to learn what is pleasing to the Lord" (Eph 5: 10). "Do not believe every spirit, but test the spirits to see whether they are of God" (I Jn 4: 1). Etc.[24]

During the year 1974, Cardinal Suenens published a book on the Charismatic Renewal, entitled *A New Pentecost?* This seems to have been the occasion of Pope Paul's allocution of Oct. 16, 1974, which, however, returned to one of his themes of predilection: that the Church lives by the Holy Spirit. This time he spoke of the two basic works of the Holy Spirit, grace and charism. His prepared text then went on:

> A great deal is said about charisms today. While taking into account the complexity and delicacy of such a subject, we cannot but hope that a new abundance, not only of grace, but also of charisms, will still be granted to the Church of God today.

The Pope set aside his prepared text, however (as he often does), to discourse at some length on the charisms, understood as the *gratiae gratis datae* of scholastic theology, or, in contemporary terms, ministry gifts. They are not necessary for the spiritual life, he pointed out, but are useful for the Church. He recalled the famous view of St. John Chrysostom and others, that the charisms had been poured out with special abundance in the beginning of the Church, in order to get it established. But instead of concluding, as many others do, that these extraordinary gifts are no longer needed, he recalled that there have always been miracle workers and exceptional persons among the saints of the Church. And he added, in language livelier than that of his text,

> How wonderful it would be if the Lord would again pour out the charisms in increased abundance, in order to make the Church fruitful, beautiful and marvelous, and to enable it to win the attention and astonishment of the profane and secularized world.

Here it is unmistakeably clear, despite all the careful reservations so characteristic of Paul VI, that he welcomes the charisms as a source of renewed vigor for the Church.

He went on to speak of Cardinal Suenens' new book on the Charismatic Renewal. The Cardinal, he says:

> ... describes and justifies this new expectation of what may really be an historic and providential development in the Church, based on an outpouring of those supernatural graces which are called charisms.

Here then can be no doubt that the Charismatic Renewal is referred to. "Providential" means that it is a work of God adapted to the needs of the present hour. "Historic" means that it is not merely of transitory interest, but marks an era in the historical development of the Church. This is the most strongly favorable language ever used by Paul VI about the Charismatic Renewal. Of course, he says only "may ... be," and he is citing the judgment of Cardinal Suenens rather than making an appraisal in his own name. Nevertheless, it is obvious that he takes this judgment very seriously and is favorably inclined toward it.

A month later, however, the Pope returned to his more usual caution:

> ... today preference is given to experience rather than to reasoning. Charismatic spirituality is preferred to rational dogmatism. We certainly will not depreciate this possible and admirable way to recover religious truth, provided this way itself is authentic. In this connection, let us listen to St. Paul, the doctor of charisms: "So, my brethren, earnestly desire to prophesy, and do not forbid speaking in tongues; but all things should be done decently and in order" (I Cor 14: 39–40).[25]

## NOTES

1. The text of their report has been published in many places, among others as an appendix to my book, *The Pentecostal Movement in the Catholic Church,* p. 291.

2. Even before Vatican II, as Cardinal Montini, he occasionally used this language. In a collection of addresses on the Church which he gave as Archbishop of Milan, while preparations for the Council were under way, the terms *charism* and *charismatic* occur five times. Once he denies the false antinomy between "the hierarchical Church and the charismatic Church" (Aug. 29, 1960; p. 100); twice he affirms the charismatic action of the Spirit in the Church (Oct., 1957 and Lent, 1962; pp. 28 and 166); twice he points out that preternatural charisms need not necessarily be attributed to bishops or even to Pope John in his summoning of the Council (April 26, 1959; Aug. 16, 1960; pp. 77 and 131). Cf. Cardinal Montini, *The Church,* Baltimore and Dublin, Helicon, 1964.

    Nevertheless, Pope Paul does not seem to have used these terms much in the first two years of his papacy. Toward the end of the Council they begin to appear occasionally in his discourses, and become rather frequent from 1969 on.

3. *OR,* Oct. 27, 1971; *ORe,* Nov. 4, 1971.

4. Apostolic Exhortation, *The Renewal of the Religious Life According to the Teachings of the Second Vatican Council. AAS* 63 (1971), pp. 497–526; *The Teachings of Pope Paul VI,* 1971 (United States Catholic Conference, 1972), pp. 375–403.

5. This language occurs frequently in addresses to religious orders, or at the canonization of their members. See, e.g., the address to the General Chapter of the Sisters of Charity of Saints Bartolomea Capitanio and Vincenza Gerosa, April 7, 1975 (*ORe,* April 24, 1975).

6. General Audience (*OR,* Nov. 13, 1969; *ORe,* Nov. 20, 1969).

7. Note that the term *charism* is used here in a somewhat different way from his address of April 26, 1959 (cited above in note 2), where charismatic powers are contrasted with those of the office of bishop.

8. This was the first of these annual conferences to be announced as "international"; it was attended by representatives of at least a half dozen other countries besides the United States. It was also the first conference in which bishops participated; Bishops Steven Leven of San Angelo, and Joseph McKinney of Grand Rapids were both active in this gathering of some 4,500 people.

9. This part of his address was discussed in the preceding chapter, p. 20.

10. Cf. Elizabeth Hamilton, *Suenens: A Portrait,* Doubleday, 1975, p. 48. Suenens

often cites Cardinal Mercier's "secret of happiness": five minutes of interior conversation with the Holy Spirit each day.

11. *Ibid.*, p. 71.

12. Vatican II, *The Church, #*12. An account of this intervention (of Oct. 23, 1963) is given in my article, "The Hidden Roots of the Charismatic Renewal in the Catholic Church," in *Aspects of Pentecostal Charismatic Origins,* edited by Vinson Synan, Plainfield, Logos, 1975.

13. *New Convenant,* June 1973, p. 4. The Cardinal is no doubt using the term *sympathetic* in the sense of the French, *sympathique.*

14. *Pneumatic* here means "inspired by the Holy Spirit" as well as "affecting the human spirit." It comes from the Greek word *pneuma* which is used throughout the New Testament for both the Spirit of God and the human spirit as sanctified by him.

15. Cardinal Suenens had gone to the States during the last two weeks of March in order, among other things, to acquaint himself personally with the Charismatic Renewal. On that occasion, he had been invited to address the Conference.

16. Not until I composed the present study did it strike me how remarkable it was that a text from the English language *Osservatore Romano* for May 31 should be reprinted and ready for distribution to 22,000 people on June 1. This paper is printed in Rome and mailed to the United States. Usually it arrives from five to eight days later than the date of publication. For example, the University of Notre Dame library did not receive its copy of the May 31 issue until June 6, as can still be seen from the librarian's stamp on it. However, it does occasionally happen that the paper is received on the very date of publication; evidently it is printed and mailed a day or two in advance. In any case, that this should have happened with the particular copy of this particular issue that went to charismatic community, True House, where it was noticed by James Byrne, the director of the Conference (who must have been so busy at that moment that it is surprising he had time to read anything!), the one person with the authority and means to have it reproduced at once, is still so implausible that I had to recheck all the dates in question before I was able to believe my own notes. It is amusing to recall that Cardinal Suenens arrived with a copy of the allocution, expecting to surprise and delight the Conference with it. Instead, he was the one who was surprised, to discover that his audience already had a copy of the text in their hands.

17. General Audience (*OR,* May 30, 1973; *ORe,* Sept. 6, 1973).

18. General Audience, Aug. 22, 1973 (*OR,* Aug. 23, 1973; *ORe,* Aug. 30, 1973).

19. More precisely, they met in the suburb of Grottaferrata. A report on this meeting is given in *New Covenant* 3/5 (December, 1973).

20. The official text of his remarks, as published in the *Osservatore Romano* on Oct. 9, 1973, evidently presumes that the statement would be made at the end of the public audience of that day, as often happens for groups taking part in a public audience. It opens with the salutation, "And now a word to the members of the Grottaferrata congress."

21. I have given a brief survey of episcopal reactions in *Perspectives on Charismatic Renewal,* University of Notre Dame Press, 1975, pp. 177 ff.

22. He goes on to add, in his most authentically Pentecostal vein: "It stretches out its arms in vain toward the latter (i.e., transcendent Reality), so long as the Holy Spirit, sent by the Father in Christ's name (Jn 14:26), does not meet it part way" (Nov. 14, 1973. *OR,* Nov. 15, 1973; *ORe,* Nov. 22, 1973).

23. Allocution of June 22, 1974 (*OR,* June 23, 1974; *ORe,* July 4, 1974).

24. General Audience (*OR,* July 4, 1974; *ORe,* July 11, 1974).

25. General Audience of Nov. 20, 1974 (*OR,* Nov. 21, 1974; *ORe,* Nov. 28, 1973).

# CHAPTER FOUR

# The Rome Conference (May 16–19, 1975)

The last and by far the richest statement by Pope Paul on the Charismatic Renewal consists in the four addresses he gave to the International Conference on the Charismatic Renewal in the Catholic Church. In previous years, this Conference had been convened annually at the University of Notre Dame; but in view of the Holy Year celebrated in 1975, the Conference was moved to Rome for that year, at the suggestion of Cardinal Suenens. The latter, who was president of the committee responsible for the International Mariological and Marian Conferences, which were being held in Rome May 12–17 and 18–21, also wanted to take advantage of this occasion to stress the mysterious relationship between Mary and the Holy Spirit.

The outcome of the Rome meeting was awaited with intense interest, but for quite diverse motives. Those involved in the Renewal naturally hoped for a strong sign of approval from the Holy Father. Others frankly and unequivocally wanted it to be censured.

Catholic opposition to Pentecostalism had never been as strong as that of the Protestant denominations during the first half of the century; nevertheless, among both clergy and laity not a few reacted to it with grave misgivings, sharp criticism, or heavy-handed ridicule. However, the first official pronouncement of any sort to appear within the Catholic Church was the cautiously affirmative report of the American Bishops, Nov. 14, 1969.[1] Over the next few years, similar statements came forth from bishops of other nations, individually or collectively.[2] At the beginning of 1975, both the American and the Canadian hierarchies[3] had issued documents more elaborate than that of 1969, but maintaining the note of approval with reservations.

This development, astounding to many, alarmed those who regarded the Renewal as a threat to orthodox Catholicism. When the Rome Conference was announced, at least one request was addressed

to several American bishops asking them to do all in their power to
dissuade Pope Paul from giving it any official recognition.[4] Rumors
circulated that some members of the Curia had been urging its condemnation. On the other hand, Cardinal Suenens, and presumably
others too, had been speaking in its favor. Right up to the opening of
the Conference, it was not sure what reception it would get.

It was in this atmosphere that planeloads of charismatic pil-
grims began to arrive at the Fiume airport in the middle of May, 1975.
Soon buses were inching their way through the congested maze of
Roman streets, heading out into the country to the catacomb of St.
Callistus, where a conference center had been set up under an awning
in an open field.

The physical handicaps did not dampen the joy and excitement
of the pilgrims, most of whom were making their first visit to the
Holy City, and all of whom seemed deeply conscious of the mo-
mentousness of this event. Speakers reminded them of their kinship
with the witnesses of the Holy Spirit, the martyrs entombed in the
catacombs beneath them. This conference was a gathering of men and
women ready to testify to the present, actual working of the Spirit
today; but their Catholic instincts were deeply stirred by contact with
the Holy City's great monuments to the uninterrupted action of the
Spirit in the Church throughout the ages. Some observers may have
anticipated that such a concentration of "charismatic power" among
the aged stone walls of Rome would have created an intolerable pressure; that either the walls would crack or the spirit would be suppressed.
In fact, however, the joyous singing and dancing of the charismatics fitted as easily and naturally into their setting as the green umbrella
pines flourishing beside the polished grey stones of the ancient Appian
Way.

On Pentecost Sunday, they gathered in the Basilica of St. Peter
for the Mass celebrated by the Holy Father. A quiet delirium of joy
rose within them as they stood there, conscious of being accepted and
welcome in the Mother Church of their religion. When the Pope arrived to celebrate the Mass of Pentecost, and still more when he returned the following day to address the Conference participants, they
thundered their applause for the man whom they recognized in the
Spirit as the Vicar of Christ, and the chief shepherd of his flock on
earth. Pope Paul, in his turn, was visibly touched by their affection.

His homily for the Mass of Pentecost was, like many previous
ones, an eloquent reminder of the overwhelming mystery of divine life
communicated to man by the gift of the Spirit. Although this Mass was
not reserved for the "Charismatics," they made up a least half of the

congregation; and the Pope had them in mind no doubt as he stressed the need of preparation for the gift of the Spirit by inner silence, prayer and confession of sins. Very likely it was his intention to warn against the pseudocharismatic attitude which expects to receive the gifts of the Spirit without moral preparation.

Pope Paul went on to recall the "miracle of tongues" that occurred on the first Pentecost. We today are heirs of this marvel he said; but "for us—it is expressed in the form of a certain ease and aptness in bearing witness to all and for all, in an apostolate that knows no bounds." He returned to this theme again shortly after the Mass, in the *Regina Coeli* message spoken from the window of St. Peter's. The Holy Spirit summons all peoples, he said, "each with its own language, that is, its peculiar genius for expressing its humanity—to make up one, sole and genuine family, the one, universal Church."[5]

Did he mean thereby to suggest that the gift of tongues is no longer realized in the literal sense? If his observations had been minted specifically for this occasion, one might well suppose that this was his intention. However, the reflection made here was not original with Pope Paul, nor was this the first time he had used it. Among the Fathers of the Church, it was already a commonplace to point out how the gift of tongues symbolized the catholicity of the Church; and this "spiritual" interpretation did not exclude, but presupposed, the literal sense of the gift. This thought is an old favorite of Pope Paul's. In the very first Pentecostal sermon preached by him as Pope, he declared that the memory of the "miracle of tongues" turned his thoughts to the Church's catholicity:

> ... that is universality, the fact that it is destined for all peoples, open to all souls, offered to all tongues, inviting all cultures, present over the whole earth, persistent in all history.[6]

He has made similar reflections on many other occasions, e.g., to the bishops of the South Pacific (Dec. 1, 1970),[7] in a General Audience (Oct. 27, 1971),[8] in his Pentecost homily of 1972 (May 21, 1972, I), and in addressing the Third Symposium of European Bishops (Oct. 18, 1975).[9] On the present occasion, therefore, he does not seem to have been casting doubt on the gift of tongues, but simply reiterating a Pentecostal theme very dear to him.

In any case, the Pope soon had occasion to observe this gift in its literal sense. At the elevation of the Mass, as he raised first the host, then the chalice, a gentle melody of prayer in tongues rose throughout the basilica. This has to have been the first time such a thing ever occurred in St. Peter's, but it was so spontaneous, so discreet and so lovely that no one seems to have made any objection. Whether Pope Paul made any comments on it is not known.

The following day, the Charismatic Conference closed with a Mass and a papal audience in St. Peter's. The leaders of the Conference had hoped that the Pope himself would celebrate the Mass. He did not; but Cardinal Suenens was allowed to do so at the High Altar reserved ordinarily to the Pope himself. This in itself was an exceptional sign of favor.

After the Mass, Pope Paul arrived to speak to the assembly. The feebleness of his age was evident as he strained under the labor of reading three formal addresses in languages not his own: first in French, then in English, and last in Spanish. But when he finally put down his texts and spoke impromptu for a few minutes in his native Italian, his warm enthusiasm was unmistakable.

What were the precise implications of this reception? Many have taken it as an unqualified approval of the Charismatic Renewal.[10] The exuberance of the Charismatics as they left St. Peter's, many of them singing and dancing, suggests that this was their impression. Others, however, have insisted that it was nothing more than a fatherly welcome such as would be extended to any group of Holy Year pilgrims.[11] The texts of the Pope's addresses are printed below, under the date of May 19, 1975, for anyone to examine and interpret for himself. Three points in their composite message need to be discussed here.

The first is that the term *Charismatic Renewal* is studiously avoided in all three of the prepared addresses. This is a remarkable fact that demands explanation. To have given three speeches, welcoming the Charismatics and commenting on their activities and aspirations, but not once pronouncing their name, is almost a feat of linguistic dexterity, and can hardly have been accidental. (What would we make of an address to the International Fellowship of Firemen, that avoided all reference to fire?)[12]

But when the Pope put down his texts and began to speak impromptu in Italian, the term *charismatic* sprang immediately to his lips. He was addressing, he said, first of all "those of you who are here with the charismatic pilgrimage." Evidently he had planned to avoid the term, but it was the one that came to him spontaneously, as soon as he was free from his prepared texts.

Instead of *Charismatic Renewal,* he uses the term *spiritual renewal* throughout these addresses. This is a more general term, which he has been using for years. His deliberate preference for it is underlined when, in his Italian remarks, he calls it "the twofold name which defines what you are." We need not see here a discreet effort to change the name of the movement, although his longstanding concern about abusive charismaticism may incline him in this direction. But his statement (in the French address) that this spiritual renewal is being stirred up by the Holy Spirit today "in such diverse regions and circles," seems to indicate the intention not to single out the Charismatic Renewal in particular, but to speak in general terms of the renewing action of the Spirit which he recognizes in other movements as well.

Nevertheless, the manifestations of the Renewal which he cites, while not identical with those listed in the Grottaferrata address, compose a very appropriate summary of some of the chief features of this movement. The first point cited in the main address (French) is: "deep communion of hearts and close contact with God." This corresponds to the experience of God in and through fellowship with one's brothers that is characteristic of the Charismatic Renewal. The second is "prayer that is often in groups, in which each one expresses himself freely, thus helping, supporting and nourishing the prayer of others." This is an exact description of a charismatic meeting. The third manifestation, called the basis of all, is "a personal conviction deriving, not only from instruction received by faith, but also from a certain personal experience, that, without God, man can do nothing, whereas with him, everything becomes possible." The difference between knowledge acquired by instruction, and that which comes through personal experience, is one of the main emphases of the Charismatic Renewal. Finally, the Pope calls attention to the "need to praise and thank (God)," which arises from this experiential knowledge. This is precisely what has caused the cry, "Praise God," to become the slogan of the Charismatics.

Experiential contact with God, holy and loving fellowship with one another, prayer meetings in which these find a common expression, and the felt need to praise and thank God—these points taken together compose a very apt delineation of the Charismatic Renewal. Several other well-known marks of this movement—a taste for prayer, attentiveness to the grace of the Holy Spirit, and more assiduous reading of Holy Scripture, which had been mentioned in the 1973 list, although not retained in the main address, are repeated in the Spanish remarks which follow it.

On the other hand, a prominent feature of the Renewal to which no evident reference is made is the controversial notion of the baptism in the Holy Spirit. But when communion of hearts and contact with God are said to occur "in faithfulness to the commitments undertaken at Baptism," there may be intended a discreet allusion to this experience, understood, as it is by most Catholic theologians, to be a release or actualization of a grace that is normally received in the sacrament. Likewise there is no allusion to the charisms themselves. We know, however, from his earlier addresses, that the Pope is completely open to them (Oct. 16, 1974), and that he believes in using prudence and discretion when pronouncing upon them (June 23, 1971). This, as well as the fact that he insists on the deeper works of grace and the virtues as the essential values of a renewal, help to explain why the Pope makes no mention of the charisms here.

In any case, it seems clear that the Pope deliberately and methodically abstained from making any judgment about the Charismatic Renewal as such, or as a whole. On the other hand, he did more than praise virtue in the abstract. He pointed out precisely those fruits for which the Renewal is famous, and acknowledged them to be signs of the renewing action of the Spirit in today's world.

The second point in the Pope's message which we must consider is what he has to say about the "spiritual renewal" thus discreetly depicted. He began his main address by declaring that in a world that is becoming more and more secularized, "nothing is more necessary than the witness of this 'spiritual renewal' which we see the Holy Spirit stirring up today." Then, after listing the manifestations noted above, he asked, "how then could this 'spiritual renewal' be anything but beneficial for the Church and for the world?"

If the abstract mode of this formal address seems to weaken its force, the concreteness and warmth of the Pope's impromptu remarks make up abundantly for that. After telling his listeners that the name, *spiritual renewal,* defines them, he adds:

> This renewal should rejuvenate the world, and put back into
> it a spirituality, a soul, a religious way of thinking. It should
> reopen the closed lips of the world to prayer, to song, to joy,
> to hymns and to witness.

While "opening closed lips to prayer, song and witness" is a remarkably apt evocation of the Charismatic Renewal, it should be noted that these effects are quite the same as those of several earlier texts (especially that of March 17, 1976)[13] which we examined in chapter 1, which described the renewal for which Pope Paul hoped and prayed. Does the present text then envisage this renewal as realized in the people who stood before him, or does it merely recall one of the great needs of our time?

The Pope continues: "It will be a great good fortune for our times . . . if there should be a whole generation of young people . . . who, on the occasion of Pentecost, cry out to the world the glory and greatness of God." When he says, "on the occasion of Pentecost," he does not mean merely "on the feast day we have just celebrated," but "in reference to the whole mystery of Pentecost," the ever-living source of the Church's life. Charismatics, otherwise known as Pentecostals, are precisely those who praise God on the occasion of Pentecost. The Pope is saying, therefore, in effect, "Pentecostals who truly live up to their name and their claim will be a blessing for the Church." But the cautious "should there be" stops this statement short of being a definite commendation of an actual movement.

Finally, what is most significant of all, the Pope turned to those pilgrims in his audience who did not belong to the Charismatic movement. He urged that they "join with (the Charismatics) in celebrating the feast of Pentecost," so that "they (the non-Charismatics) too . . . might nourish themselves on the enthusiasm and spiritual energy with which we should live our religion." This implies that the enthusiasm and spiritual energy displayed by the former represents something that all Christians ought to emulate. The reason given is one that Paul has formulated before: "Today, either you live your faith with devotion, depth, vigor and joy, or that faith dies out." Clearly, Paul recognizes in the Charismatics something much needed by the Church today.

The third point we must consider here, consists of the admonitions addressed to the Charismatics. These make up the bulk of the three prepared addresses. As in his Grottaferrata address of 1973, the Pope stressed the need for discernment. But this time, instead of merely pointing out the responsibility of bishops in this regard, he specifies three principles for discernment taken from St. Paul. The first is fidelity to the teachings of the faith. This alone, he says, can ensure against deviations, and against a fervor that "beats the air" to no purpose.

Nothing makes religious enthusiasts fret more than the restraints imposed in the name of right doctrine; but nothing is more necessary to keep a revival movement from destroying itself. For religious enthusiasm is a two-edged sword. When it adds fervor to love and vigor to action, it is invaluable; but when it is cultivated for its own sake, and above all when it becomes its own guide, it heads rapidly toward exaggeration and disorder, as Ronald Knox has shown convincingly (albeit with a one-sided inverse enthusiasm of his own).[15]

Faith is the root from which all that is authentically Christian must spring. Paul, the Shepherd of the Church, speaks like an experienced Pentecostal pastor when he affirms that only the truth of faith can preserve charismatic enthusiasm from degenerating into something useless and even harmful. The basic problem of spiritual discernment is that of judging whether a given inspiration is from the Holy Spirit or not. One of the surest signs that it is not from him is divergence from the truth of faith. If what is said or urged is in discord with the word of God, it cannot be from the Holy Spirit, who is the Spirit of truth and the inspirer of the word; for he cannot contradict himself.

Pentecostals often cite this criterion as "agreement between the Spirit and the Word," meaning by the latter Sacred Scripture. Catholics hold that not only scripture, but the doctrine of the Church is inspired by the Holy Spirit, in accordance with the teaching of John 14:26 and 16:13: "He will teach you all things, and bring to your remembrance all that I have said to you . . . he will guide you into all the truth." Hence, besides scripture, the living Magisterium of the Church is cited by the Pope as a touchstone of authenticity. Generally this is a more effective criterion than scripture alone, because false prophets are seldom so gross as to contradict scripture blatantly. But when the question arises, which of several rival interpretations is truly and deeply in accord with scripture, then the "mind of the Church" is the surest guide.

In adding, "That is why you feel the need of a deeper and deeper doctrinal formation," Pope Paul is not merely formulating his admonition in as benign a manner as possible. Charismatics notoriously experience a deep thirst to learn more about scripture, spirituality, and sacred doctrine in general. But the Pope points out that only the hierarchy can ensure that this formation will be authentic. This is not establishmentarianism; it is part of the structure of the Church that supreme responsibility for teaching resides in an office instituted by Jesus and aided by the Spirit of truth, which no purely "charismatic" teaching, however inspired, can replace. Hence, a little farther on, the Pope recalls that the primitive Christian community was not only united in love (a point of great importance for him too, as we shall see in chapter 7), but was also "devoted to the teaching of the apostles."

The second principle is that those spiritual gifts which are most useful to the community should be the most highly prized. Perhaps this point is motivated by the notorious tendency of Charismatics to exaggerate the importance of glossolalia and other 'flamboyant' gifts. More likely, however, it reflects the Pope's long-standing concern with those who, under pretext of reforming the Church 'charismatically,' follow their own whims, in disobedience to pastoral authority and without regard for the discord caused by their idiosyncracies.

The same motivation may lie in part behind the third criterion, that all the other gifts of the Spirit are ordained to charity. One who uses his gifts in a way corrosive of the ecclesial community is surely not following the lead of the Spirit. Even authentic charisms can be exercised in an unloving manner, e.g., haughtily, as a means to spiritual dominion, or as an occasion of vain self-gratification. The

Church, as Pope Paul sees it, is essentially a communion of hearts in loving faith;[16] only when contributing to this are the charisms rightly ordered.

But there is an even deeper significance to this third criterion. Charity, or love, is not to be identified with the joyous emotions, external enthusiasm, or even good works, in which it is manifested. One of the more notorious weaknesses in charismatic spirituality is the tendency to conceive of spiritual vigor largely in terms of superficial enthusiasm; singing, dancing, hugging, kissing, and vociferous witnessing to the lordship of Jesus. These all have their place as spontaneous, connatural expressions of the freedom, love and joy which the Spirit brings. But the essential values of life in the Spirit are not situated on this plane, but rather in that interior world where man shares in the quiet, eternal life of the Father, Son and Holy Spirit. This is the direction that Pope Paul, as a pastor wise in the ways of the Spirit, discreetly indicates to those members of his flock who may be excessively inclined toward Charismatic exuberance.[17]

All of the Pope's observations seem permeated with the concern that Charismatics be rightly related to the Church. He congratulates them for holding the conference in Rome as a sign of attachment to the Church and to the See of Peter, and he summons them to a communion of faith, charity and apostolate with their pastors. His three principles all involve relationship with the Church, as a communion in love, as holding the Magisterium of right doctrine, and as meant to be built up by the charisms. The sacraments of the Church are recommended as the chief sources of grace—especially Baptism, Penance and Eucharist.[18]

Are these admonitions indicative of specific apprehensions about the Charismatic Renewal? Do they reflect reports the Pope has received about disorders that have been detected in it? Or do they simply express some of his long-standing concern with inordinate charismatic views? The precision and aptness of his depiction of the Renewal would suggest that his admonitions also correspond to the specific needs and shortcomings of the movement. On the other hand, they do largely reflect warnings be had been giving long before the Renewal began. It would be futile to pursue a more definite answer to this question. What is sure is that the allocutions of May 19, 1975, represent the carefully considered advice addressed to Charismatic Catholics by their supreme pastor. On this account alone, they deserve to be studied carefully and taken to heart.

In addition, the evident aptness and soundness of these counsels commends them, and not only to Catholics, but to Charismatics of all persuasions.

In conclusion, how can Paul VI's attitude toward the Charismatic Renewal be summarized? Certainly not in any simple statement of approval or disapproval. He consistently and firmly refrained from making a global judgment about this movement which, it must be remembered, is still very new, fluid and diversified. The best statement of his mind is that which he himself drew from his patron saint: "Paul's answer to this question was typically, not yes or no, but: Prudence! Here opens one of the most difficult and complex chapters of the spiritual life, that of the 'discernment of spirits'" (June 23, 1971).[19]

Two things, however, can be said to define his position somewhat. First, when we review the statements he has made from 1969 onwards, it seems possible to detect a shift toward a more and more favorable opinion. Paul's earliest observations seem more freighted with caution; later on, the encouraging signs are more emphasized. The chief factors accounting for the change seem to have been his face-to-face encounter with people of the Renewal at the Grottaferrata Conference of 1973 and the International Conference of 1975. The impact of the latter can be measured by the difference in tone between the three addresses prepared before the Conference, and the impromptu remarks made at its end. Cardinal Suenens' book, *A New Pentecost?* (1974), also seems to have influenced the Pope's thinking considerably.

Secondly, while his studied avoidance of the name, *Charismatic Renewal,* obviously means that he is not prepared to give his blessing to the movement in its totality, it does not mean he is simply neutral. At the International Conference, he singled out seven different features that accurately characterize this movement, and then asked, "How could this 'spiritual renewal' be anything but beneficial for the Church and for the world?" Moreover, he made no express criticisms of the movement. One can legitimately wonder whether his admonitions cover some implicit criticisms, but it is not at all necessary to take them in this sense, and in any case they do not negate his declarations of esteem for the fruits of the Renewal. When, finally, with glowing face and vibrant voice, he recommended the enthusiasm and spiritual energy of the Charismatics as something from which others would do well to take nourishment, his predominantly favorable attitude was unmistakeable.

Throughout the 14 years of his pontificate, Paul had been hoping, praying, pleading and working for a renewal of the Church by the Holy Spirit. Did he, at least at this last, culminating moment of the Conference, recognize in the Charismatic Renewal the fulfillment of his aspirations? It is tempting to think so, especially since much of what he had been saying about the longed for renewal had been realized to the letter in the Charismatic Renewal. Such a conclusion, however, would go beyond the evidence.

Since the 1975 conference, the Pope has said little that may be considered relevant to the Renewal. A month after the Conference, he spoke to the College of Cardinals of various signs that the Holy Spirit is making his voice heard strongly today (June 23, 1975). In his Exhortation on Evangelization he made the statement cited in chapter 1, that "We are living in a privileged moment of the Spirit in the Church...."[20] It is likely that he had the Charismatic Renewal in mind when making these observations.

On the other hand, at the end of the Holy Year, when he came to list some of the year's "particularly intense moments" which he was "happy to recall,"[21] he did not even mention the Charismatic Conference. He did, however, name several others, including the Marian and Mariological conferences, which occurred simultaneously with it, and were much smaller than it.[22] This casual omission, in a list that was far from complete, cannot be taken as a deliberate rebuff, but is decisive evidence that the Charismatic Renewal appears to Pope Paul as somewhat less than the fulfillment of his dearest wish. A fairer estimate would be that he is pleased and encouraged by it, but remains quite conscious of its ambivalence.

## NOTES

1. See note 1 of chapter 3.
2. I have drawn up a list of such statements up to the early part of 1975 in *Perspectives on Charismatic Renewal,* Notre Dame, 1975, pp. 177–182.
3. "Statement on Catholic Charismatic Renewal," published by the Committee for Pastoral Research and Practices of the National Conference of Catholic Bishops, Publications Office, United States Catholic Conference, 1312 Massachusetts Ave., N.W., Washington, D.C. 20005.
   "Charismatic Renewal," Message of the Canadian Bishops addressed to all the Catholics of Canada (April, 1975), Publications Service, Canadian Catholic Conference, 90 Parent Ave., Ottawa, Ontario, Canada K1N 7B1.
4. Dr. William Storey, of the University of Notre Dame, one of the original leaders of the movement, wrote to the Vatican Secretary of State, the Apostolic Delegate to the United States, and several bishops, asking them to do all in their power to dissuade the Pope from showing it any kind of approval. (Cf. *National Catholic Reporter,* Aug. 15, 1975, p. 1.)
5. *OR,* May 19–20, 1975; *ORe,* May 29, 1975.
6. Homily for the Mass of Pentecost, May 17, 1964 (*OR,* May 18–19, 1964; *TPS* 10 (1964–65), p. 77).
7. This text is cited in chapter 7 at note 29.
8. *OR,* Oct. 28, 1971; *ORe,* Nov. 4, 1971.

9. *OR,* Oct. 19, 1975; *ORe,* Oct. 30, 1975.

10. Carlos Aldunate, in a booklet on the Rome Conference, comes to the following conclusions about the position of Pope Paul:
    "1. The Pope believes that "this spiritual renewal" or charismatic renewal, as it is called, is God's work, stirred up by the Holy Spirit "visibly acting today in the most diverse regions and surroundings";
    2. he approves fully of the "manifestations of this renewal," which he enumerates;
    3. he desires that this charismatic renewal, so described, continue to develop;
    4. he points to criteria and means by which the renewal can develop without deviations.
    "It is easy to understand the excitement surrounding the words of the Pope. Those present felt themselves to be perfectly understood and welcomed by Paul VI. His discourse is of extraordinary importance because it confirms that this spiritual current is actually affecting the religious world in a profound way, both inside and outside the Catholic Church.
    "The charismatic renewal was given a divine blessing by the Church, and while following the wise norms of Paul VI can count on the approval of the Pope and the sympathy of all Christians of good will" (*El Papa y los Carismáticos,* Ediciones Paulinas, Chile, 1976, pp. 33–34).

11. The late Archbishop Dwyer, retired Archbishop of Portland, Oregon, an intransigent foe of the Charismatic Renewal, declared that the Pope's discourse "was nothing that would in any way endorse Pentecostalism and nothing that could not have been given to any Christian group. The Pope merely pointed out that the Holy Spirit does dwell in the Church and through grace in every Christian heart" (*The Wanderer,* Aug. 14, 1975).

12. When 20,000 members of the GEN ("New Generation") movement, an offshoot of the Focolarini, gathered in Rome on pilgrimage on March 2, 1975, the Pope did not hesitate to commend them explicitly by name: "It seems to us that you, the Focolarini, have faced this twofold problem—Who is he, Christ? and who is he, Christ, for us? And see, the fire of light, enthusiasm, action, love, self-giving and joy has been kindled within you, and in a new inner fullness you have understood everything: God, yourselves, your life, people, our times, the central orientation to stamp on your entire existence.
    "Yes, this is the solution, this is the key, this is the formula—genuine and everlasting and, when it is discovered, new. You have understood it, and with good reason you have defined your movement as the "New Generation," GEN!
    "So, dear young people of GEN! To meet, to know, to love, to follow Christ Jesus! This is your program" (*ORe,* March 13, 1975).

13. Cited in chapter 1 at note 38.

14. Cf. the allocution, "Live the Faith with Enthusiasm," of June 2, 1974.

15. Ronald Knox, *Enthusiasm,* Oxford, 1950.

16. On this point, see chapter 7 below.

17. This may help to explain why the Pope includes "a taste for contemplation" among the signs of spiritual renewal, both at the Grottaferrata Conference of 1973, and in his English-language allocution at the Rome Conference. Although several observers have noted this as a fruit of the baptism in the Spirit, it is far from being one of the more prominent aspects of the Charismatic Renewal. But Pope Paul perceives in it a significance that others perhaps have often overlooked. At the same time, he is doing what he can to encourage a development which, though delicate and frail, is precious.

18. With the English-speaking Charismatics (mostly Americans), the Pope stressed the sacraments and good works. With the French, he lingered more on participation in the divine life. Was this in some measure an attempt to speak to each group according to its characteristic strengths?

19. Cf. p. 33.
20. Dec. 8, 1975. Cf. p. 15.
21. Address to the College of Cardinals, Dec. 22, 1975 (*ORe,* Jan. 8, 1976).
22. The 10,000 people who took part in the Charismatic Conference had to meet in an open field; no auditorium was available that could contain them. The Mariologists who gathered in the auditorium of the Franciscan athenaeum could be counted in the hundreds, and certainly did not amount to a thousand.

# CHAPTER FIVE

# Parameters of Pope Paul's Doctrine

Before going into Pope Paul's general doctrine on the Holy Spirit, we should take note of several parameters that condition it. Otherwise we may attribute false significance to aspects of it which have little to do with him personally.

The first is that as Pope, that is, as supreme pastor (under Jesus Christ) of the Roman Catholic Church, he has not the freedom to indulge in personal theological speculation. It is his office to recall, maintain and declare the official and traditional doctrine of the Church. Hence we must not expect to find him creating an original theology. A good part of his teaching simply reiterates an ancient and familiar doctrine of grace and the divine indwelling; this is to be expected.

But this does not imply that his teaching reduces inevitably to a routine repetition of commonplaces, for two reasons. In the first place, the teaching of any pastor inevitably reflects something of his personal spirituality. Those aspects of the common doctrine which have been most meaningful to him personally will naturally receive particular emphasis, and be presented with special fire. The great example of this was Pope John XXIII, whose winsome personality irradiated all the official acts of his pontificate. He probably taught the Gospel message to more people by his personal exemplification of it than by his great and widely acclaimed encyclicals, *Pacem in Terris* and *Mater et Magistra*.

In the second place, and much more importantly, it is the very purpose of the papal office to adapt the eternal truths of the Christian message to the needs of the time. This does not imply compromising in order to curry favor; quite the contrary, it means discerning those points of the Gospel which this world most needs to hear, perhaps because they have been the most sinned against, perhaps because their particular light, nourishment and strength correspond to the needs and aspirations of the given epoch.

It is the grace of a true shepherd to discern the spiritual requirements of his flock, not merely by rational analysis of the contemporary situation, but also by the charism that comes with his office. Thus the teaching of any given Pope will have (in a measure that varies indeed with the individual, but is never wholly lacking) a genuinely prophetic character, as an interpretation of his times in the light of the Gospel.

The most remarkable modern example of this function of the papacy was Pius XII. In drawing out the implications of Catholic doctrine for the enormously complex situation of modern culture, he dealt with a vast range of matters, not only directly ecclesial topics such as the doctrine of the Mystical Body, the role of biblical scholarship, or the function of the liturgy, but also the moral implications of modern political and technological developments. Although frequently treating problems which had hardly yet been assimilated by theologians, he handled them with such sureness and insight that his many-sided, constant originality came to be taken for granted. The Church of his day, in its encounter with the new problems created by the modern world, came to rely even excessively on his leadership and judgment; and while theologians have long since reacted against the inertia which then threatened their function with atrophy, they have not yet gotten an adequate perspective on the incredible range and originality of this extraordinary Pope.

Pope Paul is more in the mold of Pius who was his mentor, than of John, who was his close personal friend. He is a teacher for our times more than a personality who marks our era. Although he does not equal Pius in range and strength of knowledge, he has a more sympathetic appreciation for the spirit of our times, and a greater flexibility and tact in communicating with it. This has not been so evident to the public, because he has been caught in a crossfire between reckless reformers and rigid reactionaries, which forced him into the ungrateful position of holding a moderate position despite violent criticism from both sides. Pius XII was able to be more peremptory and decisive in his judgments, for he spoke as head of a Church that was still firmly united in obedience under him. Paul is in a position rather like that of a wise adult in a turmoil of unruly adolescents. He affirms the traditional doctrine firmly and quietly, reiterates it when necessary, but has to wait patiently and calmly for truth to prevail. The restraint with which he has refrained from condemning those in error has disappointed many who were eager for a showdown, but it is precisely the way he has kept his cool under fire that is likely to be recognized in the long run as the mark of his greatness.

Pope Paul works at his teaching with great seriousness. This holds particularly for the talks he gives each Wednesday at public audiences. These are not perfunctory words of greeting for the pilgrims, nor documents prepared by his staff. They are the deeply pondered, carefully composed instructions of a pastor for his flock. They have aptly been called the "Catechesis of Pope Paul."[1]

No previous Pope ever made such methodical use of these audiences as a means of teaching. Pope John used to speak extemporaneously at them, rambling along amiably like a country curé among his parishioners. Pius XII gave his chief teachings through encyclicals and in allocutions to special groups (e.g., the Pontifical Academy of Sciences, Oct. 22, 1951, or the Congress of Italian Midwives, Oct. 29–30, 1951). Pope Paul is the first Pope to make serious, systematic use of the weekly audience as a means of teaching. It is no accident that during his papacy many newspapers around the world began the regular reprinting of these talks, from which the majority of the texts in the present collection are drawn.

A second parameter to be noted is the continuity of Pope Paul's teaching with that of John XXIII and the Second Vatican Council. It was Pope John who conceived and summoned the Council. Paul, after presiding over the last three sessions, has been largely occupied with the implementation of the conciliar decrees. He frequently represents his work as that of carrying out the mandate of the Council. In looking back over the first eight years of his pontificate, he declared:

> We have taken up with determined fidelity the program
> bequeathed to us by the ... Council. This has determined
> and qualified the principal aspects of our pontificate.[2]

Moreover, it was Pope John who first prayed for a "new Pentecost," and who drew attention to the "signs of the times," two themes that Paul has pursued.[3]

On the other hand, the work of the Council cannot be conceived as distinct from that of Pope Paul, since he had a major hand in shaping it. As Cardinal Montini, he was one of the most important personages in the planning of the Council.[4] As Pope, he presided over the last three sessions, which were precisely those in which the doctrine of the Spirit received so much attention.[5] That he contributed notably to drawing attention to the Holy Spirit is evident from his addresses to the Council, particularly that of Sept. 14, 1964, opening the Third Session.[6]

It is, therefore, not easy to distinguish between Paul's personal contribution, and the heritage he received from John XXIII and Vatican II. But little is to be gained by belaboring such a distinction. We will point out, where possible, whatever is distinctively Pauline; but his whole teaching will be presented, whether inherited or original.

A third parameter lies in the fact that a large part of Paul's teaching on the Holy Spirit occurs in talks given on or near the feast of Pentecost. (Hence the preponderance of selections from the month of May and June in the present collection.) Since in these cases, it was the liturgical season that suggested or even imposed the theme, it would be a mistake to take all these talks as indicative of a spontaneous personal devotion. However, when due allowance is made for this fact, the texts themselves provide abundant evidence, as we have already seen, of Paul's personal concern with the Holy Spirit. Moreover, some of his most important statements were made on occasions which had nothing to do with Pentecostal liturgy.[7]

A fourth parameter has to do with the idiom in which Pope Paul expresses himself. The theology in which he was trained as a seminarian conceived the Christian life in terms of the soul's participation by grace in the divine life mediated by Christ. This pattern of thought tended to polarize around Christ and (created) grace, with little attention to the Holy Spirit. It was the result of a long, complex series of historical factors, notably the Church's laborious defense of the Divinity of Christ (against Arianism), of the necessity of grace (against Pelagianism), and of the reality of created grace (against Protestantism). Scholastic theology, which took form in the course of this process, adopted a vocabulary in which the term *grace* was referred primarily to the work of God in the human soul, rather than to the merciful love that is in God himself, which is its predominant (though by no means exclusive!) reference in the bible.

In the last few decades, however, Catholic theologians have tended to react against this pattern of thought out of several quite disparate motives. Some have a radical distaste for the philosophical precision and abstraction of the scholasticism, which they regard as dead and uninspiring. Some seek to return to a more biblical vocabulary. Some want to insist more on the person and action of the Holy Spirit. For all these reasons the term *state of grace,* in particular, has been denounced as unbiblical, impersonal and static.

In this matter, as in others, Pope Paul's policy has been one of intelligent, discriminating moderation. Like most priests of his generation he is used to thinking in Christological more than in pneumatological terms. That may not be apparent in the present selection of texts, which is focused on the theme of the Holy Spirit; but it is evident to anyone who reads a representative cross-section of his talks, addresses and letters. Likewise, he tends to think more in terms of created than uncreated grace. But these facts, which are to be expected, given his theological background, only increase the significance of the stress he lays on the personal presence and action of the Holy Spirit. On this point he has deliberately and wholeheartedly embraced the basic movement of modern theology.

He retains, however, the scholastic vocabulary. This is not just the result of his seminary training, but is a considered policy. Pope Paul is a convinced admirer of St. Thomas Aquinas, whose work he praises on every convenient occasion.[8] He has also repeatedly expressed his esteem for precision, order, firmness and rationality in theology[9]—the qualities characteristic of scholastic thought. (At the same time, he is, like the great scholastics, deeply and constantly aware of the suprarational transcendence of the divine mysteries.)

Paul's policy, which can be detected throughout his statements, is to maintain communication between these two modes of thought and styles of vocabulary. Thus, we find him repeatedly declaring that the state of grace is nothing other than the breath and action of the Holy Spirit (e.g., Oct. 12, 1966), and that the chief effect of the Holy Spirit is grace (Oct. 16, 1974). More synthetically, he gives the following description:

> Grace, that is to say, a gift *par excellence,* charity, the Father's love communicated to us in virtue of the redemption effected by Christ in the Holy Spirit... (Oct. 16, 1974).

His characteristic stance is that of welcoming new emphases, while firmly recalling that they do not displace the old:

> We call this central chapter of our religion "Christology." At present other chapters such as the one on "Ecclesiology" (so much studied by the Council) and the one on "Pneumatology," that is, concerning the doctrine on the Holy Spirit, claim our study and our spiritual life. But do not let us close the volume of our doctrine on Christ the Lord, as if he were already well known to each of us. We must open this volume again; we must always keep it open before us, for our attentive reflection and passionate contemplation. "For me to live is Christ," St. Paul says (Phil 1:21).[10]

Pope Paul is notorious for being a man of "but's" and "howevers." After presenting one side of a matter, he usually counterbalances it with others. The brief, popular statements to which his public audiences are necessarily confined are forever being brought up short by the wistful admonition that so much more would need to be said to put the matter in perspective. This trait has led journalists to speak of him, even before his election to the papacy, as a Hamlet figure.[11] They often attribute this to his intellectual temperament which never allows him to get so engrossed in one aspect of a matter as to lose sight of others. But those who lightly blame him for indecision are perhaps not sufficiently aware of the complexity of bearing pastoral responsibility for the entire Catholic Church. He has to be loyal to an ancient tradition, of which he is the preeminent witness and guardian, while keeping open to the valid insights of secular culture and the actual breath of the Spirit in the community of the faithful. In speaking to any particular issue, he is obliged to take into consideration the interpretation likely to be placed on his words by someone coming to them with entirely different preoccupations. In a Church polarized with tensions and torn by disagreements more than at any time since the Reformation, and in an atmosphere even more confused (because of its greater diversity) than that of the 16th century, Paul is called to be the sign of unity, and to give to each of many clamoring voices the attention which is its due.

As a consequence, the goal of his policies in most areas has been that of keeping balance: between the vertical and the horizontal, between the personal and the ecclesial or social, between communion with Christ and communion with one's fellows, between structure and inspiration, law and freedom, etc. This effort to maintain a balance has the effect of dulling the impact of many of his statements, and obscuring the main point he intends to make. And it is a trait to be borne in mind by anyone pondering the way his warm recommendations of charismatic fervor are tempered by a cautious warning against excess or illusion.

Paul's gift of analyzing the complex makes possible a strategy that is characteristic of him when dealing with positions at variance with his own. Instead of denouncing their errors, he tries to pick out all the good he sees in them and stress his accord with that. He can be seen doing this in the most diverse situations: with the turbulent movements of modern youth and the wise old schemers of the United Nations; with sporting clubs and feminist leaders; with Hindu yogis and Orthodox patriarchs. He is adroit at discerning the hidden motivations and authentic aspirations of very confused movements, and pointing out their correspondence with the Gospel of Christ. We have seen an example of this in regard to currents of mysticism among modern youth.[12]

The usual tone of Pope Paul's teachings is somewhat stiff, complex and academic. Even his frequent exhortations are expressed in the language of an intellectual more adept at defining emotions or analyzing the reasons for them, than at arousing them. Nevertheless, there is a perpetual flame in Pope Paul, ready to flare out and render incandescent a line or two that reveals a heart throbbing with life and uttering itself in all earnestness. At times it attains the beauty of pure poetry or the finest eloquence. Even more often, there is a flash of fresh insight, revealing, beneath, behind the conventional language, a mind at work in real and understanding touch with reality.[13]

## NOTES

1. Cf. "Paul VI's Catechesis, a Bishop's Reflection," by L. M. Neves (*ORe*, Jan. 26, 1978). At the General Audience of Dec. 29, 1967, Paul himself declared:

   "This general audience ... is becoming more and more an important, almost a preponderant part of our Apostolic Ministry." (*The Teachings of Pope Paul*, vol. 1, Vatican City, 1969.) See also the remarks of his close personal friend, Jean Guitton (*ORe*, March 20, 1975).

2. Angelus message of June 20, 1971 (*ORe*, June 24, 1971).

3. Cf. chapter 1. Pope John first drew attention to the "signs of the times" in the bull convoking the Council, *Humanae Salutis* (Dec. 21, 1961).

4. He belonged to the Central Preparatory Committee and the Technical Organizing Committee. In these capacities, he was often consulted by Pope John, who even invited him to reside at the Vatican, a privilege extended to no other Council Father. During the First Session, he was appointed to the Secretariat for Extraordinary Affairs, a post that seems to have been meant precisely to give him the opportunity to play an important role in the decisions that gave overall direction to the Council's work.

5. Cf. chapter 1, notes 19–21.

6. A citation from this address is given in Part II.

7. Thus, for example, Sept. 14, 1964; Oct. 12, 1966; Oct. 26, 1967; Nov. 29, 1972; Feb. 21 and 28, 1973; Sept. 17, 1973, etc.

8. On the seventh centenary of the death of St. Thomas, Pope Paul wrote: "The Church has commended him (i.e., St. Thomas) in the past, and continues to do so in the present, to our contemporaries as the master of the art of reasoning, as we ourself have styled him, and as a guide in establishing the relations between philosophical and theological problems, and, it may be added, by setting in due and fitting order all that belongs to higher and recondite knowledge." Letter to Vincent de Couesnongle, the Master General of the Order of Friars Preachers, Nov. 20, 1974 (*ORe*, Jan. 30, 1975). Cf. also Pope Paul's address at the International Thomistic Congress (*OR*, April 22–23, 1974), and his address to the Capitular Fathers of the Dominican Order, Sept. 21, 1974 (*ORe*, Oct. 3, 1974). Numerous other statements and examples of the Pope's stand could be cited.

9. Cf. May 23, 1973; Nov. 14, 1973 (*OR*, Nov. 15, 1973; *ORe*, Nov. 22, 1973).

10. General Audience of Feb. 13, 1974 (*OR*, Feb. 14, 1974; *ORe*, Feb. 21, 1974).

11. While he was Archbishop of Milan, the newspapers carried the story that Pope John once greeted some visitors from Milan by asking "How is your Hamlet cardinal?" William Barrett, who recalls this in his biography of Pope Paul, *Shepherd of Mankind*, (New York, Doubleday, p. 261), doubts that Pope John would actually have said this. At any rate, the name was in the air.

12. Cf. chapter 3, at note 18.

13. One of the problems with which the present book has had to grapple has been that of extracting the nuggets of precious metal from the strata of less interesting material in which they are imbedded. It is necessary to do this to get people to read Pope Paul; but it has not been possible, and would not be desirable, to confine our excerpts to the nuggets, if we are to see them in context, and to have some idea of the full range and usual tone of Pope Paul's teaching on the Holy Spirit.

# CHAPTER SIX

# The Spirit and the Individual Christian

As Pope Paul is much more concerned with the Spirit's relationship to the Church than to the individual, and as his treatment of the latter subject, although rich, is for the most part quite classical, we can afford to summarize it briefly.[1] Sometimes he is content to recall the traditional categories of scholastic theology: grace, virtues, gifts and fruits.[2] Usually, however, even in such cases, these categories are presented or retouched in a way that gives the passage a recognizably personal stamp, as in the following text which could be taken as a lively summary of Leo XIII's encyclical on the Holy Spirit. After distinguishing two fields of the Spirit's operation, the individual soul and the Church, Paul says:

> The first is the field of the individual soul, our inward life, our spiritual being, our person, which is also our self or ego, that profound cell of our own existence which is mysterious even to our own minds. The Holy Spirit's breath enters there, and spreads in the soul with that first and supreme charism which we call grace, and is like a new life. This immediately makes the soul capable of acts that surpass its natural abilities; that is to say, it confers supernatural powers or virtues upon it. Grace spreads through the network of human psychology with gentle but powerful action, the impulses of which we call gifts. It fills the soul with wonderful spiritual effects, which we call fruits of the Spirit, the first of which are joy and peace. (May 25, 1969. Similar texts at May 18, 1967, May 17, 1972 and Feb. 28, 1973).

*Grace* here refers primarily to "sanctifying" or "habitual" grace, the radical and fundamental sanctification of the soul that is a genuine participation in the divine nature (cf. 2 Pt 1:4) imparted gratuitously by the Holy Spirit to those who are open to receive him. It implies "*actual graces*" also. Taken for granted here, but mentioned in other texts, they include every form of activity by which the Holy Spirit enlightens, inspires, strengthens, moves or consoles a creature. *Virtues* are perfections of the faculties. While man can develop many virtues simply by right living, there are supernatural virtues which can only be infused by the Holy Spirit, and which are necessary to enable a person to act in a way proportionate to his Christian calling. The most important of these are faith, hope and charity, the "theological virtues," which constitute the essential axes of the Christian life in the Spirit. The term *gifts,* as used in this text, does not embrace everything that man receives from the Spirit, nor does it refer to the "charisms" (often today called "spiritual gifts") of 1 Corinthians 12:8-11. It is used in a technical sense for a set of qualities, the traditional *Sacrum Septenarium* of wisdom, understanding knowledge, fortitude, counsel, piety and fear of the Lord,[3] the distinctive characteristic of which is to make a person sensitive and amenable to the action of the Holy Spirit (May 18, 1975). This is what the above text refers to by the elliptical expression, "action, the impulses of which we call gifts." The *fruits of the Spirit,* so-called from Galatians 5:22, are traditionally conceived as activity arising from the exercise of the seven gifts—in other words, the activity of one who is moved and led by the Spirit (Rom 8:14). The charisms mentioned in I Corinthians 12:7-11 are called, in scholastic language, "gratuitous graces," as distinct from "sanctifying graces," as Pope Paul points out in another text (Oct. 16, 1974). The significance of their omission from the present list will be discussed below; for the moment, it is enough to note that this list is not intended to be exhaustive.

Paul does not find these "scholastic categories" lifeless. He introduced them with the statement that "one of the most mysterious and wonderful pages of our catechism is that which concerns the communication of the Holy Spirit to the faithful" (May 18, 1967).

Nevertheless, he generally prefers to present the activity of the Holy Spirit by a text of Vatican II that is less scholastic but more richly biblical.[4] In his weekly audiences, he repeatedly cites this passage in full, or in part.[5]

But Paul is not content merely to cite general lists of the works of the Spirit which he finds ready made. At times he composes original summaries of his own. Thus:

> Let us remember only that it is God's Spirit of Love who instills a new awareness, an insuperable energy and a lively joy into each and every one of the 120 people gathered in the Cenacle (May 21, 1972).[6]

Other effects of the Spirit on which occasional stress is laid are faith,[7] prayer and joy. Out of the Pope's abundant teaching on the interior life, we may note in particular the statement that the Spirit is the source of all prayer, from the most basic to the most mystical (May 18, 1967).

Joy (often associated with peace)[8] is a favorite topic with Pope Paul.[9] He likes to meditate on the term *alleluia,* the biblical expression of joy.[10] He composed a lengthy exhortation[11] "to remind all of us that if we are really Christians and Catholics, we must be immersed in an ever new and ever true joy, the joy that comes to us from the grace of the Holy Spirit. . . ."[12] If joy is necessary to all men of all ages, it is particularly needed in our era of technological triumphs and jaded hearts. Hence Paul dwells on Christmas joy, Easter joy, and Pentecostal joy. While open to all the natural joys of creation, this joy is properly Christian, and rooted in all the great Christian mysteries. But it is not merely the result of our awareness of the things the Lord has done; it is the joy of Christ communicated to us by his Spirit who has been given to us.

The effect of the Spirit which Pope Paul seems to stress with greatest predilection is that of making the mystery of Christ live in us, and teaching us to *know* Christ with an intimate and fruitful knowledge.

> The gifts of the Spirit are many, but they always grant us a taste of that true and intimate knowledge of the Lord (June 29, 1971).[13]

Another effect often cited is the twofold *witness* brought about by the Spirit in us, one interior and one exterior. The Spirit himself bears witness with our spirits that we are children of God; we in turn are impelled by the Spirit to bear witness to Christ:

> May God will that we today (and tomorrow, as we remember this blessed day) may have some deep spiritual fullness, some stirring from that inward testimony that assures us that we are God's adopted children (cf. Rom 8:16), and speaks inwardly to us to enable us to give our own evidence in favor of Christ (cf. Jn 15:26–27). (May 25, 1969.)[14]

The exterior witness that every Christian ought to bear to Christ is a pressing concern of the Holy Father;[15] but he sees it as rooted in the inner witness of which the Christian himself should first have had experience.

Finally, it must be noted that vocations to the priesthood and religious life are effects of the Holy Spirit[16] (May 5, 1974). In a moving prayer for newly ordained priests, the Holy Father prays to the Spirit to give them a new heart, a pure heart, a great heart (May 17, 1970).

Even though the various gifts, fruits and graces of the Spirit come to man as a benefaction that he does not deserve and cannot merit, still the Pope insists, there is much that man can and must do to prepare himself for the Spirit's action.

> We must at least open the window to let in the breath and light of the Spirit.
>
> . . .
>
> Anyone who does not have a spiritual life of his own lacks the ordinary capacity to receive the Holy Spirit, to listen to his soft, sweet voice, to experience his inspirations, to possess his charisms (June 6, 1973).

This preparation involves first of all "cultivation of a pure conscience" (May 25, 1969). Paul does not, of course, mean that one can free himself of sin prior to receiving the Holy Spirit; but rather that "in our jealous guarding of the state of grace" (March 26, 1969), which is the basic work of the Spirit in us, we do our part to cooperate with him and prepare ourselves for further gifts.

> Show him hospitality by jealously preserving that presence which he bestows on souls in the state of grace (May 9, 1975).

The Pope is well aware that such language has an old-fashioned tone, but that does not deter him. On the contrary, with a firm pastoral sense of the importance of the issue, he counterattacks:

> Grace is the communion of the divine life in us; why is it so little spoken of today? Why do so many seem to take no note of it? They seem more eager to delude themselves about the lawfulness of every forbidden experience, and to blot out of themselves the sense of sin, than they are to protect the inner witness of the Holy Spirit (Jn 15:26) in their own consciences (March 26, 1969).

Secondly, we prepare ourselves for the gifts of the Spirit by interior or spiritual life, described as one of "recollection, silence, meditation, absorbing of God's word and spiritual exercises" (Oct. 12, 1966).

Here, too, the Pope recognizes "with sorrow and amazement," that even "some beloved sons of the Church . . . act as if the interior life were an outgrown phase, a pedagogy no longer needed for a Christian life" (Oct. 12, 1966). But he insists that "the appointment for the meeting with the ineffable Guest is fixed inside the soul," i.e., in the "cultivation of interior life" (May 17, 1972; Oct. 12, 1966).

The principal element of the interior life is prayer, a subject on which Pope Paul is eloquent:

> One question arises before all others: in these times, does man pray? Where the Church is alive, he does.
>
> Prayer is the breath of the mystical Body, its conversation with God, the expression of its love and of its striving toward the Father. Prayer is recognizing his Providence in the dynamic of world events, it is imploring his mercy and aid in our weakness, it is confessing the necessity of his being and acknowledging his glory. Prayer is the joy of the People of God at being able to sing hymns to him and to celebrate everything that comes to us from him. Prayer is the school of Christian life.
>
> In other words, prayer is a flower that springs from two deep and vital roots: the religious sense, which is its natural root, and the grace of the Holy Spirit, the supernatural root. From these it gets its life.[17] One may say that prayer is the highest expression of the Church; but it is equally its nourishment and basic principle. Prayer is the classical moment in which divine life begins to stir in the Church.

The allusion to Romans 8:26 ("we do not know how to pray as we ought, but the Spirit himself intercedes for us with sighs too deep for words") appears very often in Pope Paul's treatment of prayer.

The second element of interior life stressed by the Pope is silence. Although a constant requirement of spirituality, it needs to be emphasized particularly today because of the psychological noisiness and extroversion of modern man: who, going out of himself, lost the key needed in order to return (May 18, 1975):

> Today our psychology is turned outwards too much. The exterior scene is so absorbing that our attention is mainly directed outside; we are nearly always absent from our personal abode. We are unable to meditate or to pray. We cannot silence the hubbub inside, due to outside interests, images, passions. There is no quiet, holy space in the heart for the flame of Pentecost (May 17, 1972; cp. June 6, 1973).

The practical conclusion follows:

> ... Each of us must reserve for himself moments of silence—exterior silence indeed, but particularly interior silence. Silence to reanimate the dialogue with ourselves, that is, with our personal consciousness.[18] This will be an act of personal liberation, even if only momentary. In it, other voices will make themselves heard—the very voices of silence. Among them, the voice of the interior Teacher himself will perhaps not be lacking. This is the Spirit who works in the secret recesses of the soul. Perhaps also we will

feel ourselves impelled to give inner expression to an original and enchanting voice of ours—the prayer of the heart. In this, too, Mary will be our teacher.[19]

In stressing the need for silence, the Pope certainly does not mean to exclude vocal prayer. A remarkable conference on how to meditate on Easter begins with the recommendation of silence, which may even become mystical. But because silence is not easy for everyone, the Pope points to another way that is "easier, more common, and perfectly legitimate," particularly when this feast has been duly prepared and shared. This is called "the experience of a great wave of exultation"; but it is one that the soul itself can arouse by meditation on the "dimension of Christ's love." It expresses itself in song, and in the praise of God's wonderful works, like Mary's *Magnificat;* but all of its joy, emotion and love can be condensed in the ancient biblical cry, "Alleluia" ("Praise the Lord"). This text of April 2, 1975, reads almost as though the Holy Father had a charismatic prayer meeting in mind as he wrote.

Interior life and purity of conscience pertain to what Pope Paul speaks of as "the arena of the heart" (June 6, 1973). But there is another arena of the Spirit's action which also requires its proper preparation in order that a person be open and available to the "mysterious action of the Spirit." This is the arena of *"communio,"* i.e., sincere union with our brethren and most especially with our pastors in the Church:

> . . . *communio,* that is, the society of brothers united by faith and charity in one divine-human organism, the Mystical Body of Christ. It is the Church. It means adherence to that Mystical Body, animated by the Holy Spirit, who has his Pentecostal upper room in the community of the faithful, hierarchically united, authentically assembled in the name and the authority of the Apostles.

> So we might well consider whether certain ways of seeking the Spirit, which prefer to isolate themselves in order to escape from both the directive ministry of the Church and from the impersonal crowd of unknown brethren, are on the right path. What spirit could be encountered by a selfish communion, one that arises out of flight from the true communion of ecclesial charity? What experiences or what charisms could make up for the lack of unity and of the supreme encounter with God? (June 6, 1973).

This teaching on communion with the Church will be elaborated in the following chapter.

Preparation for the action of the Spirit is, therefore, a major theme of Pope Paul's teaching on spiritual renewal. His entire pontificate could legitimately be viewed as a many-sided effort to bring about such preparation in the Church. He often calls attention to the "novena" between the Ascension and Pentecost as the classical moment in which Mary, the Apostles, and the first disciples were prepared for the coming of the Spirit (May 18, 1966; May 17, 1972. . .).

At the same time, however, he is careful to point out that the Spirit who "breathes where he wills," can dispense with this preparation and bestow his generosity where nothing seemed ready for it (May 17, 1972). He cites the astounding example of the abrupt conversion of the young socialist, Andre Frossard, whose autobiographical sketch created a religious sensation in France (Feb. 21, 1973).[20] Nevertheless, the Pope maintains that such an exception simply shows the sovereign freedom of a merciful God; it does not exempt us from the ordinary requirement of doing what is in our power to prepare to receive the outpouring of God's Spirit (May 17, 1972).

At the beginning of this chapter, we noted that the address of May 25, 1969, which surveys the work of the Holy Spirit in the individual Christian, makes no mention of the charisms. The same is true of three parallel texts referred to there in parentheses. This leads us to the general observation that Pope Paul has very little to say about the charisms of I Corinthians 12, i.e., tongues, prophecy, interpretation, and the like. The only one of these charisms about which he seems to have much to say is discernment—and he treats that, not so much as a charism, but as a function of bishops and spiritual directors in discriminating among the inspirations received by those entrusted to their care.[21]

This absence of a doctrine on the charisms is somewhat concealed by the fluidity of language in this area. One might suppose that the mention of "gifts of the Spirit" is meant to include the charisms, and possibly it does. However, as was explained above, in the usual language of the Pope, the "gifts" are the traditional *Sacrum Septenarium*. When referring specifically to the charisms of 1 Corinthians 12, Paul ordinarily uses the term *charism,* or else the scholastic expression, *gratiae gratis datae* ("gratuitous graces").

Conversely, like many other authors today, he frequently uses the terms *charism* or *charismatic* without any special reference to the "manifestations of the Spirit" cited in 1 Corinthians. Thus, farther on in the address of May 25, 1969, he says that concern for the interior life is "the mark of anyone who wishes to be led by the Spirit . . . and to benefit from charismatic inspiration." The term *charismatic* here does not refer to the Corinthian charisms, but simply to the free promptings of the Holy Spirit that are usually associated with the Sevenfold Gifts. In sum, despite his rich teaching on the workings and inspiration of the Holy Spirit in general, and his free use of the term *charismatic,* Pope Paul really has very little to say about the charisms in the narrower sense to which attention has been drawn today by the Charismatic Renewal.

As it is a principle established in Catholic theology since patristic times,[22] that charisms in this sense are not given for the sanctification of the recipient, but for the service of the Church, one might object that it is in the latter context, rather than here, that we should expect to find Paul's teaching on the charisms. Indeed this is the case; nevertheless, as will be seen in the next chapter, even there his references to the charisms are very brief and general.

The chief reason for this seems to be the fact that the Church has had relatively little experience with the charisms since the early centuries. Of course, there have been many charismatic saints; and unlike the Protestant denominations, which for the most part denied any ongoing role of the charisms in the Church, Catholicism has always acknowledged them, and has assigned them a place in the theory of grace. But as the preternatural charisms of 1 Corinthians have played little role in the ordinary, public life of the Church, theologians have not paid much attention to them.[23] Even the modern tendency, spearheaded by Karl Rahner and Hans Küng,[24] to insist that the charisms are an essential aspect of Church life, usually insists on ordinary, non-spectacular, non-preternatural charisms, and so in effect continues the neglect of those listed in 1 Corinthians. On the other hand, the great spiritual masters, such as St. John of the Cross, writing from the perspective of the spiritual life of the individual, have tended to stress the fact that extraordinary manifestations are not essential to sanctity, and ought not to be sought after or made much of for their own sake.

The teaching of Pope Paul is simply continuing this theological tradition which no doubt needs to be supplemented by a richer and more concrete doctrine on the charisms for our "charismatic" age. However, the essential wisdom of this tradition has not lost its validity today; in fact, charismatic movements make its message all the more urgently needed. This message is that the charisms are of secondary importance compared to the primary and fundamental work of the Holy Spirit, which is the sanctification of the soul by grace and solid virtue, accompanied by the gifts and fruits of the Spirit. It is on a level far deeper than the charisms that the Spirit renews the Church. This message, which can be regarded as a part of Pope Paul's response to the challenge of the Charismatic Renewal, is providential, both for the Church at large, and for the Charismatic Renewal itself.

That being recognized, we must also acknowledge that Pope Paul, like so many other pastors, had formed his ministerial habits and methods in a relatively non-charismatic Church. By that I do not mean a Church devoid of charismatic activity, but one in which a pastor would not ordinarily expect to find his ministry complemented by the work of prophets, healers, glossolalics, and the like. The surprising abundance of these charisms today suggests that they may once again become part of the ordinary dynamics of Church life, as they have not been since the first century. This does not imply a change in the essence of the Church, but it does considerably alter the tone or style of pastoral ministry. A man whose ways of thinking and operating were already formed and consolidated would not be expected to embrace such a change lightly. Paul VI was 70 years old, and 47 years a priest, when the Charismatic Renewal first made its appearance in the Catholic Church. And it is to be remembered that his personal ministry had been a highly successful one—not only in the curial offices of the Vatican, but also in caring for university students during the tumultuous years of the Mussolini era. The slightness of his treatment of the charisms is probably due largely to the simple fact that he, like nearly all other pastors of his time, had not had occasion to take them much into account. His own practical wisdom would naturally make him dubious about an enthusiastic movement that was sometimes presented as a panacea. The fact that he did not reject it outright is a tribute both to his openness of mind, and to his faithfulness to the doctrine which it is his office to expound with the impersonal detachment of a steward.

But if he speaks as one little used to the Corinthian charisms, has he a message for a movement that is imbued with them? If Pope Paul has not the gifts of tongues or prophecy or healing, can he be a pastor and teacher for those who do? This question touches on one of the deepest principles of Catholic ecclesiology, and has implications which regard not only the Pope, but everyone ordained to an office in the Church. Furthermore, whether or not the Charismatic Renewal can be wholeheartedly Catholic hinges on the answer to it. The shepherds of the Church, if they are going to be real men, will always be bound by limitations coming from their peculiar temperament, culture and experience, to say nothing of their personal flaws and graces. Nevertheless, by the grace of Christ they are appointed shepherds for the entire flock committed to them, not just for those who share their limitations. Paul VI may not have much to say about certain charisms (the workings of which can only be learned experientially); but on matters which he does treat, he speaks as the Vicar of Christ and the authentic interpreter of his Gospel.

Moreover, the charisms of 1 Corinthians are only a small part of the Gospel message. Even in the New Testament, little attention is paid to them. For their own well being, they need to be exercised in the context of the great and deep principles of Christian spirituality, about which Paul VI is a true master. He may not be able to say, like his patron, St. Paul: "I speak in tongues more than any of you" (1 Cor 14:18). He is, however, competent and does in fact teach, like St. Paul, that "still more excellent way"—the way of love that never ends, whereas tongues will cease and prophecies and knowledge will pass away (1 Cor 12:31; 13:8).

## NOTES

1. For a general survey of the Spirit's action in the individual as well as in the Church, see the address of May 26, 1971.
2. Beatitudes, once a stock part of this enumeration, but not so any longer, are seldom mentioned by the Holy Father in this context.
3. This list, which originated from Isaiah 11:1–2, has given rise to a rich doctrine on the gifts of the Spirit in Catholic tradition. Cf. Edward Leen, *The Holy Ghost and His Work in Souls* (New York, Sheed and Ward, 1939) and my own *The Gifts of the Spirit* (McGraw-Hill, 1975). Pope Paul enumerates them in his homily of April 26, 1964.
4. Vatican II, *The Church*, #4.
5. See, for example, May 18, 1966; Oct. 12, 1966; May 18, 1967.
6. Sept. 14, 1964: "Inspiration, Life and Grace."
   June 6, 1965: "...the mystery of nearness, of indwelling, of friendship, of spiritual intimacy, of interior inspiration, of sweetness and strength, of peace and joy which the Holy Spirit grants to souls through grace."
   May 17, 1970: "Wisdom and charity, consolation, joy, hope and holiness."
   May 24, 1972: "His presence, strength and grace."
   See also the texts of June 6, 1961; May 20, 1964; May 18, 1966; May 26, 1971.
7. Cf. May 26, 1968; April 8, 1970. On May 23, 1973, Paul spoke of the Spirit as the suprarational source of light we need.
8. May 18, 1967; May 21, 1972.
9. April 26, 1964; Sept. 14, 1964; April 25, 1970.
10. E.g., April 2, 1975.
11. The Apostolic Exhortation, *Gaudete in Domino,* from which excerpts are given below, under the date, May 9, 1975.
12. Address to a General Audience, May 21, 1975 (*OR,* May 23, 1975; *ORe,* May 29, 1975).
13. This passage is not included in the excerpt given in Part II.
    Cf. June 6, 1965; Oct. 26, 1967; Sept. 9, 1970. Note also inner fullness (Nov. 29, 1972) and interior contact with God (Sept. 9, 1970).
14. See also Oct. 12, 1966; May 26, 1968; May 25, 1969. On the inner witness see May 26, 1968. The fact that many "Christians" are not properly aware of their apostolic calling "indicates that the power of Pentecost has yet to be understood

and experienced as it was at the beginning of Christianity." General Audience, May 24, 1972 (*OR*, May 25, 1972; *ORe*, June 1, 1972).

15. Cf. Oct. 26, 1967.

16. Cf. Message for "Vocation Day," Feb. 15, 1974 (*OR*, April 28, 1974; *ORe*, May 9, 1974).

17. Cf. Romans 8, 26; H. Brémond, *Int. à la phil. de la prière*, p. 244, etc.

18. *Conscienza*. The English equivalent of this term is *conscience*, which usage has restricted to the "moral conscience"—that inner sense or voice that commends us when we do right and chides us when we do wrong. Pope Paul follows the Italian usage, in which *conscienza* designates a person's total consciousness or awareness, that inner domain in which he situates himself and all else that comes into his consideration. There seems to be no suitable English equivalent for this; consciousness comes as near as any, although it is admittedly awkward.

19. From the *Regina Coeli* message of May 20, 1976 (*OR*, June 10, 1976). Cf. May 17, 1972.

20. *Dieu existe. Je l'ai rencontré*, by André Frossard, Paris, Fayard, 1969. English translation, *I Have Met Him: God Exists*, New York, Herder and Herder, 1971.

21. On the subject of discernment, see especially the Grottaferrata address (Oct. 10, 1973) and the main address to the Rome Conference (May 19, 1975, I). Also interesting is the following observation about recognizing religious vocations: "It is a matter of receiving the deeply mysterious signals of the Holy Spirit. It is not easy. One must be initiated in a technique (excuse the expression) for the reading of hearts; that is, one must have '*discretio spirituum,*' the discernment of spiritual phenomenology. To use a term which is relevant today, a psychoanalyst of the Gospel is needed. We would even add, there is need of a charism (cf. 1 Cor 12,10)." From a message for "Vocation Day," dated Feb. 15, 1974, but released on April 27 (*OR*, April 28, 1974; *ORe*, May 9, 1974).

22. Cf. Appendix 2 of St. Thomas Aquinas, *The Gifts of the Spirit*, Blackfriars, 1974.

23. On this point, St. Thomas Aquinas is a remarkable exception. Cf. his *Summa Theologiae*, I–II, III and II–II, 171–178.

24. Besides the works of these theologians cited in chapter 2, see the survey of this topic in "The New Theology of Charisms in the Church," *American Ecclesiastical Review* 161/3 (Sept., 1969), 145 ff.

# CHAPTER SEVEN

# The Spirit and the Church

One of the most striking features of Pope Paul's doctrine on the Holy Spirit is his insistence on relating the Spirit to the Church. When discussing the Church, he seldom goes very far without bringing in the Holy Spirit, without whom the Church is, for him, inconceivable. But the converse is more surprising: when speaking of the Holy Spirit, almost inevitably, in season and out of season, he adds the reminder that the ordinary way of access to him is through the Church, and that to receive the Spirit, one must be attached to the Church.

We have already seen part of the reason for this. The Church is under assault from many sides, not only from without but also from within. The domestic critics often appeal to the Holy Spirit as their justification. We have examined the Pope's appraisal of their position in chapter 2.

However, it would be misleading to imagine that his emphasis is due solely to this situation. Paul has long had a lively personal interest in the doctrine of the Church, which, combined with his deep devotion to the Holy Spirit, naturally inclines him to pay attention to the connection between the two. He calls ecclesiology "the most attractive chapter of modern theology."[1] In this, he is quite in accord with the movement of his times. As the patristic era was concerned above all with the Trinity and the Incarnation, and the Reformation era with grace, the present era, not only among Catholics, but among the Protestants and Orthodox also, is interested in the Church. The age that began with Johann-Adam Moehler (1796–1838) and Cardinal Newman (1801–1890), was carried on by Mersch and Mura, and peaked around the time of Vatican II with Journet, Congar, Cerfaux, de Lubac, Rahner and Schillebeeckx, followed by an innumerable host of epigones, has been the most creative in the history of systematic ecclesiology.

At Vatican II itself, the Church was the principal topic of deliberations, the reference point of nearly all other topics, and the subject of the Council's greatest document. While the Council was still only in preparation, Cardinal Montini declared that "what everybody is most eager to know is what the Council will say about the Church itself."[2] As member of the Central Commission, and of the Secretariat for Extraordinary Affairs, he had an influential role in seeing that this actually came about. In one of the rare interventions he made during the First Session, he joined Cardinal Suenens and numerous others in advocating a thorough revision of the original schema *De Ecclesia.* Bishop De Smedt of Bruges had criticized the schema for "triumphalism, clericalism and juridicism."[3] Montini recommended that the schema be made to speak more clearly of the Church's utter dependence on Jesus Christ for its life and activity, and of the mystical and moral life of the Church, which constitute its life properly so-called.[4] Cardinal Deopfner later declared that this and other acts of Cardinal Montini during this last week of the First Session had decisively influenced the subsequent trend of the Council.[5]

As newly elected Pope, Paul opened the Second Session of the Council with the declaration that the Church had a "desire, need and duty to give a more thorough definition of itself," not perhaps in a dogmatic definition, but in a declaration which would be an explicit and authoritative proclamation of the Church's self-understanding. This he presented as the chief reason for the convocation of the Council. He added:

> The Church's understanding of itself grows clearer as it adheres with constant obedience to the words of Christ, reverences and embraces the proven teaching of Sacred Tradition, and conforms to the inner light of the Holy Spirit, who seems to be summoning the Church today to make every effort to be recognized by men for what it really is.[6]

Paul's first encyclical Letter, *Ecclesiam Suam,* which appeared a year later (Aug. 6, 1964), was devoted to the subject of the Church.

Two themes dominate the Pope's teaching on the connection between the Church and the Spirit; the action of the Spirit animating the Church, and the role of the Church as the ordinary locale and instrument of the Spirit's action. These themes will reappear in diverse relationships as we examine the various aspects of the Church treated by Paul: the Church as a mystery, a communion, an organic society, the body and bride of Christ, and the temple and vehicle of the Holy Spirit.

## THE CHURCH, A MYSTERY

The Church is not just an association of Christ's disciples; it is a profoundly mysterious reality, existing on two planes, visible and invisible, with the visible factors serving as signs and instruments of the invisible: "a single reality, resulting from two elements, one human and one divine, analogous to the mystery of the Incarnate Word."[7] It cannot be understood merely in terms of rites, dogmas and laws—those elements that can be appraised by the anthropologist. The core of its meaning, and that which gives the ultimate rationale and criterion for all the externals in the Church, is its invisible Spirit. This was one of the main burdens of a lengthy address to a meeting of the Church's canon lawyers, which declared, among other things:

> In reality, the "Spirit" and "Law," in their very source, form a union in which the spiritual element is determinant . . . any activity of the Church must be such as to manifest and promote spiritual life. What is said of any other external activity of the Church applies also to Canon Law: while being a human activity, it must be informed by the Spirit.[8]
>
> . . .
>
> If Church law has its foundation in Jesus Christ, if it has the value of a sign of the internal action of the Spirit, it must therefore express and foster the life of the Spirit, produce the fruits of the Spirit. . . .[9]

From another point of view, this means that the Church "was born on Pentecost," as Paul repeats over and over. This traditional expression, which is not concerned merely with chronology, implies that the Church cannot adequately be explained as the result of Jesus' earthly activity, or of the human initiatives of his followers. It is a living being that received its animation and vital energy for all times from the descent of the Holy Spirit, as the following panorama shows:

> We reflect on the mystery of the Spirit's "mission." Originating in the bosom of the most Holy Trinity, he falls in an altogether new measure and form on the little group of Apostles and disciples gathered together with Mary in the Cenacle. Our memory contemplates the extraordinary phenomena which made the event perceptible: the stormy wind and the tongues of fire, followed by the outpouring of words. As in a vision, we see the stream of the Church's life and history gushing forth from that first Christian community, born with its heart already throbbing. We see it swell and spread throughout the inhabited world, the "*oikoumene.*" It traverses peoples and centuries, still full

of the limpid, life-giving sap of its origins. With supreme
wonder and sublime joy, we see it come right up here to
ourselves. . . .

What is this light which diffuses and spreads through all the
earth? It is Christ, perpetuating himself in the humanity
which he has vivified by the Holy Spirit; it is his Church,
dwelling in time and extended in the world (June 6, 1965;
cf. June 26, 1974).

Other texts make more explicit and definite what is implied
above: that Pentecost is not an event that happened merely once, at the
origin of the Church, but a perennial and constant outpouring of the
Spirit.[10]

## THE CHURCH AS COMMUNION

As the teaching examined in the preceding chapter makes clear,
the Christian life is life in the Spirit. It is not merely observance of a
rule of behavior left by Jesus to his disciples, it is a life given us by the
energy of the divine Spirit whom Jesus has imparted to us. It is therefore essentially spiritual and interior.

But this does not make it solitary. It is not meant to be a private
life of isolated individuals, but to be lived in community. This community, which is the Church, needs to be contemplated at several
successive levels, of which the most fundamental is that of communion. In the first instance, the Church is a communion with the persons
of the Trinity. It is:

... a vital communion which the Father in his infinite and
transcendent goodness wanted to establish through Christ in
the Spirit with the human soul, and with believing and redeemed mankind. (Oct. 12, 1966; cf. May 18, 1966; Feb.
28, 1973; June 6, 1973, etc.)

Communion with the Divine Persons leads to a second communion, with our fellows:

... *Communio,* that is, the society of brothers united by
faith and charity in one divine-human organism, the mystical Body of Christ. It is the Church. (June 6, 1973; cf. May
21, 1972 II; Jan. 11, 1975; May 25, 1969.)

Authentic spirituality ''will make us enjoy and live communion'' (Feb.
28, 1973).

An older ecclesiology tended to define the Church in the first
instance as a society, i.e., as a multitude of human beings unified by a

common goal and government. In recent decades, there has been a growing tendency to assert that before the Church can be regarded as a society, and in order for its societal structure to be rightly appreciated, it must be seen as a communion.[11] Pope Paul heartily embraces this approach and appeals to it often. But he insists that in order for this communion to exist as a social reality, and to have an effective influence, the ministry of the hierarchy is required (Sept. 17, 1973, #4); hence communion in the Church implies also communion with the hierarchy (Jan. 11, 1975). With some sharpness, the Pope draws attention to the ironic contradiction in the procedure of those who belittle the institutional aspect of the Church in the name of communion, but by their idiosyncratic and insubordinate styles of apostolate or excessive criticism, violate the very exigencies of communion:

> Never before has so much been said about communion, and often by those very people who promote forms of association which are the opposite of true communion.[12]

As a communion, the Church is a replica of the Trinity, in which the divine life is lived in a community of persons; but a replica translated into the complex idiom of a full human existence.[13] And the "grace of the Holy Spirit," animating and unifying all its members, is the ultimate grounds of this communion. But before going into this, we must take note of the organic structure of the Church.


## ORGANIC SOCIETY

Proceeding from the fundamental aspect of communion, the Pope affirms that the Church is also an organic society, with different charisms, different functions and different responsibilities.[14] It is not an amorphous entity resulting simply from the spontaneous coming together of believers under the impulse of the Spirit.[15] It does not adapt itself, amoeba-like, to the demands of circumstances, having unity and continuity solely from the divine breath that creates it. The Church has a firm structure of law, doctrine and sacred rite, that is the basis, support and defense of its vital communion.

Moreover, this structure itself is not simply the product of the Spirit's action, e.g., through charismatic leaders stirred up by him, as some theorists of the early Church would have it. Its essential shape and elements were fixed for it by the earthly ministry of Jesus, who determined the essential forms which were to endure thereafter. He fashioned a body for himself before breathing into it the Spirit which would make it live. By instructing disciples in the elements of his Gospel, appointing Apostles to proclaim it with power and to act as shepherds over the others, and by consecrating those simple human symbols of water, bread and wine, oil, etc., which were to be the sacraments of his grace, Jesus fashioned the basic and immutable structures of his Body which his Spirit was to animate.

That the Church, like other living beings in this world, has greatly developed in the course of its history, Pope Paul is well aware. That its offices and functions have not only undergone profound modifications, but have even, in many cases, been brought into being under the stresses and demands of history, he does not deny. On the contrary, he maintains that such developments themselves have occurred under the inspiration of the Spirit, for example, in the case of the college of cardinals.[16] Nevertheless, by comparison with the basic structures of the Church, these developments are still only modifications and adaptations, such as are to be expected in any living being. Jesus did not leave the shaping of his Church entirely to the pressures of history or even to the impulses of the Spirit, but instituted certain elements as permanent, fundamental and normative for all subsequent developments.

This position is not, of course, new; it is a reiteration of the classical position which distinguishes "catholic" (including Orthodox and Episcopalian) from Protestant Christianity. What is to be stressed is that this position (like its contrary) has profound implications for the constitution of the Church, not merely in its beginnings, but in every period of its existence, and not only in its essence but in its sacraments, laws, doctrines, institutional developments, charismatic impulses and almost every detail of its being and activity.

This can be seen in a very significant text in which Pope Paul shows how the nature of the primitive Christian community has implications for communities in the Church today:

> How was the Church formed, historically speaking, if not through communities founded by the Apostles and their co-workers? Spontaneous communities in the strict sense of the word are not in the original line of the Church. The first Christian communities were born from the word, the ministry and the direction of persons who had been sent and authorized (for this purpose). As soon as a nucleus was organized around such persons—or rather, one such person, the apostle or bishop—it was at once called the "church" of that place where the nucleus was legitimately established. A visible and regular community required at its center, its heart, a living authority derived from an apostle or his representative or successor.[17]

The sense of this text is not to suggest that "spontaneous communities" are in any way antithetical to the Church. On the contrary, they are a sign of spiritual vitality:

> ... we have noted with satisfaction the hope furnished by
> small communities and the reminder they give of the work
> of the Holy Spirit. But this hope would be truly stunted if
> their ecclesial life, in the organic unity of the single Body of
> Christ, were to cease or to be exempted from legitimate
> ecclesiastical authority or be left to the arbitrary impulse of
> individuals.[18]

Here, as in so many other instances, the Pope seeks to encourage new
energies that have been released in the contemporary Church, while at
the same time cautioning against a spirit of autonomy that would not
only deprive the Church of their contribution, but would also cut them
off from their proper root, that life of the Spirit which has its proper
locale in the Church.

But the text on the primitive Christians is intended to affirm
that the Church itself is more than a spontaneous community. The first
nucleus of the Church consisted of men empowered and authorized by
Jesus Christ, around whom other believers gathered. St. Luke says of
the first Christians: "They devoted themselves to the Apostles' teachings and to fellowship, to the breaking of bread and the prayers" (Acts
2:42). The living faith, hope and love of this first community, for all its
spontaneity, was expressed publicly and socially in acceptance of the
pastoral authority instituted by Jesus. As Christianity spread to places
apart from Jerusalem, other communities, likewise called churches,
were formed; but the same essential pattern is maintained. At the head
of each community stood an elder or group of elders (perhaps known
by some other name, e.g., bishop), whose authority derived from the
original Twelve Apostles.

Pope Paul does not go into the intricate and elusive question of
the historical process by which the structure of bishops, elders and
deacons emerged toward the end of the first century.[19] Much less does
he enter into the debate about the meaning of *apostolos* in the New
Testament, which has gone on more or less ever since Rengstorf's
article in the first volume of Kittel's *Wörterbuch* (1933). The Pope's
intention is only to insist on the doctrinal principle (which could be
reconciled with various historical theses) that the universal Church, as
well as a particular local church, is constituted not merely by the
spontaneous gathering of believers but also by a pastoral authority
deriving from that first band of twelve commissioned by Jesus to speak
and act in his name (Mk 3:13 ff; Mt. 28:18 ff.). Later on, spontaneous
communities of Christians did arise, such as the cenobitic monks or the
later religious orders. These did not constitute new churches, but *communities within the Church*, which they presupposed and to which they
adhered and submitted.

## TWOFOLD CONTINUATION OF CHRIST

In treating the twofold nature of the Church, Pope Paul draws heavily on an essay by Yves Congar, O.P., "The Holy Spirit and the Apostolic Body, Continuators of the Work of Christ."[20] Congar sees the Church as originating in two missions: the visible mission of Jesus Christ and the invisible mission of the Holy Spirit. Christ was sent to call and instruct disciples, and to commission some of them as apostles to perpetuate this same function. The Spirit was sent to give an interior realization to the exterior institutions of Christ. Thus, from the very origin of the Church there are two principles which essentially define the twofold nature of the Church as a visible society and an invisible communion. Despite the tension between them which is inevitable in this world of sin, the two aspects are both indispensable to the Church and complementary to each other.

However, the mission of the Spirit was not merely parallel to that of Christ as that of "another Paraclete"; the Spirit himself was sent by Christ. Thus one can carry the twofold nature of the Church back to Christ himself, who sent the Apostles exteriorly, and the Spirit interiorly. It is this second view of things that furnishes the name of Congar's essay, which stresses the fact that the Church has been built up by the joint witness and joint (sacramental) action of the apostolic ministry and the Holy Spirit; and that even the free "charismatic" impulses which take the Church by surprise fit nevertheless into its official and institutional framework like the woof into the warp of a fabric.

Finally, it is by the Spirit that men are vitally conjoined with Christ so as to become his Body, and by the Spirit that Christ remains present and alive in the Church, governing it effectively as its head. From these various approaches, Congar maintains the inseparability of the two aspects of the Church, as opposed to two inadequate schemes: that which would relate the Church to Christ and neglect the Spirit, by insisting mainly on canonical legitimacy, and that which would relate the Church to the Spirit, to the neglect of duly constituted authority and sacramental fidelity. Pope Paul repeatedly cites this vision of Congar's, which must be regarded as one of the leitmotifs of the Pope's own doctrine.

## TEMPLE OF THE SPIRIT

In describing the role of the Spirit in relationship to the Church, Pope Paul uses three chief notions: the Spirit dwells in the Church as in a temple, he animates it as the soul does the body, and he uses it as his instrument or vehicle.[21]

The idea of the Church as temple of the Holy Spirit is mentioned frequently, but usually without much development. Its most important implication is that the Holy Spirit does not merely enter into intimate relations with the individual believer, but also has a presence proper to the community of believers as such. Paul repeatedly cites passages of scripture in which the communities of Christians are told that they (together) constitute one temple of the Holy Spirit[22] or that they as individuals have been built into it as living stones.[23] This indwelling of the Spirit in the Church is not distinct from that of Christ; on the contrary, it is by the Spirit that Christ himself abides in the Church (May 25, 1969).

## BODY OF CHRIST

Paul makes much greater use of the idea of the Church as the Body of Christ, in which the Holy Spirit is the animating soul.[24] (*Animation* is perhaps the term he uses more than any other to characterize the Spirit's action in the Church.) For the Church, as a community, has a life of its own; it is not just a federation of living individuals. The life of the Church, like that of its individual members, comes from the Holy Spirit. "The Church of Christ lives by the Spirit of Christ" (May 1, 1964). This is why "the Church's first need is always to live Pentecost."[25] As a corporately vivified community, the Church is the Body of Christ, because the Spirit of Christ gives it a vital union with its head (May 25, 1969).

Two aspects of this life-giving influence of the soul on the Body of Christ which Pope Paul likes to single out are unification and the imparting of energy. The soul unifies the body, so that its diverse members, tissues and organs, in spite of their diversity, compose a single living whole. So the unity of the Church, composed of many different persons, is the work of the Spirit. Deeper than the acts of agreement and the affection which unite them psychologically, there is the action of the Holy Spirit who both inspires them to unity by the faith which he generates and the love he pours forth in their hearts, and also makes that unity ontological and vital because he, the one, same Divine Spirit, is present and life-giving in each individual.

The constitution of the Church calls for unity, declared the Pope, not only in the sense that Christ intended that there be but one flock and one shepherd (Jn 10:16):

> Also, and above all, it calls for interior and brotherly unity in the Holy Spirit. What would a Church divided within itself be? The Church *is* unity.[26]

In a homily preached at a celebration in a parish church near Rome, the Pope gave a colorful statement of this unity:

> What is the Church? It is the place where people can meet, join one another, unite, gather, in order to feel that they are one family, the People of God.

> This new reality is the greatest thing that can happen in the history of mankind. God came down from heaven to make this family one thing: the mystical Body of Christ. There is a new energy, a mysterious presence—the presence of the Spirit, that makes us feel that we are one heart and one soul.[27]

The unity of the Church is not only that of a multitude of persons brought into concord and collaboration; it is also that of diverse gifts, charisms, functions and ministries associated with one another in an organic whole, as noted above. Hence, clergy and laity, bishops and Pope, the Roman congregations and the various councils at parish, diocesan, national and regional levels, must see their roles as one of positive collaboration with distinct contributions coming from each.

Pope Paul likes to dwell on this Spirit-given unity of the Church especially in conjunction with its catholicity: the fact that it is not only open to all mankind, but that it embraces within itself a diversity of cultures respecting the genius of each even while giving them a superior unity and harmony in Christ. We have already noted how he sees the Pentecostal gift of tongues as a symbol of this unity amid variety.[28] In an address given in the course of his visit to Australia in 1970, he said to an assembly of Bishops of the South Pacific Islands:

> How can Catholicism, so firm and so jealous about its unity, embrace all men, who are so different from one another? Does it perhaps demand absolute uniformity in all manifestations of life? Is there perhaps only one practical and historical way of interpreting the true and unique faith of Christ?

> You know, brothers, how easy and clear is the answer to this disturbing question. It was given by the Holy Spirit himself on the day of Pentecost, when those who had been filled by the divine outpouring sent from heaven by Christ in fire and in wind began to speak foreign languages so that each of their listeners heard them "in his own native language" (Acts 2:6), although they belong to different races.[29]

Besides unifying the Body of Christ, the Holy Spirit, as its soul, is also the source of all its energy (April 26, 1964; May 21, 1972). He is the life-giving sap that makes it grow (June 6, 1965), the wind in its sails (Nov. 29, 1972). Because of the very comprehensiveness of this subject, only a few indications can be given here.

As source of energy in the Church, the Spirit impels it to works of charity (Nov. 29, 1972) and apostolate (May 25, 1969), and of evangelization in particular (Dec. 8, 1975). He is source both of the word proclaimed by the apostle and of the assent given by the believer (Dec. 8, 1975; cf. May 28, 1975). From another point of view, the inner witness he gives to the faithful (May 26, 1968; May 24, 1972) is the basis of the external witness that the Church in turn has to give to others (Jan. 11, 1975). He raises up ministers and apostles (June 6, 1965; cf. Jan. 11, 1975); pastors receive their power and authority from him (Feb. 13, 1972). As Paraclete, he gives the Church light and guidance (Oct. 26, 1967). The laws which the Church imposes on its members for the sake of order and peace derive ultimately from the Spirit (Sept. 17, 1973, #4). The Pope frequently cites a dense paragraph of *Luman Gentium* on the Spirit as guiding the Church in the way of truth, equipping and directing it by his various gifts, adorning it with his fruits, and renewing it constantly.[30]

An instructive example of the Spirit's action in the concrete development of the Church can be seen in the history of the College of Cardinals:

What we see is a progressive "institutional" development in the Church, which we may well regard as something motivated and inspired by the Divine Paraclete himself. For it flows from the very life of the Church and its continuing effort faithfully to preserve its original form over the course of history.

This development is a product of the natural growth process of the Church. But it is most important not to overlook the secret and hidden powers that inspire and guide the progress of the institutions of Holy Church. The Gospel of Christ must be regarded as a kind of seed. Christ is the one and only supreme head of the Church, although he is invisible. In like manner, the Holy Spirit is the Church's Patron, Sanctifier and Paraclete—the wellspring of its vitality, consolation, trust and joy.[31]

In a similar vein the Pope declared to an assembly of canonists:

Everything that is imposed to guarantee order and peace in the community of Christians—here we have Canon Law on the external plane—proceeds in the last analysis from the Spirit (Sept. 17, 1973, #4).

These important statements were not intended as an apologia to justify all the developments that have occurred in the course of the Church's history. As will be seen shortly, Pope Paul is too frank in acknowledging the human shortcomings in the Church for his words to be taken in that sense. But his point is to affirm that the action of the Spirit may not be confined, for example, to purely sacramental actions, nor reduced to some impotent intentionality. Whenever the Church is at work, in its most ordinary, routine functions, in its juridical processes or institutional developments, the Spirit too is at work. "The Holy Spirit is present and working in the Church throughout the whole range of its life" (Sept. 17, 1973, #2). If not everything is to be hallowed by his influence, neither is the latter so hidden as to be impossible to discern.

Having this perennial source of life and energy within itself, the Church does not age like other human institutions and human beings.

> Time does not make the Church grow old; it makes it grow, and arouses it to life and fullness. . . . The human part of the Church may . . . undergo the inexorable laws of history and time. . . . But the Church has within itself not only an invincible, supernatural, ultrahistorical principle of immortality, but also incalculable energies of renewal (June 12, 1974).

Hence, to those men of today, especially youth, who are likely to be turned off from the Church by the very fact that it is so old, for whom its ancient pedigree is a liability rather than a guarantee of authenticity, he points out the amazing vigor and the perennial youth which the Church has from the Holy Spirit, who is like a mighty current of water that keeps the jet of a fountain springing high (*ibid*).

## BRIDE OF CHRIST

The Spirit also sanctifies and beautifies the Church. In spite of the flaws with which men disfigure her countenance, the Bride of Christ is very beautiful, with an unearthly, heavenly beauty.[32] In spite of the sins of which its members and representatives are guilty, the Church is holy in two ways: by reason of the grace diffused within it by the presence of the Spirit, and inasmuch as it is used by the Spirit as the organ by which he communicates himself to the world (May 20, 1964).

Esteem for the Church is not a matter of closing one's eyes to its deficiencies in responding to the divine call. Paul is candid in acknowledging the unedifying pages in the history of the Church,[33] and

took the unprecendented step of asking pardon publicly of non-
Catholic Christians for any of the ways in which Catholics were to
blame for the separation between them.[34] But he calls on us also to
open our eyes to the deepest, truest reality of the Church, which is not
merely an unreal ideal or unattained goal, but the fact of Christ's actual
gift to her:

> Let us look at the Church as Jesus saw her, and still sees her
> from heaven, pervaded, enkindled, sanctified by his
> Spirit. . . . Christ sees his Church clothed in white robes . . .
> because "the Holy Spirit has come down from heaven in his
> beauty."[35]

We can choose whether to look at the Church with a hostile
attitude, looking for defects, bent upon contention and disparagement,
or with a friendly and filial attitude which, without losing its objectiv-
ity, starts, like Christ, from love.[36] Paul repeatedly summons his hearers to love the Church:

> Our first, new attitude in this spiritual and historical season
> (the Holy Year) must be to love the Church. We will love
> the Church both in its mystical and in its earthly reality; in
> its mysterious and divine aspects, but also in its human and
> therefore limited and defective ones. We will love the
> Church in its concreteness, such as it is: perfect in the
> thought of Christ (Eph 5:23), capable of perfection in our
> thought and desire. We will love the Church without seek-
> ing to escape in the distinction between a charismatic
> Church, conjured up by our own gratuitous idealism, and an
> institutional Church, in which we can hardly recognize
> either its identity or the need it has of our humble and filial
> adherence, in order for it once more to appear beautiful as
> the Bride of Christ.[37]

There is a close connection between loving the Church and receiving
the Spirit: "We must love the Church if we want the Spirit of God to
live in our midst."[38] Even beyond loving the Church, Paul urges us to
"delight in the Church." This is part of the charism of joy that should
be the lot of every Spirit-filled believer.[39]

Finally, the Pope makes it clear, the link between the Spirit and
the Church will never be broken. "The Church already and forever
possesses the Holy Spirit" (Oct. 12, 1966). There is no grounds for
anxiety that perhaps, because of the infidelities of its members, the
Church may have lost the Spirit.

> The fire of the Holy Spirit will never again be quenched in
> the living Church of Christ; . . . even if, in certain moments

of crisis and times of trial, it remains hidden beneath the ashes of human fraility, it is not thereby extinct. It still burns, and in every sacramental act, in every humble prayer, the "good Spirit" is present and operative (May 21, 1972, I).

This conviction, often expressed in the view that Pentecost continues forever, and is a perennial miracle,[40] is not based on any complacent assurance about the members of the Church, but on the fidelity of the Divine Spirit, who "does not forsake his Church, does not forsake his chosen ones" (May 21, 1972, I).

## NOTES

1. General Audience of June 5, 1974 (*OR*, June 6, 1974; *ORe*, June 13, 1974).

2. Cardinal Montini, "Let Us Think About the Council" (Pastoral Letter to his diocese for Lent, 1962), in Cardinal Montini, *The Church* (Baltimore & Dublin, Helicon, 1964), p. 176. See also his homily for the feast of St. Ambrose, Dec. 7, 1962, cited in *Paul VI*, by James Gonzalez and T. Perez, (Boston, St. Paul, 1964) pp. 271–273. In his years as Pope, he has frequently pointed out that the Church was the chief subject of the Council. See, e.g., May 26, 1971.

3. General Congregation XXXI, intervention 8, Dec. 1, 1962. *Acta Synodalia Sacrosancti Concilii Oecumenici* Vaticani II, vol. I, pars iv, p. 144.

4. Congregation XXXIV, intervention 2, Dec. 5, 1962. *Acta* I, iv, p. 292.

5. James Gonzalez and T. Perez, *Paul VI* (Boston, St. Paul, 1964), p. 277. Xavier Rynne, *Letters from Vatican City* (New York, Farrer, Straus & Giroux, 1963), p. 227. Besides his statement on the Council floor, Montini had given an interpretation of the Council's work in a letter to his diocese (Dec. 2, 1962), which he amplified in a homily for the patronal feastday of Milan on Dec. 7. Both of these acts received widespread attention.

6. Address for the opening of the Second Session of Vatican II, Sept. 29, 1963 (*AAS* 55 (1963), p. 849; *TPS* 9/2 (1964), p. 132).

7. Apostolic Exhortation, *Reconciliation Within the Church* (*OR*, Dec. 16–17, 1974; *ORe*, Dec. 26, 1974).

8. Sept. 17, 1973. This passages comes near the end of ch. II, #5.

9. *Ibid.*, ch. III. Similar sentiments were expressed by the Pope in his allocution to the Roman Rota Feb. 4, 1977; cf. *ORe*, Feb. 24, 1977.

10. Some of these texts have been cited in chapter 1.

11. One of the more important tokens of and influences on this development was the book, *The Church Is a Communion* by the French Dominican, Jerome Hamer (New York, Sheed and Ward, 1965). The French original, which appeared in 1962, the year the Council opened, is frequently cited in Pope Paul's discourses.

12. General Audience, Aug. 29, 1973 (*OR*, Aug. 30, 1973; *ORe*, Sept. 6, 1973).

13. Cf. the text cited below, at note 27.

14. General Audience, Nov. 12, 1969 (*OR*, Nov. 13, 1969; *ORe*, Nov. 20, 1969). Cf. Nov. 14, 1971; May 17, 1972.

15. To a group of Pentecostal theologians and leaders in Rome for a meeting sponsored by the Secretariat for the Promotion of Christian Unity, the Pope declared: "You have spoken together of how faithful souls participate in the reality of God. We believe this is a reality which establishes itself among the faithful as a visible

communion, so that they are united not only by a spiritual relationship on the level of mystery and the invisible, but also on the visible level of human realities transformed by the Spirit.'' May 26, 1976 (*ORe*, June 3, 1976).

16. Cf. the text cited below at note 31.

17. At a General Audience of Aug. 18, 1976 (*OR*, Aug. 19, 1976; *ORe*, Aug. 26, 1976).

18. From the address concluding the Synod of Bishops which met in Rome Sept. 26–Oct. 6, 1974, on the topic of Evangelization (*OR*, Nov. 27, 1974; *ORe*, Nov. 7, 1974).

19. For an introduction to this question, cf. Andre Lemaire, *Les ministères aux origines de l'Eglise,* Paris, cerf, 1971. The best introduction to this question in English is perhaps still that of Gregory Dix, ''The Ministry in the Early Church, A.D. 90–410, in *The Apostolic Ministry,* ed. by K. Kirk, London, Hodder and Stoughton, 1946.

20. First published as the fifth essay in *Esquisses du Mystère de l'Eglise (Unam Sanctam* 8), Paris, Cerf, 1953, p. 129 ff. In the English translation, *The Mystery of the Church* (Baltimore, Helicon, 1960), it originally appeared as chapter vi. In the heavily revised edition of 1965, which has been used here, it again becomes chapter 5.

   The other two works of ecclesiology most frequently cited by Pope Paul are J. Hamer, *L'Eglise est une communion,* Paris, Cerf, 1962 (*The Church Is a Communion,* New York, Sheed & Ward, 1965) and H. De Lubac, *Méditation sur l'Eglise,* Paris, Aubier, 1952, (*The Splendour of the Church,* New York, Sheed & Ward, 1956).

21. Sometimes these three are reduced to two: the Church is temple and vehicle of the Spirit (May 14, 1967).

22. 1 Cor 3:16 f., 2 Cor 6:16.

23. Eph 2:19ff., I Pt 2:5.

24. May 18, 1966, May 20, 1964. Nov. 29, 1972.

25. Oct. 12, 1966. Cf. Nov. 26, and 29, 1972, as well as the texts cited in chapter 1.

26. Angelus message of June 16, 1974 (*ORe*, June 27, 1974).

27. From an address at the parish church of St. Francis Xavier in the Roman suburb of Garbatella, April 4, 1976 (*ORe*, April 15, 1976).

28. Cf. ch. 4, at note 5 ff.

29. From an address given (in English) to the Bishops of Oceania on Dec. 1, 1970 (*OR*, Dec. 2, 1970; *ORe*, Dec. 10, 1970).

30. Vatican II, *The Church,* #4. Cf. chapter 6 at note 5.

31. From an address to the College of Cardinals, April 30, 1969 (*OR*, May 2–3, 1969; *ORe*, May 14, 1969).

32. Cf. note 35 below.

33. May 20, 1964. Cf. June 7, 1972 (*OR*, June 8, 1972; *ORe*, June 15, 1972), June 5, 1974 (*OR*, June 6, 1974; *ORe*, June 13, 1974). Etc.

34. Opening address for the Second Session of Vatican II, Sept. 29, 1963. *AAS* 55 (1963), p. 853; *TPS* 9/2 (1964) p. 136.

35. General Audience, June 7, 1972 (*OR*, June 8, 1972; *ORe*, June 15, 1972).

36. *Ibid.*

37. From an address at a General Audience, Sept. 12, 1973 (*OR*, Sept. 13, 1973; *ORe*, Sept. 20, 1973).

38. From an address to the College of Cardinals, June 24, 1967 (*OR*, June 25, 1967; *TPS* 12 (1967), p. 208).

39. April 25, 1970.

40. See chapter 1.

# CHAPTER EIGHT

# The Sacraments, the Hierarchy and the Virgin Mary

The present chapter groups together three topics characteristic of the Catholic and, in particular, the Roman Catholic understanding of the Church. The teachings of Pope Paul presented in the previous chapter would probably be acceptable on the whole to most Christians of other denominations, whereas the three points treated here would be found objectionable, alien or perplexing by many of them. Even Catholic Charismatics not rarely have a difficult time relating the sacraments, the hierarchy and the Blessed Virgin Mary to the action of the Holy Spirit.

All three of these topics pertain to the subject of the Church, and there is no way they can be understood adequately except in the light of the great mystery of the Church. The basic principle behind them is that the Holy Spirit makes use of human realities as channels or vehicles through which he imparts his gifts and his personal presence to believers. This is true already of the world of nature, on which account the beauties and powers of nature are sometimes called "natural sacraments." It holds more particularly for the institutions of Christ, and in the first place for the Church itself. Not only does the Spirit draw the faithful together into the community of the Church, and dwell within that community as in a temple; he also uses the community, as well as particular persons, events and gestures in it, as the instrument of his action.

St. Paul suggested this truth in speaking of himself as father (1 Cor 4:15) and even mother (Gal 4:19) of his disciples, because of the life of the Spirit which had come to them through him. The same idea applies with even greater reason to the Church, the community of believers, which is the vital matrix through which the Spirit is normally communicated, and which continues to nourish and support the life thus imparted. The Church's title of "Mother of the faithful," accred-

91

ited by a very ancient tradition, does not designate a foster mother, who merely protects and nourishes the life entrusted to her care, but a real mother, through whom life itself is first imparted through the gift of the Spirit.

This sacramental view does not imply that the Church has any power or control over the Spirit. It is nothing but his servant and instrument. What is implied is that the Spirit does in truth make use of the institutions of Christ as privileged instruments, contrary to the view that would regard the functions of the Church as mere ceremony and organization. The Divine Spirit can be given by God alone; but just as the sacred humanity of Jesus was made the fountain from which the life-giving waters of the Spirit pour out over all the earth ("If any man thirst, let him come to me and drink . . ." Jn 7:37), so mankind, taken up into the Body of Christ, can likewise, in subordination to Jesus, be used to impart the Spirit. Again, this does not conflict with the principle that Jesus is the unique mediator between God and man (1 Tm 2:5); it affirms simply that, in pouring out his Spirit upon all flesh, Jesus associated with himself in this life-giving function those whom he has incorporated into his Body.


## SACRAMENTS

The most important instance of this sacramental principle lies in those seven sacred rites which, since the 12th century, have been designated specially as sacraments. Rituals expressive of man's worship, and symbolizing the spiritual realities with which it is concerned, are to be found in all religions, except perhaps for a few which have deliberately undertaken (successfully or unsuccessfully?) to expunge them. The Christian sacraments use some of the most elemental realities of human life—water, oil, bread, wine, and speech—to represent the elemental action of the Spirit of God, cleansing, healing, nourishing, refreshing, comforting, etc. The Catholic understanding of the sacraments, which Pope Paul of course takes for granted, is that the Holy Spirit uses the sacramental signs as instruments or channels through which he imparts his graces, so that the efficacy of the sacraments comes, not from the splendor of the ceremony, nor from the holiness of the minister, nor from the fervor of the recipient, but properly from the Holy Spirit himself.

This concept, designated by the famous but often misunderstood theological term, *ex opere operato*, was rejected by the greater part of Reformation Christianity, in favor of other views, e.g., that the effect of the sacrament is simply to excite the faith of the recipient, to which the Spirit responds by his gracious action. This led inevitably to a relative devaluation of the sacraments in Protestant Christianity, which, without abandoning them altogether, puts far more emphasis on the word of scripture. The modern Pentecostal denominations show a curious ambivalence on this point. On the one hand, they have reacted massively against the formalism and vain ceremonies which they claim to see even in the great Protestant denominations.[1] On the other hand, however, not only do they retain Baptism and the Lord's Supper, in obedience to the commands of Jesus,[2] but they have rediscovered what might be called the deepest foundation of Catholic sacramentalism in their experience of the communication of the Spirit through the laying on of hands. Roman Catholic Pentecostals or Charismatics, in turn, have experienced some of this same ambivalence. Although the predominant effect of the renewal among them has been to reanimate appreciation of the sacraments, a serious number have been drawn to neglect the sacraments in greater or lesser measure, in favor of a purely charismatic worship.

As if in response to this temptation, Pope Paul stressed the sacraments when he addressed the Rome Conference on the Charismatic Renewal. His English-language address mentioned the four sacraments of Baptism, Confirmation, Eucharist and Reconciliation (May 19, 1975, III). There is a briefer reminder of the sacraments in the French address of the same day.

In an early homily in preparation for Pentecost, he said that the sacraments are "the ordinary but certain way in which the Holy Spirit is infused into souls from Pentecost onwards," and that resurrection to divine life "takes place especially in the sacramental ministry, which is a fountain of grace and an infusion of the Holy Spirit."[3] A year later, he mentioned that the Holy Spirit is given in Baptism and returns in Confirmation and, in a different way, in Holy Orders. "Always the Holy Spirit," he added; "Do we realize this?" (June 6, 1965).

Confirmation is the sacrament which tradition has associated most particularly with the gifts of the Spirit. But since the fundamental imparting of the Spirit occurs in Baptism, it has always been something of a theological problem to define the effect proper of Confirmation. The medieval view of it as the sacrament of Christian adulthood,[4] making the recipient a witness and soldier of Christ, has fallen into disfavor with many liturgists today. When the new ritual for Confirmation was promulgated in 1971, in conformity with the decrees of Vatican II,[5] Pope Paul declared in the accompanying letter that this sacrament: "in a certain way perpetuates the grace of Pentecost in the Church," explaining that this new gift of the Spirit imparts special strength, a more perfect union with the Church, and a stricter obligation to spread and defend the faith in word and deed as true witnesses to Christ'' (Sept. 30, 1971). Even though the terms soldier and adult are not used, this text basically supports the traditional conception. And as it occurs, not just in a homily or routine allocution, but in the Apostolic Constitution that promulgated the new ritual, and since each of the three effects listed is substantiated by a reference to the decrees of Vatican II (indicated in the footnotes), it is a text of considerable gravity.

## PASTORAL AUTHORITY

We have seen Pope Paul's teaching that the work of Jesus is carried on conjointly by the Holy Spirit and the apostolic hierarchy, both of which were sent by him, one interiorly and the other exteriorly.[6] Now we must examine what he has to say about the inner relationship between the Spirit and the hierarchy. It is summed up in the principle:

> The Spirit of Jesus uses this hierarchy as his ordinary instrument in the ministry of word and sacrament (Sept. 14, 1964).

Thus the role of the clergy in the Church is comparable to that of the sacraments, all the more so since it is by a sacrament that priests and bishops are ordained, and as ministers of the sacraments that they exercise a major part of their ministry.[7]

The Pope seldom neglects to mention that the Spirit, who ''breathes where he wills,'' has no need of this human instrumentation. (The breath of the Mystical Body can do without its human diaphragm, he observes, May 18, 1966.) Nevertheless, he insists untiringly that together with the sacraments of which they are the ordinary ministers, the clergy constitute the vehicle, chosen by Christ, to communicate the Holy Spirit to us (May 26, 1971).

His insistence on this point is due no doubt to the restiveness toward ecclesiastical authority that has grown during his pontificate.[8] Some object to any person possessing religious authority over others; some to the understanding of this authority as coming directly from Christ rather than through the community; some to the belief that it involves spiritual powers not shared equally by all believers; some to the undemocratic (or, more often today, ''uncollegial'') manner in which ecclesiastical authority appears to them to be exercised.

As the chief authority figure in the Church, the Pope inevitably bears the brunt of the attack. Is he to some degree responsible for this by the way he has exercised his office? Or would any human being, even John XXIII, or even Jesus Christ himself, have been able to avoid the confrontations that have sprung out of Vatican II? No matter what position we take on these more or less futile questions, it is obvious that Paul VI has been compelled to speak in defense of an authority of which he is the principal subject.

At a deeper level, however, the issue is not whether the sheep have been insubordinate or the shepherd authoritarian; it has to do with the rediscovery of the dignity, liberty and responsibility of the layman, and his reinsertion into a heavily clericalized Church. Although the Church, from the very beginning, was under the direction of a pastoral authority appointed by Christ (Acts 1:42), it took several centuries for the concept of Catholic priesthood as a distinct power of ministry to be articulated clearly and invested with a social form. The Middle Ages, Renaissance, Reformation and early modern periods produced a succession of trials in which first the liberty and authority of bishops and popes, and then the spiritual power of priests, have been challenged and reaffirmed. The notion of the priest as "another Christ," as one who acts "in the person of Christ," summarizes this development which perhaps reached its apex in the French spirituality of the 17th century.

Concomitantly, initiative, authority and responsibility in Church activities have passed predominantly into the hands of the clergy. Whether this came about chiefly through the excessive self-assertiveness of the clergy or because of the apathy of the laity is a question that cannot be settled a priori (as it commonly is), and does not in any case alter the universally admitted fact of atrophy of lay Christian life at the beginning of the modern era. The resultant impotence of the Church in civic life finally started the pendulum swinging back during the 19th century. In his book, *Lay People in the Church,* Yves Congar has pointed out some of the great lay leaders of this period.[9] One who deserves to be cited among them was Giorgio Montini, father of the present Pope. A follower of Giuseppe Tovini (one of the first organizers of Italian Catholic Action), he served for 31 years as fearless and effective editor of a Catholic journal in Brescia, during a period of intense Italian anticlericalism and antiecclesiasticism. He was one of the first Catholics to enter Italian politics after Benedict XV relaxed the *Non Expedit* of Pius IX, and was elected to the Chamber of Deputies. As president of the Electoral Union of Italian Catholics, he helped Don Luigi Sturzo found the Italian Popular Party, which the Fascists suppressed in 1926, but which revived after the Second World War as the Christian Democratic Party.[10]

During the 20th century, most of the ideas and energy for the role of the layman in the Church have galvanized around the concept of Catholic Action, i.e., the organized lay apostolate. Meanwhile, however, the pendulum has swung so fast that, at least in the realm of ideas, the final quarter of this century threatens to become an epoch of declericalization. Whereas the early manuals of Catholic Action emphasized the essential role of the priest for the apostolate of the laity, much of today's ecclesiology has radically challenged or questioned the traditional concept of the Catholic priesthood. Arguments drawn from scripture and early Church history have represented it as a late institutionalization and unification of the pluriform charismatic ministries of the primitive Church. The development of "political" and especially "liberation" theology has fostered a humanistic and democratic mentality that can ill accommodate a "representative of God," and has little appreciation of his spiritual functions. Widespread dissatisfaction with the lack of spirituality of so many of them has led some spiritual movements to react into truculent independence of the clergy. Loss of confidence in their own vocation, and loss of a sense of identity on the part of many (especially the younger) priests, has been both a result and a contributing factor to this situation.

All his life long, Paul VI has been an enthusiastic promoter of the lay apostolate. As a youth, he himself had originally intended to serve the Church as a lay journalist like his father; not until the age of 19 did he announce his intention to enter the seminary.[11] During his early years in the priesthood (which occurred under the pontificate of Pius XI, the great architect of Catholic Action), he devoted much of his free time to aiding an organization of Catholic students at the University of Rome. His success in this work led to his appointment as National Moderator of the Italian Federation of Catholic Students.[12] As Archbishop of Milan and as Pope, he has continued to give his warm support to all forms of Catholic Action; we have already noted his prophetic vision of it (ch. 2). Two of the texts cited in Part II of the present book are taken from his frequent addresses to Catholic Action congresses (Jan. 11 and July 3, 1975).

But in the changed theological climate of the post-war period, Montini, the promoter of the lay apostolate, has had to become Paul, defender of priestly authority. The tension between the two attitudes is almost palpable in the addresses to the Catholic Action congresses, in which, while continuing to support the lay apostolate, he has had to reaffirm the pastoral power of the ordained priesthood.

He treats this subject more often in reference to bishops than to simple priests; but with the understanding, of course, that the episcopate is nothing other than the fullness of that priesthood in which every priest shares.[13]

> The gift of the Holy Spirit is conferred at the moment of episcopal ordination, and that Spirit, dwelling in the

Bishops, sustains and nourishes the whole life of the ecclesial communion through them. There can be no doubt that
the Bishops, at the time of their episcopal ordination, receive the pastoral gifts of sanctifying, teaching and ruling,
by which they, acting in the person of Christ, the pontiff,
teacher and pastor, become the instruments of the Spirit of
Christ to carry out their ministry within the ecclesial communion.[14]

Similarly, in speaking of the ordination of every priest, he said that by
the imposition of the Bishop's hands in the sacrament of Holy Orders,
Christ pours the Holy Spirit into those being ordained (May 17, 1970).
This graphic expression is not of course meant in a materialistic sense,
nor to suggest that the ordaining bishop has control over the gift of the
Spirit, but intends to stress the reality of that gift of the Spirit through
which a man is ordained to represent Jesus Christ to the Christian
community.

In speaking once about the meaning of Pentecost for priests, the
Pope declared that "the one chosen for the sacred ministry" is:

... transformed into an instrument for distributing the divine gifts. The priest not only receives grace, but imparts it;
he is not only sanctified by grace, but by it is likewise made
into a worthy instrument of sanctification[15] (May 14, 1964).

Hence the priesthood is like a fountain to which one goes "in order to
draw the water of salvation" (*ibid.*). The Holy Spirit gives priests
power "to bring him to the faithful in ... preaching, in directing the
People of God, and in the ministry of the sacraments" (May 25, 1969).

In speaking at an ordination, Paul declared that the efficacy of
this sacrament was the focal point "not only of the present ceremony,
but of the mystery of the Church":

It is nothing less than the transmission of spiritual powers,
powers which the Holy Spirit himself infuses into the chosen disciple, who is raised to the rank of minister of God,
for Christ, in the Church. Remember the Risen Christ
speaking to the disciples and breathing upon them: "Receive the Holy Spirit" (Jn 20:22). At that moment, a contact, an impression, a character formed the one receiving the
sacrament of Holy Orders, as it does still today: he is ena-
bled to dispense "the mysteries of God" (1 Cor 4:1; 1 Pt
4:10). Brothers and sons, let us never forget this most special relationship that priestly ordination creates between us
and God: we become vehicles of the divine action.[16]

Pope Paul's teaching on the priesthood and episcopate is quite
traditional, and fully conformable with the doctrine set forth richly and

forthrightly by Vatican II. Chapter III of the Constitution on the Church declares that in the Bishops, "Our Lord Jesus Christ, the supreme High Priest, is present in the midst of those who believe ... preaching the word of God to all nations, and constantly administering the sacraments of faith. ... By their wisdom and prudence he directs and guides the people of the New Testament in its pilgrimage toward eternal happiness." For the discharge of these duties, Christ enriched the apostles by a "special outpouring of the Holy Spirit," which they in turn passed on to their successors. "By means of the imposition of hands and the words of consecration, the grace of the Holy Spirit is conferred, and the sacred character so impressed, that bishops in an eminent and visible way undertake Christ's own role as Teacher, Shepherd and High Priest, and act in his person" (#21). Christ himself created the distinction "between sacred ministers and the rest of the People of God"; but "this very diversity of graces, ministries and works gathers the children of God into one, because 'all these things are the work of one and the same Spirit' (1 Cor 12:11)" (#32).

While staying completely within the limits of the Conciliar teaching, Pope Paul introduces the term *charism,* which the Council did not use in this context. In opposition to those who "have recently ventured to place the charismatic and the hierarchical Church in opposition" (Feb. 13, 1972), he affirms that the charisms are given by preference to those who hold speical directive functions in the Church (March 26, 1969). The "charism of pastoral power," received by every bishop through his ordination, "consists in his being called to leadership of that part of the flock which has been entrusted to him." In this pastoral power, charism and authority are one. The bishops share "both charismatic gifts and hierarchical offices in a unique way" (Feb. 13, 1972). They have received "the charism of teaching the word of God authentically, and of being the principle of unity in the Church" (Jan. 11, 1975). The Holy Spirit illumines them in their teaching; hence the teaching authority of the Church should be obeyed, not merely because of the reasons which may be advanced in support of any particular decision, "but still more because of the light of the Holy Spirit, which is given to the pastors of the Church in a particular way, in order that they may illumine the truth."[17]

In insisting on the authority and spiritual power that come with the charism of the hierarchy, Pope Paul is not guilty of the charge so often formulated today, of conceiving of office in terms of power rather than of service. He himself often recalls the principle that every office and power in the Church exists for service. But the point he has to maintain is that the service rendered by the Church's pastors is not one of impotence! Christ gave real spiritual power—a supernatural power (Sept. 14, 1964)—to those who were to shepherd his flock.[18] To deny this power under the pretext of democracy, or of humility and love, would be to emasculate the pastorate, which Christ made strong for the sake of his flock (2 Cor 10:8; 13:10). "Strike the shepherd and the sheep will be scattered" (Mt 26:31). The Pope's firm maintenance of authority at the papal, episcopal and priestly levels is not motivated by a spirit of domination, but by fidelity to the word of Christ. This can well be seen in his description of his own office. The Successor of St. Peter, he says, is one:

> ... to whom the Lord has entrusted the weighty, permanent and loving office of tending his lambs and his sheep (Jn 21:13–17), of strengthening his brethren (Lk 22:32), and of being the foundation and sign of Church unity (Mt 16:18–20). ... We say with trepidation, by reason of the responsibility that falls upon us, that the Successor of Peter is and remains the ordinary pastor of the Church in her unity and entirety. "By virtue of his office, that is, as vicar of Christ and Pastor of the whole Church, he has full, supreme and universal power in the Church. And he can always exercise this power freely" (*Lumen Gentium* #22). It is not a question here of a dialectic of powers, but of a single desire— that of following the will of the Lord with total love—with each one contributing by the faithful accomplishment of his own task.[19]

Elsewhere, he points to the First Letter of Peter to show that "Peter's special position is that of a vicarious sacrament of the true and first living stone, Christ himself" in that mystical abode in which every stone is alive (Feb. 13, 1972).[20] Likewise the Bishops are "the successors to the apostles not merely juridically, but also as heirs in an ever-living communion of life-giving and ministry." Similarly, after reminding candidates for the priesthood of the marvelous work which the Holy Spirit is about to accomplish in them, he adds:

> Never forget that this marvel happens in you, but not for you. It is for others, it is for the Church. ... Your power is one of function, like the power of a special organ working for the benefit of the whole body. You become instruments, ministers at the service of the brethren (May 17, 1970).

## CHARISMS OF THE LAITY

Pope Paul's insistence on the charisms of the hierarchy does not involve any minimizing of those of the laity. The doctrine of Vatican II on this subject, which Paul occasionally cites, (e.g., Jan. 11, 1975) he also reaffirms in his own terms: "The laity," he says,  ... has its own peculiar charism for giving a Christian inspiration to temporal realities" (July 3, 1975). Moreover, the laity receive "particular gifts or charisms ordained to the good of men and the building up of the Church" (Jan. 11, 1975).

Elsewhere, speaking in terms of ministry rather than of charism, the Pope writes:

> It is certain that, alongside of the ordained ministries, by which certain people are appointed pastors and consecrated in a special way to the service of the community, the Church recognizes the role of unordained ministries suited for special services to the Church.[21]

As examples of such ministries, catechists, choir directors, prayer leaders, Christians devoted to the service of God's word or to the assistance of the needy, heads of small communities and others charged with responsibility for apostolic movements, are mentioned. Paul insists that the specific character of all the diverse charisms be respected (Jan. 11, 1975).

His overriding preoccupation, however, is that the many charisms and functions in the Church be exercised in harmonious unity, complementing one another in a united apostolate. This, he maintains, can be achieved only on condition that the charisms of the laity are exercised under the direction of the hierarchy.

> There are different ministries, but unity of missions around the pastors given to the Church by the Holy Spirit.[22]

Another statement on lay ministries declares:

> These ministries will have a real pastoral value to the extent that they are established with absolute respect for unity, and adhere to the directives of the pastors. It is the latter who are responsible for the Church's unity and are builders of it.[23]

This subordination of charisms comes from the very principle of respect for the specific nature of each; for the bishop's charism is that of leadership in the Church (Feb. 13, 1972). Pope Paul cites St. Paul as his authority that:

> ... the charisms granted to the faithful are subject to discipline, which only the charism of pastoral power, acting in charity, can maintain (Feb. 13, 1972).

In his first direct message to the Charismatic Renewal, the Pope pointed out that the discernment called for in every work of renewal belongs especially to those who are in charge of the Church (Oct. 10,

1973). This was amplified in his main address to the Rome Conference on the Charismatic Renewal (May 19, 1975, I).

When the American Bishops issued their "Statement on Catholic Charismatic Renewal" at the beginning of 1975, they gave a felicitous expression to this doctrine in calling the priest's special function in the renewal that of "Coordinator of the gifts of the Spirit."[24]

On the other hand, the Pope also reminds bishops that they must be sensitive to the action of the Spirit in the hearts of their flock:

> Pastors, therefore, should strive to ensure that their zeal, even in the juridical sphere, be pastoral, informed by the Spirit. . . . "Do not quench the Spirit" (1 Thes 5:19), for "the Spirit breathes where he wills" (Jn 3:8). The Holy Spirit grants his gifts to both pastors and faithful that they may help to build the Body of Christ. It is true that everything must be tested (1 Thes 5:21); but the heart which tests them must lie open to every genuine prompting of the Holy Spirit. "He that has an ear, let him hear what the Spirit says to the Churches" (Apoc 2:7).[25]

Consequently, in speaking to the Roman Rota on the subject of Church law, the Pope insisted that "the faithful . . . are not to be regarded merely as subjects of, but rather as collaborators with, the hierarchical order. . . ." Hence the new Code of Canon Law is to be designed in such a way as to "leave to individual Christians their necessary and (as it is called) responsible freedom for the building up of the Body of Christ" (*ibid.*).

## MARY

Whereas the sacraments and pastorate are part of the structure that gives firmness and stability to the Body of Christ, making of his followers an organic People, rather than an amorphous mass, the role of the Virgin Mary must be understood in an entirely different perspective. She exemplifies the unofficial and informal, the most personal and intimate values in the Church, almost at the opposite pole from structure. Christ structured the Church around the Apostles; but Mary was not an Apostle, nor had she any other ecclesiastical title or office. When Pope Paul reminds us over and over (as Pius XII and John XXIII also had done, but less insistently) that the Apostles were "together with Mary" at the original Pentecost, it would be a mistake to interpret this as a covert attempt to attribute a quasi-official position to her. The meaning is almost the very opposite: namely, that the apostolic ministers were filled with the Spirit, not for their own sake, but for the sake of the People of God, who are here represented in their supreme exemplification, the holy Virgin Mary.

In most of the texts selected for the present collection, little is said to explain their brief but frequent allusions to the Blessed Virgin. This is due largely to the fact that these texts have been selected for their doctrine about the Holy Spirit, not Mary. But it also seems to be a deliberate policy of Pope Paul to encourage devotion to Mary by example (e.g., by his pilgrimages to the Marian shrines of Fatima and Ephesus in 1967), more than by argument and discussion. However, these unexplained allusions to Mary may appear as disconcerting divagations to anyone not imbued with the rich doctrine on the Blessed Virgin that has developed in Catholic tradition. It will, therefore, be useful to indicate the main outlines of what Paul calls "the mysterious connection between the Holy Spirit and Mary" (Feb. 2, 1974) which he has at times explained at length. The chief source for his teaching on this subject is the Apostolic Exhortation, *Marialis Cultus,*[26] which deals with how Marian devotion can and must be adapted to the mentality of the present day. It should be read, however, in conjunction with the letter to Cardinal Suenens of May 13, 1975.[27] Although not so solemn and authoritative as the preceding document, this letter is much richer and more specific about Mary's relationship with the Holy Spirit. Other texts of major importance are the Apostolic Exhortation, *Signum Magnum,* (May 13, 1967), on the title, *Mother of the Church*[28] and the address of Oct. 25, 1969, to the Bishops' Synod, on Mary's relationship with the Church.[29]

Although Pope Paul takes for granted the whole Catholic tradition about the Mother of Jesus, he lays greatest stress on what we may call Mary as the eminent biblical exemplar of the Spirit-filled Christian. The Holy Spirit is given to those who believe in Christ (Jn 7:39). At the Annunciation, Mary became the first to believe in him, and in consequence, the first to be filled with his Spirit: blessed because she believed (Lk 1:45).

Being filled with the Spirit, she was "full of grace," and therefore incomparably beautiful:

> Mary is the Creature "all beautiful." She is the flawless mirror, the supreme ideal of perfection which the artists of every period have endeavored to reproduce in their works. She is the "woman clothed with the sun" (Apoc 12:1), in whom the purest rays of human beauty mingle with those sovereign inaccessible rays of supernatural beauty. And what is the reason for all this? It is that Mary is the one "full of grace," that is, we can say, full of the Holy Spirit, whose light shone forth in her with incomparable splendor. Yes,

we need to look to Mary, to focus on her unsullied beauty
these eyes of ours, too often hurt and blinded by the deceitful images of this world's beauty.[30]

. . .

We need to know the Madonna better as the authentic and
ideal model of redeemed humanity. Let us study this limpid
creature, this sinless Eve, this daughter of God in whose
innocent, stupendous perfection the original, creative
thought of God is mirrored intact. Mary is human beauty,
not only aesthetic, but essential, ontological, in synthesis
with divine love, with goodness and humility, with the
spirituality and the clear-sightedness of the "Magnificat."
She is the virgin, the Mother in the purest and most genuine
sense. . . .[31]

Such stress on the beauty of Mary comes from a deliberate,
pondered choice on the part of the Pope, who regards this as the best
way to present her to the mentality of our time, as he once mentioned
to a congress of theologians and pastors meeting in Rome to discuss the
theme, "Mary and the Holy Spirit."[32] However, the beauty attributed
to her is not a fiction of pious rhetoric, but the sober implication of the
scriptural teaching that she is "full of grace," "pleasing to God," and
one on whom the Holy Spirit came (Lk 1:28, 30, 35). She is simply the
supreme instance of the "new creation" or "new man" that is the
work of the Holy Spirit in human nature (Ti 3:5). This is brought out in
rich detail in the letter of May 13, 1975, to Cardinal Suenens. What is
honored in Mary is, therefore, the Holy Spirit, just as the Holy Spirit is
honored in the Church and in the individual Christian. After a pilgrimage to the great Marian shrine of Fatima, the Pope urged his listeners in
Rome:

We invite you to honor the Holy Spirit in the Madonna; she
was filled by him and from him received her divine
motherhood. Let us honor the Holy Spirit in the Church,
which is his temple and the vehicle which ministers him to
souls. Let us honor the Holy Spirit in each person who has
received him, in your own persons, who have been elevated
by him to the Christian life.[33]

But the holiness of this "incomparable dwelling place of the
Spirit"[34] was not merely the work of the Holy Spirit. Mary had to
respond personally to the action of the Spirit, to cooperate with his
inspirations. In this respect, also, therefore, she is a model. Contemplative though he is, Pope Paul has a tenacious practicality and almost
an activist bent that leads him to add with some force that Mary's
holiness:

... was also a result of the fact that she freely and earnestly heeded the interior promptings of the Holy Spirit at all times. It was this perfect harmony between divine grace and her own human activity that gave honor to the Blessed Trinity and made her the crowning glory of the Church.[35]

Mary is a special model for the priest, who receives in the sacrament of Orders a grace, not only for his own sanctification, but to minister to the sanctification of others:

Consider the fullness of grace that makes her "*tota pulchra*," blessed and immaculate. Do we not find some correspondence between that and the rich store of grace that was conferred on us when sacred ordination assimilated us to Christ through the charisms of holiness and ministerial grace? We would always do well to make Mary the mirror of our priesthood, our *speculum justitiae*.[36]

Mary is not only a model for individual believers and ministers in the Church; according to a venerable tradition, formulated by St. Ambrose and recalled by Vatican II,[37] she is a type or figure of the Church itself:

Her virginal procreation of Jesus is mystically reproduced in the Church's maternal and supernatural procreation of the faithful.[38]

Mary's status as model and type, either of the individual believer, the priest, or the Church as a whole, once it is rightly understood, does not seem to involve any major theological difficulties. But Pope Paul's understanding of her "mysterious connection" with the Holy Spirit goes much farther than that. He strongly reaffirms the Catholic tradition that sees her collaborating in the work of human salvation:

Here there opens before us a great theological panorama, characteristic of Catholic doctrine, in which we see how the divine plan of salvation, offered to the world by the one mediator between God and men, the one who is efficacious by his own power, Christ Jesus (I Tm 2:5, Heb 12:24), is carried out with human cooperation marvelously associated with the divine work.[39] And what human cooperation has been chosen in the history of our Christian destinies, if not that of Mary? First in function, dignity and efficacy, not merely instrumental and physical, her cooperation is that of a predestined, yet free and perfectly docile factor (cf. *Lumen Gentium*, 56).[40]

This text refers primarily to Mary's part in the Incarnation, when she was called upon to consent freely to becoming mother of the Son of God. But coming in a talk on how Mary can help the Church obtain the effects desired from the Holy Year, and which culminates in the recommendation to "have confidence in recourse to the intercession of the Blessed Virgin," this statement is obviously meant to imply that Mary's collaboration in the saving work of Jesus still goes on today.

The basis of this belief (not discussed by Pope Paul) is the doctrine of the communion of saints, according to which there is a communication of graces among the members of Christ's Body. That is to say, Spirit-filled Christians share the gift of the Spirit with one another and serve as channels to mediate his charisms to one another. Thus, St. Paul longed to visit Rome, so that he might impart some spiritual gift (*charisma*) to the brethren there, to strengthren them (Rom 1:11). This is the deepest level of the fellowship (*koinonia*) or sharing with one another, that was a prominent characteristic of the infant Church (Acts 2:42) and has been so joyously rediscovered in the Charismatic Renewal.

In contradistinction to most other Christian denominations, Catholic tradition holds that this communion is not cut off at death; rather, those who are "at home with the Lord" (2 Cor 5:8) remain in living union with their brethren in the world, and those who have "finished the race" (2 Tm 4:7) are all the more able to assist those who are still running (1 Cor 9:24).

Here, as in the preceding case, Mary is simply the most eminent example of a principle that applies to all. The work of bringing the grace of Christ to mankind is one in which everyone is called to take part. All such cooperation is totally subordinate to and dependent on the unique and sovereign work of Jesus Christ. Hence also "in the Virgin Mary everything is relative to Christ and dependent upon him."[41] Although this point might go without saying, it needs to be emphasized because of the spiritual temper of our time (*ibid.*). In any case, no one has a role so exalted or so universal in its influence as the one who, by her faith, received the Savior himself into the human world. And the role that she continues to play in the life and history of Christ's mystical Body is somehow typified by the role she played in regard to his physical body.

In describing more concretely what this present role amounts to, Pope Paul usually speaks in terms of intercession.

> We must have confidence in recourse to the intercession of
> the Blessed Virgin. We must pray to her, invoke her. She is
> admirable in herself, she is lovable to us. As in the Gospel

(cf. Jn 2:3, ff.), she intervenes with her divine Son and
obtains from him miracles that the ordinary course of events
would not admit. She is kind, she is powerful. She knows
human needs and sorrows. We must renew our devotion to
the Blessed Virgin[42] if we wish to obtain the Holy Spirit and
be sincere followers of Christ Jesus.[43]

Many Catholic theologians would be prepared to go farther, attributing
a kind of instrumental mediation of graces to Mary. In support of their
view, they could perhaps appeal to the widespread use of the title,
*mediatrix,* which occurs even in the documents of Vatican II.[44] Pope
Paul never seems to go this far when giving an explanation of Mary's
action in support of the faithful on earth; he speaks only of intercession. But there are allusions or brief remarks of his that suggest at least
an openness to something more, as when he prays to her: "Remember
all your sons; support their prayers to God, preserve their faith,
strengthen their hope, increase their charity,"[45] or when he cites the
text of St. Bernard, "When the Holy Spirit came upon her, he filled
her with grace for herself; when, coming again, he pervaded her, she
overflowed with superabundant grace for us also."[46]

The term which most appropriately sums up Pope Paul's teaching on Mary is the title, "Mother of the Church," which he proclaimed
in closing the Third Session of the Vatican Council.[47] This ancient but
little used title had not been employed in the Council documents, for
which reason the Pope's action provoked a small storm of protest by
commentators who felt that he was proceeding uncollegially.[48] But in
fact, this title does no more than capsulize the declaration of the Council that "the Catholic Church, taught by the Holy Spirit, honors her
with filial affection and devotion as a most loving mother."[49] It is
further explained that Mary "is a mother to us in the order of grace,"
and that "by her maternal charity, she cares for those brethren of her
Son who are still journeying on earth amid dangers and difficulties."[50]
The motherhood attributed to Mary implies that, over and above her
status as type or exemplar of the Christian life, she also contributes
actively and positively to the reception and pursuance of the life of
grace.

The Pope explained the rationale behind this term in the Apostolic Exhortation, *Signum Magnum* (May 13, 1967).[51] He points out
that a mother bears, nourishes and educates her child. Mary fulfilled
this role in regard to the Apostle John, according to the words of Jesus,
"Woman, behold your son" (Jn 19:26), and now she continues the
same role in regard to all mankind. This is a doctrine of faith, the Holy
Father points out, and can be explained in two ways. On the one hand,
her virtues make her a model of the Christian life. With greater reason

than St. Paul, she can say, "Be imitators of me as I am of Christ." On the other hand, she fosters the development of the life of grace in us "by her unceasing supplications, prompted by her deep love." Thus her motherhood sums up the two aspects of Mary's role regarding the Church that we have already discussed.

Over and above the explanation given by Pope Paul, we may note that the term *mother* immediately situates Mary in the sphere of life given and fostered. This is the life of which the Holy Spirit is the intrinsic and essential principle. Mary does not in any way supplant the Holy Spirit in this work; every quality in her and every grace she obtains for others, is itself the work of the Holy Spirit (Feb. 2, 1974). Like Paul and Apollos, she only plants and waters, while God gives the growth (1 Cor 3:6). Surely we can adapt to her the words of St. Paul, "You have countless guides in Christ, but not many fathers" (1 Cor 4:15), or still more aptly, "My little children, with whom I am again in travail until Christ be formed in you" (Gal 4:19).

The connection between Mary and the Holy Spirit is illustrated in a statement the Pope made for Pentecost, 1967, immediately after his pilgrimage to the Marian shrine at Fatima:

> Back from Fatima, we bring you the blessings of the Madonna. These seem to us to consist principally in good inspirations which ought to guide each one of us, and the whole of society as well, on the right paths of justice and peace. We believe that these inspirations come to us, in the final analysis, in so many forms, from the Holy Spirit, whose greatest feast we celebrate today, the feast of Pentecost.[52]

There are those who fear that devotion to Mary will distract from the Holy Spirit or from Christ. Pope Paul, in the great speech which declared that "our primary devotion should be to the Holy Spirit," added that "devotion to the Blessed Virgin leads us to this, as it leads us to Christ" (Nov. 29, 1972). His strongest statement, however, was made when he led the 1969 Synod of Bishops in a Mass concelebrated at St. Mary Major, the great Marian basilica of Rome:

> Mary obtains love. She conceived Christ through the action of the Holy Spirit, who is living love, God-love. She who presided over the birth of the Church on the day of Pentecost, when the Holy Spirit filled the group of disciples—the Apostles being first among them—and breathed a life of unity and charity into the mystical and historical body of Christians, into redeemed mankind. And we have come here to implore, through Mary's intercession, the never-

ending continuance of this same miracle; to obtain from her, as from a spring, a new outpouring of the Holy Spirit.[53]

The Pope is keenly aware that Catholic devotion to Mary is the cause of some difficulty for the ecumenical movement. But he replies:

> ... since it is the same power of the Most High which overshadowed the Virgin of Nazareth (Lk 1:35) and which today is at work within the ecumenical movement, making it fruitful, we wish to express our confidence that devotion to the humble Handmaid of the Lord, in whom the Almighty has done great things (Lk 1:49) will become, even if only slowly, not an obstacle but a path and a rallying point for the union of all who believe in Christ. We are glad to see that in fact a better understanding of Mary's place in the mystery of Christ and of the Church on the part also of our separated brethren is smoothing the path to union. Just as at Cana the Blessed Virgin's intervention resulted in Christ's performing his first miracle (Jn 2:1–12), so today her intercession can help to bring to realization the time when the disciples of Christ will again find full communion in faith.[54]

## NOTES

1. W. J. Hollenweger, *The Pentecostals* (Minneapolis, Augsburg, 1972), ch. 30.
2. *Ibid.*, chapter 27.
3. General Audience of May 14, 1964 (*OR*, May 14, 1964).
4. Cf. St. Thomas Aquinas, *Summa Theologiae*, III, 72.
5. Vatican II, *The Liturgy*, #71.
6. Cf. the preceding chapter in the sections, "Organic Society" and "Twofold Continuation."
7. On the other hand, as free agents, the clergy can act contrary to the inspiration of the Spirit, whereas the sacraments cannot.
8. Cf. what was said on this subject in chapter 2.
9. Westminster, Newman Press, 1965, pp. 359–360.
10. Cf. *Pope Paul VI*, by John Clancy (New York, Kenedy, 1963), chapter 1 and *Shepherd of Mankind* by William Barrett (New York, Doubleday, 1964), chapters 3–5.
11. Barrett, chapter 5.
12. Characteristically, he insisted that the members of the movement make a weekend retreat each year. Cf. William Barrett, *Shepherd of Mankind* (New York, Doubleday, 1964), p. 100.
13. Cf. Vatican II, *The Church*, #26 and 28.
14. From an address to the Roman Rota, Feb. 4, 1977 (*ORe*, Feb. 24, 1977).
15. General Audience of May 14, 1964 (*OR*, May 14, 1964).
16. From a homily at the ordination of 359 priests from all five continents, June 29, 1975 (*OR*, June 30–July 1, 1975; *ORe*, July 10, 1975).
17. Encyclical Letter, *Humanae Vitae* (July 25, 1968), #28.

18. General Audience of Nov. 12, 1969 (*OR*, Nov. 13, 1969; *ORe*, Nov. 20, 1969).

19. Address of Oct. 26, 1974, closing the Synod of Bishops (*OR*, Oct. 27, 1974; *ORe*, Nov. 7, 1974).

20. This sentence is not included in the excerpt cited in Part II. Cf. the General Audience of June 25, 1975 (*OR*, June 27, 1975; *ORe*, July 3, 1975).

21. Apostolic Exhortation, *Evangelization in the Modern World*, #73 (*OR*, Dec. 19, 1975; *ORe*, Dec. 25, 1975).

22. Address to the World Meeting on the Lay Apostolate, Oct. 11, 1975. (*OR*, Oct. 12, 1975; *ORe*, Oct. 23, 1975).

23. Apostolic Exhortation, *Evangelization in the Modern World*, #73 (*OR*, Dec. 19, 1975; *ORe*, Dec. 25, 1975).

24. P. 5. This document, drawn up by the Bishops' Committee for Pastoral Research and Practices at the request of the National Conference of Catholic Bishops, was published by the latter (Washington, D.C.).

25. Audience for Judges and other officials of the Sacred Roman Rota, Feb. 4, 1977 (*Ore*, Feb. 24, 1977).

26. Feb. 2, 1974. (*OR*, March 23, 1974; *ORe*, April 4, 1974). A simpler, more personal presentation of Marian devotion can be found in the homily for Aug. 15, 1964 (*TPS* 10, 1964–65, 55–59).

27. *OR*, May 19–20, 1975; *ORe*, June 5, 1975.

28. *AAS* 59 (1967) 465–475; *OR*, May 13, 1967; *TPS* 12 (1967) 278–286.

29. *OR*, Oct. 27–28, 1969; *ORe*, Nov. 6, 1969.

30. Address of May 16, 1975, to the Marian and Mariological Congresses meeting in Rome (*OR*, May 18, 1975; *ORe*, June 5, 1975).

31. General audience of May 30, 1973 (*OR*, May 31, 1973; *ORe*, June 7, 1973).

32. Reference as in note 30.

33. *Regina Caeli* message for the feast of Pentecost (*OR*, May 15–16, 1967). Translation by Thomas Bonaiuto.

34. Apostolic Exhortation, *Gaudete in Domino*, May 9, 1975, #4. (This passage is not included in the excerpt given in Part II.)

35. *Signum Magnum*; reference in note 28.

36. Reference in note 29.

37. Vatican II, *The Church* #53.

38. Reference in note 29.

39. Cf. H. De Lubac, *Méditation sur l'Eglise* (Paris, Aubier), p. 241 ff. (The note to the Pope's text does not indicate which edition of this work is referred to; presumably it is the original, published in 1953.—Editor's note.)

40. From an address at a General audience, May 30, 1973 (*OR*, May 31, 1973; *ORe*, June 7, 1973).

41. *Marialis Cultus*, #25.

42. Cf. Vatican II, *The Church*, #67.

43. From an address at a General audience, May 30, 1973 (*OR*, May 31, 1973; *ORe*, June 7, 1973).

44. Vatican II, *The Church*, #62.

45. Reference in note 47.

46. *Signum Magnum*, as in note 28. Cf. St. Bernard, Homily 2,2; *PL* 183:64.

47. *AAS* 56 (1964) 1007–1018. *TPS* 10 (1964–65) 131–141. An English translation of this address is also appended to *The Third Session*, by Xavier Rynne (New York, Farrar, Straus & Giroux, 1965), p. 381.

48. Cf. Xavier Rynne, *op. cit.*, p. 267 f.

49. Vatican II, *The Church*, #53.
50. Vatican II, *The Church*, #61 and #62.
51. Reference in note 28.
52. *Regina Caeli* message for the feast of Pentecost, May 14, 1967 (*OR*, May 15–16, 1967). Translated by Thomas Bonaiuto.
53. Reference in note 29.
54. *Marialis Cultus*, #33 (reference in note 26.)

# CHAPTER NINE

# The Spirit and Ecumenism

Pope Paul has said many times that the ecumenical movement is the work of the Holy Spirit.[1] In closing the Week of Prayer for Unity among Christians, he spoke of the quest for reconciliation among Christians as "the work of the Holy Spirit and an expression of that 'wisdom and patience' with which the Lord 'follows out the plan of his grace on behalf of us sinners.' "[2] He has often cited the aspiration toward unity which has arisen all over the world in diverse Christian denominations, as one of the signs that the Spirit is at work in the world today.[3]

The Spirit demands unity of us, he teaches, and is actually bringing unity about among us. Whatever unity is actually to be found in the Church is the work of the Holy Spirit, and it is to the Holy Spirit that we must look for its complete realization. To a delegation from the Orthodox Patriarchate of Moscow, he said:

> We pray that the divisions of centuries will be overcome in the truth and charity of Christ, and that the Holy Spirit will bring to completion a work that has been begun under his inspiration—a work that is indeed manifested among the signs of the times.[4]

The Pope's most important statement associating ecumenism with the action of the Holy Spirit is the address of Oct. 26, 1967, which is cited in Part II.

But Paul does not leave it to the Holy Spirit to bring about this unity by a purely divine action. In keeping with his teaching on the responsibility of man to cooperate with the action of the Spirit, he has done everything in his power, both by dramatic gestures and by practical measures, to prepare for the reunion of Christians, and to urge others to do so. The image which may well stamp this Pope's place in

111

history is that of his meeting with Patriarch Athenagoras of Constantinople, the head of the Greek Orthodox Church. This was the first direct contact between the bishops of Rome and Constantinople since the schism of 1054. Their meeting in the holy city, Jerusalem, Jan. 5 and 6, 1964, was not just a formal gesture, but a warm and moving encounter between two brothers in Christ, both devoted to recovering unity between their divided flocks. After they had embraced one another affectionately, the Patriarch addressed his "most holy brother in Christ, the Pope of Rome," while the Pope spoke of the two of them as "pilgrims from Rome and Constantinople" who had "been able to meet and join in common prayer."[5]

The following year (Dec. 7, 1965), the Pope and the Patriarch issued a common document lifting the sentences of excommunication which Romans and Greeks had leveled against one another in the schism of 1054. Acknowledging that this gesture of justice and mutual pardon was not sufficient to end the differences between the two churches, they declared their assurance that:

> Through the action of the Holy Spirit, those differences will be overcome through cleansing of hearts, through regret for historical wrongs, and through an efficacious determination to arrive at a common understanding and expression of the faith of the Apostles and its demands.[6]

The cause of Christian unity is a matter of very high priority with Pope Paul. "He has," says Yves Congar, "made ecumenism the most comprehensive and dynamic idea of his pontificate."[7] Even before becoming Pope, he declared that ecumenism would be one of the chief aims of the Council.[8] In opening the Fourth Session, he announced his intention to "promote that mystical unity which Christ left to his Apostles as the most precious and authentic heritage and as his supreme exhortation."[9] In actual fact, he has pursued this end tirelessly.

Three years after the meeting in Jerusalem, he went to Istanbul for another visit with Athenagoras. The usual protocol would have called for the latter to visit the Pope in Rome first—something the Patriarch was more than willing to do. But in one of those dramatic, precedent-shattering gestures characteristic of him, Paul took the first step. He set the unity of the Body of Christ above questions of rank and dignity, and demonstrated his readiness to go to every possible length to heal the divisions of the past.[10]

In 1975, when a delegation from the Patriarchate of Constantinople came to Rome to celebrate the tenth anniversary of the lifting of the excommunications, Pope Paul again startled the ecclesiastical world by kneeling down before Archbishop Meliton and kissing his feet.[11] This gesture expressed both the humility of one who, holding the highest office in the Church, regards himself as the servant of all, and the contrition of one who, as head of the Catholic Church, acknowledges that Catholics have been guilty of their share of the wrongs that have divided Catholics and Orthodox from one another. The Patriarch of Constantinople said that "by this manifestation, the most venerable, and our most beloved brother, the Pope of Rome, Paul VI, has excelled himself, and has shown to the Church and the world who the Christian bishop and above all the first bishop of Christendom is and can be, namely, a force of reconciliation and unification of the Church and the world."[12]

These dramatic actions have been accompanied and followed by a long series of others, less colorful, but no less important for the steady progress toward unity. Besides his own visit to the World Council of Churches in Geneva (June 11–12, 1969), the Pope has received visits from representatives of innumerable other Christian churches and non-Christian religions. Archbishop Michael Ramsey, Archbishop of Canterbury, came in 1966,[13] as did his successor, Archbishop Donald Coggan, in 1977. In between them (as well as before and after them), has come a long line of patriarchs, archbishops, bishops and their counterparts in the various churches. Pope Paul's most important work for ecumenism may well have been the unfailing friendliness, respect, openness and warmth with which he has encountered them all.

Most of these meetings have been the occasion of public statements on Christian unity. For example, together with the Catholicos of the Apostolic Armenian Church, Paul issued a statement which said:

> Conscious of their duties as pastors, they (the Pope and the Catholicos) invite all Christians, especially those of the Catholic Church and of the Apostolic Armenian Church, to respond with ever greater fidelity to the call of the Holy Spirit, which urges toward a more profound unity which will accomplish the will of our common Savior, and will make the service of the world by Christians more fruitful.[14]

In addition to public gestures and statements of policy, Paul has also acted on the practical level to eliminate obstacles and move toward actual union. He has approved the erection of several theological commissions to study the doctrinal, liturgical and disciplinary differences between the Catholic Church and other churches. He has encouraged work on a Common Bible, intended to enable the various denominations to work from the same text. He has reformed the

Catholic discipline concerning mixed marriages, in order to remove the offense given by the previous Church regulation. He has given permission, in cases of need, for Catholics to receive Communion in the Orthodox Church, or for non-Catholics, under certain conditions, to receive Communion in the Catholic Church.[15]

Pope Paul's ecumenism has not been confined to the Christian churches. Leaders and representatives of innumerable non-Christian religions have also gotten a very warm reception from him. Paul's own position is expressed in the following statement he made about the teaching of Vatican II on non-Christian beliefs:

> The Fathers (of the Council) saw in them, in fact, a very significant, even if incomplete, expression of the religious genius of mankind, a testimony of the secret action carried out in the course of the centuries by the grace of the Holy Spirit (which fills the whole earth; cf. Wis 1:7 and Is 6:3) in order to bring forth in upright souls the "seeds of the Word which lie hidden in them," so that those religious manifestations, in spite of the differences, "often reflect a ray of that Truth which enlightens all men."[16]

The ecumenical activity of the Pope is characterized by the assumption that the Holy Spirit is present and active in all men of good will, inspiring in them a desire for that unity willed by Christ, and impelling them inexorably toward it. It is the responsibility of churchmen, therefore, not to produce the unity of the Body of Christ, which only the Spirit can create, but merely to foster and support on the institutional and theological planes the interior action of the Spirit.

At the same time, however, the Pope is convinced that Christian unity does require a definite institutional and theological configuration. This unity does not consist simply in an inner communion of hearts, nor in an unknown kingdom of the future, the form of which is still quite indeterminate. It is realized in the Church, founded by Christ, preserved by him through the Spirit up to the present time, and guaranteed by him to remain until his return. This side of Paul's teaching accounts for certain statements and stands of his that may at first seem inconsistent with the humility, openness and generosity of the foregoing sentiments. For example, he repeatedly cites texts of St. Augustine insisting that the Holy Spirit can be had solely in the Body of Christ, which is identified with the Catholic Church. The sharpest of these passages is from a letter on the Donatists, in which Augustine says, "Only the Catholic Church is the Body of Christ. . . . Outside this body the Holy Spirit does not vivify anyone. . . . Those who are outside the Church do not have the Holy Spirit."[17]

Such texts, however, are used by Pope Paul in what we may
call a very different *mood* from that which they had in the work of
Augustine. While we cannot here deal adequately with the richness of
the thought of this great Father of the Latin Church, it can be said,
speaking simply and grossly, that he was a pioneer, affirming a fundamental principle of the Christian economy which the Church of
subsequent eras has maintained, but with more nuances. This principle
(already dealt with in the preceding chapter) is that the Church is the
human matrix in and by which Jesus intends for the life of the Spirit to
be nurtured. Deliberately to reject the Church, therefore, or to cut
oneself off from it, is to close oneself to the Spirit.

What theologians did not come to recognize until long after
Augustine's age is that not everyone who remains "outside the
Church" is guilty of rejecting the economy instituted by Christ. The
saving grace of Christ attains even those who have not been reached by
a missionary. Furthermore, it is possible (and is presumably a frequent
occurrence) for someone who does know something of the Church to
fail to recognize in it the authentic People of God. He may be of good
will; and if he cooperates loyally with the grace of God by which "all
mankind are called to salvation," he will be saved—which implies that
he has been animated by the Holy Spirit. This teaching of Vatican II[18]
was supplemented by the formal recognition that Christian churches
and ecclesial bodies separated from the Holy See do nevertheless retain
authentic elements of the Church and are used by the Holy Spirit as
means of salvation.[19]

Pope Paul, who presided over the publication of these declarations, takes them for granted when speaking of the connection between the Spirit and the Church. His citations from Augustine are
aimed, not at the Orthodox or the Protestants, but at those Catholics
who, by their contentiousness, contempt and disobedience, are wound-
ing the Body of Christ.[20] He uses a strong statement from a weighty
authority to give force to his admonitions; but the spirit of his message
is better represented by another text of Augustine which, in fact, he
uses much more often: "We have the Holy Spirit if we love the
Church; we love the Church if we abide in its structures and in its
charity" (June 6, 1965). The Pope's personal attitude toward the
churches separated from Rome is illustrated by the message he sent to
representatives of the Orthodox Churches meeting in Geneva to prepare for a Pan-Orthodox Conference. Paul assured them of his fervent
prayers, "that the Holy Spirit may enlighten and guide your assembly
for the best service of the venerable Orthodox Church."[21]

It remains true, however, that the Pope regards the Catholic
Church not merely as one among several alternative forms of Chris-

tianity, nor even as merely the best of the various historic achieve-
ments of Christian community, but as truly and simply the one Church
founded by Jesus Christ, and the only one that can properly be said to
be animated by the Holy Spirit. He does not hesitate to call it "the one
true Church" (May 17, 1964), "the only one that is complete and
perfect in its conception."[22] By this, of course, he does not mean that,
in its actual human reality, the Church lives up perfectly to the call of
Jesus. The Pope's entire program of renewal is based on the keen
awareness that this is not the case; and no one is readier than he to
acknowledge failures. His point is that the Church founded by Jesus
Christ still exists today in what is called the (Roman) Catholic Church,
which, thanks to the Spirit of Jesus, retains the essential vitality of the
Body of the Lord, along with all the means of sanctification with which
it was initially endowed. Other churches, even if they have much of the
substance of the Church, such as scripture and some or all of the
sacraments, suffer from constitutive defects. At the very least, they
lack the unity which Christ wished to bestow on his followers, which
comes through the pastoral direction of the Apostles and their successors, under the headship of Peter.

This understanding of the Church is not, of course, original
with Pope Paul. It is the classical Catholic ecclesiology, which was
firmly, even though gently and tactfully, maintained by Vatican II.[23] It
is not motivated by the intention of belittling other denominations.
Vatican II exerted itself to give credit in every way possible to the
authentic Christian realities preserved by those separated from the
Catholic Church, and to recognize them as brothers who "have a right
to be called Christians."[24] The acts of Pope Paul sketched above make
it more than obvious that he has maintained this same attitude.

Likewise, the doctrine on the "one, true Church" is not
motivated by smug complacency or self-glorification. On the contrary,
as the Pope himself acutely notes, "it takes wisdom and humility to
adhere to the Church in its human, concrete, and sometimes faulty
manifestation" (May 20, 1964). What he says is perhaps more true
today than ever before in history; for the intellectual atmosphere of our
world, even more than its physical atmosphere, is polluted with
acidulous criticism of sacred institutions. "We are not being trium-
phalistic," the Pope says in explanation of his teaching:

... We are seeking to interpret the historical and social, that
is to say ecclesial system, that the Lord laid down for the
spread of the Gospel and the building up of his Church.[25]

This must be the starting point of any authentically Christian
concept of the Church. Ecclesiology is not just sociology; it cannot

take its principal directives from even the noblest social ideals such as democracy, liberty or fraternity. If mankind is to be brought together under the headship of Christ, and if the unity of the Church willed by Christ is to be recovered, this will never be achieved on the basis of plans devised by the cleverest human intelligence, but solely by compliance with the mind of Christ. Before we have the right to denounce a strong doctrine on the Church as, e.g., "a demonic pretension," we must ask, What did Jesus himself intend for his Church to be?

There is, of course, a school of thought which contends that Jesus did not envision a church; that his expectation of an imminent end of the world left no room for the organization of a religious society. Without entering into a debate on the matter, Pope Paul proceeds from the assumption that the Church is the work of Jesus, and must be construed according to his plan.

If this assumption be granted, the essential question posed by his position, which is the traditional Catholic position, is whether the Church of Christ can be identified in the world as a real, historical, human society that can be traced through history; or whether the "true Church" is something that transcends each and every religious association that seeks to realize it in society.

In identifying the Church with a concrete human society, Paul is not of course reducing it to its visible or social components. That which is primary in the Church is spiritual and mystical, as we have seen in the preceding chapter. The Church is, if you will, like an inverted iceberg, the greater part of which is hidden in the heavens. But Paul is maintaining the position which he and Vatican II inherited from Plus XII,[26] that the Church's visible, social embodiment is an integral part of it, giving it an identity in the world and in history.

Because the Church is not merely a natural, human society, there is the possibility, not paralleled elsewhere, that people who are not members of it on the human, social level, may nevertheless be in profound and vital communion with it through the Holy Spirit. But when all that is granted, it remains that the Body of Christ is embodied in a definite community of human beings who give it an historical identity and a recognizable countenance. This is what the Catholic Church understands itself to be.

Even when thus modestly restricted, the claim of a particular human reality to enjoy a privileged and exclusive relationship with the divine is difficult to admit. However, it should be noted that this difficulty is characteristic of the whole order of the Incarnation. It is difficult to believe that a given human being could be the unique Son of God. It is difficult to believe that one little race should have been chosen by God as his peculiar people, and anointed as his witnesses and the bearers of his blessings to the entire world. For precisely the same reason it is difficult to believe that one society should be uniquely his Church, the Body of his Son and the temple of his Spirit.

To conceive of the "true Church" as transcending all particular human societies is much less obnoxious to human reason (human pride?), but the question to be asked is whether such a concept corresponds to the teaching of Jesus and the portrait of the Church traced in the New Testament. Such a church is usually envisioned either as an invisible, spiritual entity, of which visible societies are merely symbols; or an ideal, at which the real churches aim without being able to attain it; or a future goal, not to be realized until the end of history; or a nebulous spirit, embodied in a multitude of disparate particular traditions.

All of these views are current, often combined with one another, in the ecclesiological and ecumenical thought of our day.[27] All of them contain elements of truth which Pope Paul would undoubtedly acknowledge; e.g., that all sincere believers do belong in some hidden way to the Church; that as it now exists, the Church realizes only imperfectly the ideal which Christ set for it; that there is a plurality of legitimate traditions within the Church; that it will not attain its perfection until the *parousia*; etc. But the New Testament pictures the Church as a concrete fellowship of real people who were identified by the faith they professed and the Baptism they had received. They knew the identity of one another and of their pastors, by whom they were directed. Their neighbors were so aware of their distinct identity that they soon invented a name for them—Christians (Acts 11:26). The primitive Church in Jerusalem was nothing other than that community of men and women who "were together and had all things in common"; who "devoted themselves to the Apostles' teaching and fellowship, to the breaking of bread and the prayers" (Acts 2:42–44). The churches in Corinth, Ephesus, Thessalonika, etc., were definite communities to which Paul could address letters. And when the captivity epistles give the term *Church* to the brotherhood of all the local communities, the mystical attributes applied to it, as "Body of Christ" and "dwelling place of God in the Spirit," do not dissociate the Church from these particular communities with their idiosyncracies so well known to the Apostle. Thus, for example, to have the peace to which they were called "in the one body," they are admonished that they must practice meekness, patience and forbearance with one another (Col 3:12–15).

We can study the question at a deeper level by asking whether the Church is properly the work of Christ or the work of men. (In this case, of course, we refer the term *Church* to the historical human community, as was without a doubt the reference of the Hebrew *qahal* and the Greek *ekklesia*.) That the Church in this sense is the work of men is tacitly assumed by much ecclesiological literature and ecumenical activity today. From such a standpoint, no absolute claims can be made for any particular church. There can be at best only relative superiority in one or another respect, and that usually only transitory.

The position espoused by Pope Paul stands on the assumption that the Church is properly the work of Jesus Christ himself. Without a doubt, it is the work of men also. Through their actions, the Church has been constructed; the wisdom of their projects, the mistakes they have made, the options they have taken, have really shaped its development. Nevertheless, in and through human activity, and also above and beneath it, and even, if need be, apart from it, Christ has built his Church. He founded it; but he did not then leave it to make its own way through history. He promised to remain with it until the end of the world (Mt 28:20), and by his presence he sustains, strengthens, teaches, inspires, guides, animates, purifies and sanctifies it; one day as sovereign Lord, he will perfect it. This does not provide a cover for the obvious errors committed by its members or its pastors; it does not relieve us of our responsibility to build up, and if need be to reform, the Church in the measure of our ability. But it does mean that the life and development of the Church follow a different dynamic from that of any other human society.

How the infallible action of Jesus has its way amid the fallible actions of his servants is a mystery we do not have to resolve. What is essential is the faith that, just as Yahweh Elohim took slime of the earth and molded it into a living body, so Jesus builds us as living stones into the temple of his Spirit. How so a holy a temple can be made out of such sinful materials is a question that can be debated in the tract on justification. It does not shake the certainty that "We are, if we hold fast, the house of God, of which Jesus is the builder" (Heb 3:2–6). "I will build my Church," he says in the Gospel of Matthew (16:18); and this statement, regardless of form-critical speculations about the original circumstances in which it was uttered, expresses the deepest truth about the relationship of Jesus to his Church: he is its builder. This is the basis of Pope Paul's ecclesiology.

When, therefore, Paul supposes that the Church has retained its authentic identity amid the changing but unrelenting pressures of external situations and the unabating ferment of interior sinfulness, he is not affirming this as a human achievement over which anyone could boast, but is witnessing to a sovereign work of Jesus Christ, before which every human being must be humbled. His assurance comes from reliance, not on the history of a juridical structure but on the promises of Christ. He does not attribute to the Church a (monopolistic) hold on the Spirit; he sees the Church as sustained by the power of the Spirit:

> Yes, we have hope, we have confidence. . . . This confidence springs from the divine promises: both because the Holy Spirit is in the Church, is the soul of the Church, vivifies, supports and guides it and does not abandon it because it belongs to him; and also because Christ's words are true: "and behold, I am with you all days, even to the consummation of the world" (Mt 28:20); "you are Peter, and upon this rock I will build my Church, and the gates of hell shall not prevail against it" (Mt. 16:18).[28]

The basic principle of Pope Paul's ecumenism, therefore, may be summarized thus: the unity of the Spirit demands the unity of the Body. And the Body of Christ is nothing other than that Church which, founded on the Apostles, has maintained its identity throughout the vicissitudes of history, and still exists today as the Catholic Church. Whatever formulas may be elaborated for the restoration of full communion between the Church of Rome and other denominations—an area in which the Pope seems disposed to make every possible concession—there is no way that this basic supposition can be given up. Paul's overall stand was outlined in a statement made at Bethlehem about his first meeting with the Patriarch Athenagoras:

> This is the historic hour in which the Church of Christ must live its deep and visible unity. It is the hour in which we must heed the wish of Jesus Christ: "May they become perfectly one, so that the world may know that you (O Father) have sent me. . ." (Jn 17:23). We repeat that we are disposed to consider every reasonable possibility to smooth out the path of understanding, reverence and charity, as preparation for a future and, God grant, early meeting with the brethren presently separated from us. The door of the fold is open. All are waiting sincerely and eagerly. The desire for this meeting is strong and patient. There is abundant room. The step to be taken is preceded by our affection and can be carried out with enthusiasm and mutual happiness. We shall refrain from requiring any acts which may not be free and based on conviction, that is to say, moved by the Spirit of the Lord, who breathes where and when he wills. We shall await this happy hour. For the present, we shall merely ask our most beloved brethren to do what we propose to ourselves: may the love of Christ and his Church inspire every eventual gesture of reconciliation and dialogue.[29]

Here, the warm and open friendliness, so characteristic of Pope Paul's human relations, is coupled with the unflinching consciousness that he speaks as chief pastor of the flock of Christ: only as such can he declare, "The door of the fold is open," and, "We shall refrain from requiring any acts which may not be free and based on conviction." Although Paul regards the papal office as one of service to the unity of the Church, he is well aware, and has said so,[30] that it is seen by many as one of the chief obstacles to ecumenical reunion. Nevertheless, he maintains it uncompromisingly, convinced that no one has the right to alter the structure laid down by the Prince of Pastors, the Lord of the Church himself.

It would not be fair to say that his position demands the capitulation of other churches to the Catholic vision. There is no question of capitulation to anyone but Christ himself (cf. 2 Cor 9:13; 10:5). Paul is bound in conscience to uphold what he believes to be the will of Christ; and he calls on others likewise to be loyal to the truth as they see it:

> The search for unity also calls for complete loyalty to all the demands of truth.[31]

Does this make the goal of Church unity impossible? The various churches are presumably convinced already that their way is that of truth; what power on earth can ever bring them into agreement? Pope Paul, who has unrelentingly pursued the cause of unity on all fronts since the beginning of his papacy, is as aware as anyone of the "serious obstacles still to be overcome"[32]—the immense and complex difficulties that still block the way.

> If there is any project which forces us to acknowledge the impotence of our human powers to produce any good results, and their essential dependence on the mysterious, powerful action of the Holy Spirit, it is that of ecumenism.[33]

In spite of the obstacles, Paul remains steadfastly optimistic.

The basis of his optimism is the same Holy Spirit who summons us to unity. In a meditation for the 1977 Week of Christian Unity, he took for his theme the text of Romans 5:5: "Hope does not disappoint us." Declaring that "hope is the moving spirit of the ecumenical cause," he called upon all those who still hesitate to embrace this cause, those who have wearied of laboring for it, those whose interest has changed into routine, and those who are tempted to be satisfied with incomplete results, all to take hope. He added:

> This is the Christian's supreme hope, which he knows "will not disappoint" him, because he has within himself the

active presence of the Holy Spirit who has been given to us
(Rom 5:5). In fact the outpouring of the Spirit in our hearts
brings about in Christians a change which is slow and hard
won, but certain. It is a change which leads toward the
formation of the new man, "until we all attain to the unity
of the faith and of the knowledge of God, to mature man-
hood, to the measure of the stature of the fullness of Christ"
(Eph 4:13).[34]

That Paul's hope has not been in vain is evidenced by the
ecumenical progress already made. Ten years after the Joint Declaration issued by himself and the Patriarch Athenagoras, it was possible to
declare:

> The Holy Spirit has enlightened our intelligences and has
> brought us to see with greater clarity that the Catholic
> Church and the Orthodox Church are united by such a deep
> communion that very little is needed to reach the fullness
> that would authorize a common celebration of the Lord's
> Eucharist... may we be able to progress together in iden-
> tifying the divergencies and difficulties that still separate
> our Churches, and finally overcome them by a reflection of
> faith and docility to the impulses of the Spirit.... It is the
> Divine Spirit himself who asks us to carry out the task.[35]

## NOTES

1. "The pursuit of unity among Christians . . . is the work of the Holy Spirit," Dec.
   22, 1975 (*ORe*, Jan. 8, 1976).
2. Jan. 25, 1975 (*OR*, Jan. 27–28, 1975, *ORe*, Feb. 6, 1975). See also his remarks
   to the College of Cardinals, Dec. 22, 1975 (*OR*, Dec. 22–23, 1975; *ORe*, Jan. 8,
   1976).
3. Cf. pp. 13–14.
4. July 3, 1975 (*OR*, July 5, 1975; *ORe*, July 10, 1975).
5. Cf. *Paul VI* by J. L. Gonzalez and T. Perez (Boston, St. Paul, 1964), p. 123. See
   also A. Wenger, *La deuxième session* (Centurion, Paris, 1964), ch. XI.
6. W. Abbot, *Documents of Vatican II*, p. 726.
7. "Paul VI and Ecumenism" (*ORe*, Sept. 29, 1977).
8. Address of April 27, 1962, to the Institute for the Study of International Politics,
   in G. B. Montini, *The Church*, Helicon Press, 1964, pp. 209 f.
9. Sept. 14, 1965.
10. Detailed discussions of the Pope's visit to Turkey can be found in the *Osservatore
    Romano*, Italian edition, from July 25 to August 3, 1967. See also the illuminat-
    ing commentaries of R. Laurentin and C. J. Dumont in *Informations Catholiques
    Internationales* 293–294 (Août 1967), pp. 4–5, and that of D. Caloyeras in the
    English *Osservatore Romano* for Aug. 18, 1977.
11. *ORe*, Jan. 1, 1976.
12. *ORe*, Jan. 8, 1976. Paul also adopted the term, *sister Churches*, in reference to
    the Orthodox. See, e.g., his communication to Dimitrios I, June 29, 1977 (*ORe*,

July 14, 1977). This term had already been in use among the Orthodox as including the Church of Rome.

13. This visit was not unprecedented. Archbishop Geoffrey Fisher had already paid an epoch-making visit to Pope John in 1960.

14. Statement of May 12, 1970 (*OR,* May 13, 1970; *ORe,* May 21, 1970).

15. The most important documents on all these points are published in *Vatican Council II,* edited by Austin Flannery (Collegeville, MN, 1975), # 33–44.

16. Address of July 6, 1974, to Cardinal Sergio Pignedoli together with the Officials of the Secretariat for non-Christians (*OR,* July 7, 1974; *ORe,* July 18, 1974). The quotations are taken from Vatican II, *The Missionary Activity of the Church,* #11. The Pope gives the Latin text of the Conciliar decrees, but for the sake of simplicity they are translated here into English. Cf. also the address to Catholic missionaries of Jan. 6, 1974 (*OR,* Jan. 16, 1974).

17. Cited by Pope Paul on June 12, 1974. See also the texts cited on May 20, 1964; May 18, 1966; April 25, 1970; Nov. 29, 1972; etc.

18. Vatican II, *The Church,* #13–16.

19. Vatican II, *Ecumenism,* #3; cf. *The Church,* #15.

20. Cf. chapter 2 above.

21. Message to His Eminence, Meliton, Metropolitan of Chalcedon, on the occasion of the First Pan-Orthodox Conference in preparation for the Great Holy Council of the Orthodox Churches, Chambesy (Geneva), Nov. 21–30, 1976 (*ORe,* Dec. 20, 1976).

22. General Audience of Aug. 29, 1973 (*OR,* Aug. 30, 1973; *ORe,* Sept. 6, 1973).

23. Vatican II taught that Jesus Christ founded one and only one Church, shepherded by the Apostles under the headship of Peter. This Church "subsists" today in the Catholic Church, in which the Apostles have been succeeded by the bishops, and Peter by the Pope. All men are called to belong to this Church, which is necessary for salvation, at least for those who are aware of it. The "unity of the one and only Church, which Christ bestowed on his Church from the beginning . . . still subsists in the Catholic Church as something she can never lose." The Catholic Church is the "all-embracing means of salvation," the "universal sacrament of salvation." It and it alone possesses the fullness of the means of salvation instituted by Christ. While authentic elements of the Church have been retained in those churches and ecclesial bodies that have separated from Rome, and while the latter are indeed used by the Holy Spirit for the salvation of their members, even these elements "belong by right to the one Church of Christ." (Cf. Constitution on the Church, #3, 8, 13–16, 48; Decree on Ecumenism, #3, 4; Decree on the Pastoral Office of Bishops, #2, 3; Decree on the Church's Missionary Activity, 4–6. Pope Paul cites some of these texts in an important document, the *Apostolic Exhortation, Reconciliation Within the Church,* Dec. 8, 1974 (*OR,* Dec. 16–17, 1974; *ORe,* Dec. 26, 1974).

  When the statement that the Church of Christ *is* the Catholic Church was reworded to read "subsists in," in *Lumen Gentium,* #8, the Theological Commission responsible for the change explained that this was done in order to accord better with the affirmation that elements of the Church are to be found elsewhere. Thus the Council in no way detracted from the identity of the Catholic Church as the Church of Christ; it simply acknowledged that authentic elements of the Church are to be found "outside its visible boundaries." Cf. *Acta Synodalia Sacrosancti Concilii Oecumenici Vaticani Secundi, Vol. III, pars 1 (Vatican City, 1973) p. 177.*

24. Vatican II, Decree on Ecumenism, #3.

25. Homily at a Mass for Missionaries on the Feast of the Epiphany, Jan. 6, 1974 (*ORe,* Jan. 16, 1974). A few months later Paul wrote of "the quest for the visible unity of all Christians in the way determined by Christ, in one and the same

Church." (*Apostolic Exhortation, Reconciliation Within the Church*, Dec. 8, 1974 (*OR,* Dec. 16–17, 1974; *ORe,* Dec. 26, 1974).

26. On this see chapter 2 at notes 21, 22 and 23.

27. A recent example is Langdon Gilkey's allusion to "...the various communions: Orthodox, Roman Catholic, Anglican, the forms of Protestantism, each expressing historical and relative interpretations and perspectives on the infinite richness of the faith, each embodying the true Church in its own way, but in fragmentary, partial, historical form" (in *Experience of the Spirit,* edited by Bassett and Huizing, New York, Seabury, 1977, p. 65).

28. Address to the College of Cardinals, June 21, 1976 (*OR,* June 21–22, 1976; *ORe,* July 1, 1976).

29. Address of Jan. 6, 1964, at Bethlehem (*OR,* Jan. 7–8, 1964). I have not found any translation of this address in English. The citation given here, translated by Bishop Edward L. Heston, C.S.C., appeared in *Paul VI,* by J. L. Gonzalez and T. Perez (Boston, St. Paul, 1964) pp. 127f.

30. In the address of April 28, 1967, to the Secretariat for the Promotion of the Unity of Christians (*OR,* April 30, 1967; *TPS* 12 (1967), p. 101).

31. Address of Nov. 12, 1976, to the Secretariat for the Promotion of the Unity of Christians (*OR,* Nov. 13, 1976; *ORe,* Nov. 25, 1976). This document, which cannot be reproduced here for want of space, is one of the most important of Pope Paul's statements on ecumenism.

32. *Ibid.*

33. Address of April 28, 1967, as in note 30.

34. General Audience of Jan. 19, 1977 (*ORe,* Jan. 27, 1977).

35. Address of Dec. 14, 1975, to Patriarch Dimitrios I (*OR,* Dec. 15–16, 1975; *ORe,* Jan. 1, 1976).

# PART 2
# Texts of Pope Paul VI

# The Paraclete*

The Pope observed that the day's Gospel[1] gives matter for much reflection and meditation. However, he chose for consideration only a single word in it, a word that is full of profound meaning, and one that has become commonplace in our catechesis— the word *Paraclete*. Our Lord, he said, seems to pronounce this name as though sharing a confidence or revealing a secret. It came to his lips during the farewell discourse at the Last Supper, when Jesus was trying, with a gentle but profound message, to prepare the Apostles for the great events in the history of the Gospel and of the world that were soon to take place.

The Passion was about to begin, and Jesus felt the duty, we may say, of taking leave of his own. In the act of departing, he reveals the relationship that will exist between him and them from this point on. He announces that he is going to leave their physical sight, and that he is concerned about them, about those who have listened to and believed his words. He is concerned with how the great certitude of the Kingdom of God, which he had initiated and founded, was to endure among them in his absence.

He proclaims a new relationship between himself and man, a relationship that will become an interior conversation between God and souls. Seeing his disciples sad and bewildered, he declares that he will send them the Holy Spirit, the Paraclete. This word has many meanings: advocate, aid, help, defender, consoler, one who stands close by and comes to give assistance, to infuse energy, to bring something new. This is precisely what the catechism calls grace, the presence of God operating within us in order to make our souls holy and good.

For those who know how to listen and to follow, who seek that ineffable and wonderful interior conversation, the Paraclete becomes the active voice of God in the depths of souls. For the Christian, spiritual life is not merely an unfolding of his natural energies, but the development of the Holy Spirit's indwelling within us, in what might be called a symbiosis or union of lives.

This is the relationship that our Lord wants to establish with those who follow him and are sustained by him, a relationship that is not sensible, but is nevertheless real, new and above our natural faculties. Today's Mass invites us to this communion with God by the Gospel revelation that is offered for our meditation. (If we reflect on the way this meditation fits into the course of the liturgical year, the thought occurs that the feast of the Ascension will ensue, and that Christ will vanish from the historical sight and presence of our devotion.)

Thus, the Church tells us: cultivate devotion to the Holy Spirit, and you will be in communion with Christ. You will understand that from an exterior teacher, our Lord

*Homily preached in the Vatican Basilica for the Fourth Sunday after Easter. The actual text of the Pope's homily is not available: what is given here is a reporter's summary of the homily, which appeared in the *Osservatore Romano* of April 27, 1964. The translation is by Thomas Bonaiuto. A comparison of this text with the authentic texts that follow gives us every reason to suppose that this was a very accurate report of what was actually said. It is in fact remarkable how many of Pope Paul's favorite themes are touched upon here: the interior voice of God, the Christian life conceived as a dialogue or conversation with God, exhortation to cultivate devotion to the Holy Spirit, the Seven Gifts, the experience of grace, the joy and energy that comes from the Spirit, etc.

has become, as St. Augustine says, the interior teacher, the inspirer of our good thoughts and good will through the language of the Paraclete. The Paraclete makes us capable of virtue that we would not know how to exercise of ourselves. He is the source of the Seven Gifts, as anyone who has been confirmed will remember. These energies of wisdom, understanding, counsel, fortitude, knowledge, piety and fear of the Lord cause the soul to glow with spiritual life, to reflect the divine life above it, thus becoming a mirror for those rays which come down from heaven, and which Christ shines on souls that are receptive to this light.

Pope Paul went on to remind the faithful of an episode narrated in the Acts of the Apostles.[2] St. Paul asked a group of early Christians in Ephesus whether they had received the Holy Spirit. Because these faithful had not yet heard of the Holy Spirit, Paul conferred on them the baptism instituted by Jesus, and laid hands on them. They too were filled with the Holy Spirit and began to prophesy, to exalt our Lord, and to experience[3] that interior fullness of grace which permeated them with the presence of God.

The question asked by St. Paul (which can also be a reprimand!) addresses itself to many Christians, perhaps even to ourselves. The spiritual life is not a soliloquy, a closing of the soul in on itself, but a dialogue, an ineffable conversation, a presence of God that is not to be sought for only in heaven, or in church or outside ourselves, but within. What joy, what energy, what hope comes with abandoning oneself to this interior embrace which God gives to souls that are truly faithful and devoted.

The Holy Father exhorted everyone to do at least this much: to remember the Holy Spirit. Our first and supreme devotion, he said, ought to consist in invoking him, especially at this time which prepares us for the feast of Pentecost. We should seek to become capable of recognizing this quiet, inner voice and presence of God. This conversation, which is known as the Christian spiritual life, contains a foretaste of that eternal conversation in paradise, to which we are invited.

## NOTES—APRIL 26, 1964

1. Jn 16:5-14, including the line, "...if I do not go away, the Paraclete will not come to you; but if I go, I will send him to you."
2. Acts 19:1-7.
3. *Avere,* literally, to have.

# Pentecost and Catholicity*

Venerable brothers and beloved sons! We have invited you to this most holy ceremony so that we might celebrate together the feast of Pentecost, the source of all the other Christian feasts; so that we might commemorate together the coming of the Holy Spirit in his fullness, and offer to this Divine Person an act of worship (love in return for Love!) that is as sublime and alive as possible; so that, united in song and in silence, we might taste a moment of genuine spiritual inebriation through the absorbing presence of the invisible divine Guest; so that we might perceive in a single glance, in an instant, as in a flash of lightning, the visible, historical and human result of the Paraclete's entrance into the world.

This result is nothing other than the Church, ourselves, mankind, taken up into the authentic and effectual current of redemption; the Church, launched on the way to its eschatological destiny, living and journeying from that day until this! We have invited you so that together we might feel and know that we are enveloped by this current of grace—light, strength, sweetness, prophecy and hope—flowing from Christ and leading to him; this supernatural charism and virility of virtue that can bring about in us a holiness surpassing all our expectations, and can instill in us—yes, in us!—the simplicity and daring to witness to Christ in the formidable conditions of our age. We have invited you so that we may meditate, pray, and enjoy together a day that will stand out among the many days of our weary, prosaic life, as full and blessed.

. . .

We want to speak to you for a moment about the Church; about that Mystical Body that had its gestation in the Gospel story, and was born in the Cenacle at Jerusalem, alive with the Holy Spirit, just as it is today. We ourselves knelt in that very same place a few months ago, trembling with emotion as if bowing low before the crib of the Church of God.[2] We think you know all this, and we leave it for your devout meditation. What we intend to offer you now is a view of that native property of the Church that has shone forth from its very first day as a wonderful characteristic note: its *catholicity,* that is, universality, the fact that it is destined for all peoples, open to all souls, offered to all tongues, invites all cultures, is present over the whole earth and persists throughout history.

What invites to such thoughts (as always happens on this blessed day) is the memory of the first wonder that took place, in virtue of the event of Pentecost itself more than by the intention and power of those in whom it occurred: *the miracle of tongues.* The account in the Acts of the Apostles is very precise, with a long list of peoples that seems to us to be intentionally ecumenical:

> Now there were dwelling in Jerusalem Jews, devout men from every nation under heaven. And at this sound the multitude came together, and they were bewildered, because each one heard them speaking in his own language. And they were amazed and wondered, saying, "Are not all

---

*From a sermon for the feast of Pentecost (*OR*, May 18–19, 1964). Translated by Thomas Bonaiuto. (A complete translation of this sermon will be found in *TPS* 10, 1964–65, pp. 76–81.)

these who are speaking Galileans? And how is it that we hear, each of us in his own native language? Parthians and Medes and Elamites and residents of Mesopotamia, Judea and Cappadocia, Pontus and Asia, and the parts of Libya belonging to Cyrene, and visitors from Rome, both Jews and proselytes, Cretans and Arabians . . . (Acts 2:5–11).

In other words, representatives of the whole known world of that time. And what a magnificent echo to this list of peoples would be sounded by the roster of nationalities of those of you listening to us here today. The name *Catholic* is still affirmed, still celebrated.

The habitual use of words often drains them of power and wonder. We use this term *Catholic* with great ease and practically without adverting to the fullness to which it refers, the dynamism that comes from it, the beauty that it envisions, the obligations that it imposes. Often in common speech it becomes a term that defines and hence attempts to circumscribe and limit the one true Church, the Catholic one, to distinguish it from other divisions that are respectable and still endowed with immense Christian treasures, but separated from the Catholic fullness. Sometimes we prefer the word *Christian* to *Catholic,* and practically forget that in theory and in practice the latter is supposed to contain the whole of the former, whereas the reverse is not always true.

We need to have a clear idea of this name *Catholic.* We need to hold it dear, for it bespeaks the transcendence of the Kingdom of God that Christ came to inaugurate on earth and that the Church is in the course of establishing in the world. This kingdom penetrates like a leaven, or like a supernatural energy, into every soul and every culture that welcomes it, without appropriating any part of the earthly kingdom to itself. It hovers over the temporal plane, not to dominate but to illuminate and compose it in a panorama of living and universal harmony.

We need to hear in the term *Catholic* the undying echo of the mysterious and loving vocation of God who calls all men to an encounter with his mercy, and who uses this call to form the new people, his people, who are defined precisely as a people who have been called together, the *congregatio fidelium,*[3] the Church. If you were to take away the Church's quality of being catholic, you would be changing the face that the Lord wanted it to have and that he loved. You would be going against the ineffable intention of God, who wanted to make the Church the expression of his unbounded love for mankind. . . .

## NOTES—MAY 17, 1964

1. As the first Pentecost homily preached by Paul after becoming Pope, this sermon is of special interest here. But since it is rather long, and is devoted chiefly to the Catholicity of the Church, we are reproducing only a representative selection, drawn especially from those portions which refer to the Holy Spirit.
2. The allusion is to the pilgrimage which Pope Paul made to Jerusalem Jan. 2–4 of this same year.
3. "Congregation of the faithful"—a traditional definition of the Church.

# The Sanctifier*

The feast of Pentecost, which we have recently celebrated and in the light of which this large audience takes place, obliges us to recall to you the mystery of the descent of the Holy Spirit, a mystery begun on the day the Lord inundated the nascent Church with his Spirit. *"Baptizabimini"*—"you will be baptized by the Holy Spirit," Jesus said, as he took leave of his Apostles (Acts 1:5). However, it did not end on that day; it is a mystery which still continues, the mystery which at one and the same time both conceals and reveals the secret of the life of the Church. The Holy Spirit is the divine animating principle of the Church. He is vivifying, as we sing in the Credo of the holy Mass. He is unifying. He is illuminating. He is acting. He is consoling. He is sanctifying.

In a word, he confers on the Church this note, this prerogative, of being holy. And holy in two senses: holy because receptive of the Holy Spirit, that is, pervaded by grace, by supernatural life, which makes every soul in the grace of God a temple of the divine presence and makes the whole Church the dwelling, "the house of God,"[1] on earth. The Church is holy, moreover, because the Holy Spirit makes use of it as his organ, as his instrument, for communicating himself to souls, to the world. He does this especially by forming in the Church a ministry, a vehicle, a service by means of which the Holy Spirit, through the action of the sacraments and the exercise of the magisterium, normally diffuses himself throughout the Church itself, animating and sanctifying that humanity which is taken on to form the mystical Body of Christ.

This is a great doctrine. It is the great and mysterious reality of the vital relations established by Christ between man and God. This is religion in its essence, profound and ineffable. This is the true religion, the true relationship which, in the Holy Spirit and through the merit of Christ, unites us to the Father.

How could We fail to take advantage of this simple allusion by recommending to all of you, who here and now are seeking the highest and most authentic expression of religious life, the supreme and loving worship of the Holy Spirit? *Sine tuo numine, nil est in homine,* says the very beautiful sequence of the holy Mass of these days: "without your divine assistance, O Divine Spirit, nothing is left in man."

As you already know, We desired to insert among the Divine Praises[2] an acclamation to the Holy Spirit also, "Blessed be the Holy Spirit, the Paraclete," precisely in order to fill a gap which, unfortunately, is rather common in popular piety, that gap which forgets to offer express and fervent praise to the Holy Spirit, God, the Third Person of the most holy Trinity, who is communicated to us as the supreme gift of God's love. Let us try to give more worthy expression to the worship of the Holy Spirit.

And, again, how can We fail to remind you all that this ineffable encounter with the Holy Spirit is normally and authoritatively conditioned for us by adherence to the visible and hierarchical Church, i.e., the ecclesiastical ministry, mentioned above? The Holy Spirit can pour himself forth as he wishes: *Spiritus ubi vult spirat,* "the Spirit

---

*Address at a General Audience (*OR* May 21, 1964). Translated by Thomas Bonaiuto.

breathes where he wills'' (Jn 3:8). But we must wait for him and look for him there where Christ promised that he would be communicated and conferred. It is always worthwhile to recall the very wise words of St. Augustine which remind us of the essential connection between the visible and human body of the Church and her invisible and divine animation. The holy doctor says: "The Christian ought to fear nothing so much as separation from the body of Christ. If, indeed, one is separated from the body of Christ, he is no longer his member; if he is not his member, he is no longer nourished by his Spirit."[3]

If we have the wisdom and humility to adhere to the Church in her human, concrete, and sometimes faulty manifestation, we will have the happiness of receiving from her, the ever faithful and inexhaustible source of truth and grace, the incomparable and indispensable gift of divine life.

## NOTES—MAY 20, 1964

1. Gen 28:17; cf. Eph 2:22.
2. The Divine Praises, beginning, "Blessed be God," are a set of ejaculatory prayers which originated at the end of the 18th century to make reparation for blasphemy and profanity. They became widely used during Benediction of the Blessed Sacrament, and after low Mass.

   Since people seldom blaspheme the Holy Spirit (the forgotten Person of the Trinity!), no ejaculation in praise of the Holy Spirit was included among them originally. But in the course of time, the motive of reparation for blasphemy gradually gave way to a more general spirit of praise of God, his mysteries and his saints, in the popular use of these prayers. Hence, other ejaculations came to be adopted, and it was in this spirit that Pope Paul added, "Blessed be the Holy Spirit, the Paraclete." This was done by a decree emanating from the Sacred Congregation of Sacred Rites, April 25, 1964. (Editor's note.)
3. St. Augustine, *Homilies on the Gospel of John*, tr. 27, #6 (*PL* 35:1618; *NPNF*, new series, vol. 7, p. 176).

# The Spirit and the Apostolic Office*

Under the sign of the Holy Cross, in honor of which we have just concelebrated the Eucharistic Sacrifice, we begin today the third session of the Second Vatican Council.

Truly the Church is present here!

. . .

But if the Church is here, then the Holy Spirit is also here, the Paraclete whom Christ promised to his Apostles in the work of building the Church: ". . .I will ask the Father and he will give you another Paraclete to dwell with you forever, the Spirit of truth whom the world cannot receive, because it neither sees him nor knows him. But you shall know him, because he will dwell with you, and be in you" (Jn 14:16-17).

### The Holy Spirit and the Apostolic Office

For Christ, as we know, promised us the activity of two—the Apostolic Office[1] and the Holy Spirit. And in different ways he sent them forth to carry on his work, to spread his kingdom in time and space, and to assemble the people redeemed by him into his Church. This Church, his mystical Body, was to be the full measure of Christ while mankind awaited his triumphant return at the end of time.

The Apostolic Office operates externally and in the objective order. It is, so to speak, the material body of the Church which provides her visible, social structure. The Holy Spirit, on the other hand, operates from within. He works on the souls of individuals and on the community as a whole, providing inspiration, life and grace.

Both are active together. The Apostolic Office has been passed on to the sacred hierarchy, and the Spirit of Jesus uses this hierarchy as his ordinary instrument in the ministry of word and sacrament. On the day of Pentecost they joined forces in a wondrous way to begin the extensive work of Christ the Lord. He was no longer visible to sight, but was to remain present forever in his Apostles and their successors "upon whom he conferred the role of pastors, vicars for his work."[2] Both, working in different but complementary ways, render testimony to Christ; and the bond between them gives supernatural power to the activity of the Apostolic Office.[3]

### Still at Work Today

Do we believe that this plan of salvation, bringing Christ's redemptive work to us and accomplishing it in us, is still operative? Yes, indeed, Venerable Brothers. As a matter of fact, we are to believe that this plan is being carried on and brought to fulfillment through the power conferred on us by God, who "has made us fit ministers of the new covenant, not of the letter but of the Spirit; for . . . the Spirit gives life" (2 Cor 3:6). If anyone were to doubt this, he would cast aspersions on Christ's fidelity to

*From the Address opening the Third Session of the Second Vatican Council (*OR*, Sept. 14-15; *TPS* 10, pp. 106-109).

133

his promises, he would be stinting our apostolic mandate, and he would strip the Church of her indefectibility—a quality guaranteed by God's word and confirmed by the lessons of history down through the centuries.

### Attention to the Presence of the Spirit

The Spirit is present here, not to add sacramental grace to the work we undertake at this Council, but to illumine and guide this very work for the benefit of the Church and the whole family of man. The Spirit is here, and we invoke him, wait for him, follow him. He is here, and we advert to this fundamental doctrine, to the reality of his presence, chiefly for this reason: that once again we may appreciate fully and completely our communion with the living Christ. For it is the Spirit who unites us to him.

We advert to this fact also so that we may stand before him with hearts anxious but ready, humbly recognizing our own wretchedness and nothingness; so that we may feel the need to call upon his merciful help; so that we may hear the words of the Apostle echoing in the deepest recesses of our own hearts: "Discharging . . . this ministry in accordance with the mercy shown us, we do not lose heart" (2 Cor 4:1).

In this period of the Council we are called to make our hearts docile, to accept the word of God obediently as loyal sons should, to offer fervent acts of prayer and love, and to enkindle our minds with spiritual fire. The poetic vision of St. Ambrose fits in quite well with this singular event: "Let us drink joyously the sober libation of the Spirit."[4] That is the call which sounds for us during the sacred time of the Council.

### The Church Defining Her Own Nature

And finally we advert to the Spirit's presence because the Church, which is represented by us and receives her form and structure from us, has reached a significant moment in her history. Today she is examining herself and formulating the things which Christ, her founder, thought and willed concerning her; the things which have been pondered earnestly and devoutly over the centuries by the Fathers, Doctors, and Pontiffs of the Church. Now, the Church must define her own nature. From the depths of an enlightened self-knowledge she must articulate the teaching imparted to her by the Holy Spirit in accordance with the Lord's promise: "But the Advocate, the Holy Spirit, whom the Father will send in my name, he will teach you all things, and bring to your mind whatever I have said to you" (Jn 14:26). In this way the Church will complete the doctrinal work which the First Vatican Council had intended to enunciate. . . .

NOTES—September 14, 1964

1. The Apostolic Office (*apostolatus*) spoken of here refers to the office conferred initially on the Twelve Apostles, and by them transmitted to the Bishops. It is the office of proclaiming the faith authoritatively, and of shepherding the flock of Christ. Pope Paul's teaching here is mainly inspired by an essay of Yves Congar, "The Holy Spirit and the Apostolic Body, Continuators of the Work of Christ," which was published in French in the book, *Esquisses du mystère de l'Eglise* (Paris, Cerf, 1956), and in the English translation, *The Mystery of the Church* (Baltimore, Helicon, 1960). Pope Paul cites it expressly in several of his addresses. (Editor's Note.)
2. From the Preface of the Apostles in the *Roman Missal*.

3. Cf. 1 Pt 1:12: "...the things which have now been announced to you by those who preached the good news to you through the Holy Spirit sent from heaven..."
4. St. Ambrose (*PL* 16:1411). For another citation of this text, see the Italian remarks at May 19, 1975.

# Pentecost: Source of the Church and of the Priesthood*

Two facts and two thoughts engage Our brief but intense meditation at this moment.

The first fact and first thought has to do with this celebration of Pentecost, the feast of the Holy Spirit, "*Omnium festivitatum maximum*" (the greatest feast of all), as Eusebius of Caesarea defined it, as long ago as the fourth century.[1] This feast is at the source of the other feasts. In fact, it would not be possible to celebrate any feast—if feast signifies the joyful remembrance of persons or events recalled and honored by a perennial tradition—so long as at the origin of the tradition there were lacking the vital principle which engenders it and gives it coherence and vigor.

### Pentecost and the Spread of the Church

Right now we have time only for a very rapid glance at the great Pentecostal event and what followed it. We recall the words of Christ revealing and promising the Holy Spirit. We reflect on the mystery of the Spirit's "mission." Originating in the bosom of the most Holy Trinity, he falls, in an altogether new measure and form, on the little group of Apostles and disciples, gathered together with Mary in the Cenacle. Our memory contemplates the extraordinary phenomena which made the event perceptible: the stormy wind and the tongues of fire, followed by the outpouring of words. As in a vision we see the stream of the Church's life and history gushing forth from that first Christian community born with already throbbing heart. We see it swell and spread throughout the inhabited world, the "*oikoumene.*" Still filled with the limpid, animating sap of its origins, it traverses peoples and centuries. With supreme wonder and sublime joy, we see it come right up here to ourselves. History, if we examine it well, presents us with nothing more full of meaning and mystery, nothing more human and more transcendent, nothing more lively and more serene, nothing more bound up with the past and more oriented to the future, than this. What is this light which diffuses and spreads through all the earth? It is Christ, perpetuating himself in the humanity which he has vivified by the Holy Spirit; it is his Church, dwelling in time and extended in the world. Upon encountering mortal men, the Church infuses into them a spark of glorious immortality; she finds them agitated, unhappy, and corrupted by sin, and she regenerates them in joy and holiness. She encounters them, mad, lost wayfarers in the desert and twilight of this life, and she gathers them, redirects them, and puts them back on the road. She knows their destination, but weariness she knows not.

### Receiving the Holy Spirit

The picture is fascinating and would require endless contemplation. Let us observe the last phase, the one which concerns us. Let us strain the ear of the soul to

*From the homily at the Mass of Pentecost (*OR*, June 7–8, 1965). Translation by Thomas Bonaiuto.

hear the well-known but mysterious words which brought the Holy Spirit to each of us: *"Exi ab eo, immunde spiritus, et da locum Spiritui Sancto Paraclito"* (Depart from him, unclean spirit, and give place to the Holy Spirit). With this first exorcism, performed over us by the minister of the Church, our being became capable of housing the Holy Spirit, of being his tabernacle. St. Paul reminds us: *"Nescitis quia templum Dei estis, et Spiritus Dei habitat in vobis?"* (Do you not know that you are God's temple, and that God's Spirit dwells in you—1 Cor 3:16). Thus we received Baptism, and were consecrated children of God, members of Christ, holy for the worship of the New Testament. The Spirit returned with the sacrament of Confirmation, *"ut perfectio fiat,"* as St. Ambrose says, *"quando ad invocationem sacerdotis Spiritus Sanctus infunditur"*[2] (so that the work would be completed when the Holy Spirit is infused at the invocation of the priest): by means of the chrism a new resemblance to Christ was impressed upon our souls.

### The Holy Spirit and the Priest

And for those of us who were ordained priests for the ministry of the People of God there came, and for those of you dear clerics and Levites whom the grace of the Lord will call to the altar of God through perseverance in his invitation, there will come, the loftiest and most transfiguring moment of our lives, the moment marked by the powerful words: *"...innova in visceribus eorum Spiritum sanctitatis"* (renew in their hearts the Spirit of holiness), followed by those others, faithfully echoing the word of the Gospel: *"Accipite Spiritum Sanctum..."* (Receive the Holy Spirit...).[3] Always the Holy Spirit! Do we realize this?

In those of us who have been chosen for the sacred ministry, the solemnity we are celebrating should revive the memory of this very personal investiture conferred upon us by the Holy Spirit. It should inflame our awareness of it. This feast ought to be celebrated in the inner sanctuary of our souls. If the Christian religion has the secret of drawing God near to man, our vocation should make us understand and savor more than other Christians the mystery of nearness, of indwelling, of friendship, of spiritual intimacy, of interior inspiration, of sweetness and strength, of peace and joy which the Holy Spirit grants to souls through grace. And if grace is defined as the supernatural initiative of God, elevating and sanctifying the human being, who can bring nothing to this ineffable encounter except the humility of his nothingness, his faith, and his willing availability; how much more is the mystery of the unilateral gratuity of grace and of the operative presence of the Holy Spirit, realized in the one chosen for the sacred ministry so that he be transformed into an instrument for distributing the divine gifts! The priest not only receives grace, but imparts it; he is not only sanctified by grace, but by it is likewise made into a worthy instrument of sanctification.

### Ordination in Rome

The second fact, the second thought, is, therefore, connected with the first. It is of the Holy Mass which we are concelebrating with the rectors of the seminaries and ecclesiastical colleges of Rome in the presence, and with the participation, of all the students of these institutions. Some of these students have already been marked with the seal of the priesthood; others are waiting for it eagerly and ardently. If ever a feast of the priesthood gladdened the Roman and universal Church, this is the fullest and most beautiful. If it is really the Holy Spirit who animates the Church, and raises up within her ministers and apostles with the mission and power to call upon the Holy Spirit to vivify and sanctify the Church, this wonder has its richest and most moving expression here. Do not let the fullness of this moment escape us.

Beloved sons, we would like this spiritual moment to have for each of you a decisive efficacy in your ecclesiastical formation and the power to infuse into your souls an inextinguishable fervor—a fervor free from the anxiety which pervades so many beautiful and generous souls of priests and ecclesiastical students in our days; a fervor deriving from the certainty that your education is authentic and wise; a fervor that will not diminish your interior and exterior cohesion with your bishops and with this Apostolic See, but rather one capable of reinvigorating such cohesion, making it a spring of spiritual and pastoral energy; a fervor which would make you just as impervious to the profane and vicious suggestions of the world, as sensitive to its moral necessities and lovingly desirous of its salvation. We would like the vision of this unique assembly, praying and rejoicing in the celebration of the mystery of Pentecost, to remain in your souls as an inspiring and guiding light. Let it remind you, as worthy to perpetuate the benefits of this superlative liturgical encounter, of the words of St. Augustine which say everything: *"Habemus ergo Spiritum Sanctum, si amamus Ecclesiam; amamus autem, si in eius compage et charitate consistimus"* (We have the Holy Spirit if we love the Church; we love the Church if we abide in its structure and its charity).[4]

## NOTES—June 6, 1965

1. Eusebius of Caesarea, *Life of Constantine,* IV, 64 *(PG* 20:1219).
2. Ambrose, *The Sacraments,* III, 2, 8 *(CSEL* 73:42).
3. Cf. the *Roman Pontifical* at the Rite of Ordination and Jn 20:23.
4. Augustine, *Homilies on the Gospel of John,* 32:8 *(PL* 35:1646; *NPNF,* new series, vol. 7, p. 195).

# The Spirit, the Church and the Hierarchy*

In these weekly encounters, these general audiences, we have been talking about the Church. The Council offers us material for this and almost obliges us to do so, by the abundance and authority of the doctrine on the Church herself which it has taught. Your visit gives us the opportunity to touch on this doctrine, without claiming to examine or explain it adequately, but only with the purpose, and we might say with the pleasure, of giving you a fleeting glimpse of some aspect worthy of particular consideration.

### The Holy Spirit: Soul of the Church

And do you know what is, to our mind, the most interesting and at the same time the most mysterious aspect of the doctrine on the Church? The relationship between the Church and the Holy Spirit. In a wonderful and dense page of theology, the Council says:

> When the work which the Father gave the Son to do on earth (cf. Jn 17:4) was accomplished, the Holy Spirit was sent on the day of Pentecost to sanctify the Church perpetually. Thus all who believe through Christ would have access to the Father in one Spirit (cf. Eph 2:18). He is the Spirit of life, and the fountain of water springing up to eternal life (cf. Jn 4:14; 7:38–39). Through him the Father gives life to men dead in sin until the day when he will bring their mortal bodies to life in Christ (Rom 8:10–11). The Spirit dwells in the Church and in the hearts of the faithful as in a temple (cf. 1 Cor 3:16; 6:19). He prays in them, bearing witness to the fact that they are adopted sons (cf. Gal 4:6; Rom 8:15–16; 26). He guides the Church in the way of all truth (cf. Jn 16:13), unifies it in communion and ministry, equips and directs it with various hierarchical and charismatic gifts, and adorns it with his fruits. (Cf. Eph 4:11–12; 1 Cor 12:4; Gal 5:22). By the power of the Gospel he maintains the Church in the freshness of youth, constantly renewing it and leading it to complete union with its Bridegroom. Both the Spirit and the Bride say "Come!" to the Lord Jesus (cf. Apoc 22:17).[1]

This is a long page, and one full of references to the bible which would need explaining. But here we only wish to delineate the relationship between the Holy Spirit and the Church, and we must content ourselves with quoting a phrase from a great German Catholic thinker of the last century. On the first page of his famous book on the unity of the Church, he writes, with synthetic vigor: "The Father sends the Son; and the Son sends the Holy Spirit. It is thus that God has come to us. And it is in the inverse direction that we reach the Father. The Spirit leads us to the Son, and the Son to the Father."[2] It will be enough for us to think of the Holy Spirit as the divine animating principle of the Church, its uncreated soul.[3] He produces the created anima-

---

*Address at a General Audience (*OR*, May 19, 1966; *Papal Addresses*, May 18, 1966).

tion of our Lord's mystical Body. That is, he produces grace, the gifts of the Holy Spirit, and the fruits of the Holy Spirit. St. Paul enumerates the latter thus: "Charity, joy, peace, patience, kindness, goodness, longanimity, meekness, faith, temperance, continency, chastity."[4] Moreover, isn't the sacramental character an effect of the Holy Spirit? And his inspirations which guide the soul on the way to sanctity; and the assistance of the Holy Spirit, which gives the ministry of the Church its orientation and its certainty—aren't these also the work of the Holy Spirit?

### The Spirit and the Hierarchy

One point of special importance in all this marvelous doctrine is that which refers to the hierarchy of the Church. Isn't the Holy Spirit free to exercise his mysterious action directly—"*Spiritus ubi vult spirat*" (The Spirit breathes where he will—Jn 3:8)? Certainly he is. The Council expressly and repeatedly affirms it.[5] Then isn't the service which the ecclesiastical hierarchy undertakes for the teaching, sanctification and guidance of the faithful superfluous and an interference? Don't the faithful receive the Holy Spirit directly without this, his human diaphragm, this intermediary institution? This is an essential point of the doctrine on the Church. We must have recourse to the thought of Christ.

Christ has entrusted the fulfillment of his work in mankind to two different factors: the Holy Spirit and the Apostles. He promised to send the Holy Spirit, and He sent the Apostles. Both these missions proceed equally from Christ. The incontestable design of the divine Founder of the Church wills the Church to be constructed by the Apostles and vivified by the Holy Spirit. The Apostles construct the body of the Church, the soul of which is the Spirit of Christ. These two different agents are so closely knit that St. Augustine affirmed that the work of one was coextensive with the work of the other. He did so with these famous and incisive words: "*De Spiritu Christi non vivit, nisi corpus Christi . . .* ; *Vis ergo et tu vivere de Spiritu Christi? In Corpore esto Christi*" (Only the Body of Christ lives by the Spirit of Christ . . . ; Do you also wish to live by the Spirit of Christ? Then be in the Body of Christ).[6] And he wrote further: "The Christian should fear nothing so much as being separated from the Body of Christ. If he is in fact separated from the Body of Christ, he is not his member. If he is not his member, he is not nourished by his Spirit."[7]

We should always remember that the work of the visible hierarchy is ordained to the diffusion of the Holy Spirit among the members of the Church. Its ministry is not indispensable for God's mercy, for he can bestow mercy as he pleases. But normally it 's indispensable for us, who have been ordained to the good fortune of receiving the word, the grace and the guidance of God from the Apostles—that is, from the ministers of this supernatural religious life that comes from Christ.[8]

It gives us pleasure to recall this luminous truth on the vigil of the beginning of the novena—the great novena of Pentecost. We would ask that the celebration of this "metropolis of feasts," as St. John Chrysostom calls Pentecost, be preceded by the preparation which our Lord himself instituted:[9] in recollection, prayer, and reflection on the mystery of the Church, both in its inward depths and in its exterior manifestations. It is a limitless meditation. We would like the beautiful Encyclical of Leo XIII, *Divinum illud munus* (1897) to be recalled and studied. We would that the cult and the love of the Holy Spirit were more ardent and more widespread among all Christians! We entrust this to you, for your good and for that of the holy Church, with our Apostolic Blessing.

NOTES—May 18, 1966

1. Vatican II, *The Church*, #4. (Translation by the present editor.)
2. Johann-Adam Moehler, *Die Einheit in der Kirche,* Tübingen, 1825.
3. Cf. Charles Journet, *The Church of the Word Incarnate,* vol. I (New York, Sheed and Ward, 1955), p. 515.
4. Gal. 5:22. (Pope Paul is here citing the text according to the Vulgate tradition. A translation from the commonly accepted Greek text is cited above, in note 4.— Editor's note.)
5. Vatican II, *The Church,* #12–16; *Ecumenism,* #3, 4, 21, etc.
6. Augustine, *Homilies on the Gospel of John,* tr. 26, #13 (*PL* 35:1612–1613; *NPNF* vol. 7, p. 172).
7. *Ibid.* tr. 27, #6 (*PL* 35:1618; *NPNF* 7, 176).
8. Cf. Yves Congar, ''The Holy Spirit and the Apostolic Body, Continuators of the Work of Christ,'' in *The Mystery of the Church* (Baltimore, Helicon, 1960), ch. 5.
9. Cf. Acts 1:4, 12: ''And while staying with them he charged them not to depart from Jerusalem, but to wait for the promise of the Father, which, he said, 'you heard from me'.... Then they returned to Jerusalem from the mount called Olivet, which is near Jerusalem, a sabbath's journey away.'' Acts 2:1: ''When the day of Pentecost had come, they were all together in one place.''

# The Church Lives by the Holy Spirit*

... Now pay attention to this: What makes the Church live? . . .The question is about the internal principle of its life; the original principle which distinguishes the Church from every other society; an indispensable principle, just as breathing is indispensable for man's physical life; a divine principle which makes a son of earth a son of heaven and confers on the Church its mystical personality: the Holy Spirit. The Church lives by the Holy Spirit. The Church was truly born, you could say, on the day of Pentecost. The Church's first need is always to live Pentecost.

Listen to what the Council says:

> ...The Holy Spirit was sent on the day of Pentecost to sanctify the Church perpetually. Thus, all who believe through Christ would have access to the Father in one Spirit (cf. Eph 2:18). He is the Spirit of life and the fountain of water springing up to eternal life (cf. Jn 4:14; 7:38–39). . . . The Spirit dwells in the Church and in the hearts of the faithful, as in a temple (cf. 1 Cor 3:15; 6:19). . . . He guides the Church in the way of all truth (cf. Jn 16:13), unifies it in communion and in ministry, equips and directs it with various hierarchical and charismatic gifts, and adorns it with his fruits.[1]

It is in the Holy Spirit that the Church's twofold union is perfected—union with Christ and God, and union with all its members, the faithful. It is the Holy Spirit who gives life to the whole body of the Church and to its individual members by means of that intimate action which we call grace. We are all firmly convinced of this theological truth of our faith, even if it isn't easy for us to form an adequate concept of the ontological and psychological reality to which it corresponds.

### The Church's Need of the Holy Spirit

But this is enough for us now, and we can say: If the Church lives on the illuminating and sanctifying inspiration of the Holy Spirit, then the Church has need of the Holy Spirit: a basic need, an existential need, a need that cannot be satisfied with illusions or substitutes, a universal need, a permanent need.'' *Sine tuo numine nihil est in homine''* (without your grace there is nothing in man), as the beautiful Pentecost sequence puts it.

At this point, someone might raise the objection: But doesn't the Church already possess the Holy Spirit? Isn't this need already satisfied? Yes, of course, the Church already and forever possesses the Holy Spirit. But first of all, his action admits of various degrees and conditions, so that our action is needed too, if the activity of the Holy Spirit is to be free and full. Secondly, the Holy Spirit's presence in individual souls can diminish or be missing entirely. This is why the word of God is preached and the sacraments of grace are distributed; this is why people pray and why each indi-

*From an address at a General Audience (*OR*, Oct. 15, 1966; *The Pope Speaks*, v. 12, pp. 79–81).

vidual tries to merit the great "Gift of God," the Holy Spirit, for himself and for the whole Church.

### The Guideline of Vatican II

For this reason, if we really love the Church, the main thing we must do is to foster in it an outpouring of the divine Paraclete, the Holy Spirit. And if we accept the ecclesiology of the Council, which lays so much stress on the action of the Holy Spirit in the Church—as we note likewise in the traditional Greek ecclesiology—then we should be glad to accept its guideline for fostering the Church's vitality and renewal, and for orienting our own personal Christian lives along these lines.

Where does this guideline lead us? Toward the Holy Spirit, we repeat. This means toward the mystery of the Church, toward the vital communion which the Father in his infinite and transcendent goodness wanted to establish through Christ, in the Spirit, with the human soul and with believing and redeemed mankind, the Church. In other words, it leads us toward the search for and the attainment of God; toward theological truth, toward faith, which discloses to us the religious order of salvation.

### Horizontal Orientation

Some people have preferred to see in the Council an orientation of the Church in what might be called a horizontal direction—toward the human community that makes up the Church; toward the brothers still separated from us who are the object of our longing and are called to the same perfect communion; toward the world around us, to which we must carry the message of our faith and the gift of our charity; toward earthly realities which must be recognized as good and worthy of being taken up in the light of the kingdom of God.

### Vertical Orientation

All this is very true and very beautiful; but we must not forget what we might call the vertical orientation, which the Council reaffirmed as primary for interpreting God's design for the destiny of mankind and for explaining the Church's mission in time. God—his mystery, his charity, his worship, his truth, the expectation of him— always remains in first place. Christ, mediator between man and God, is the necessary Redeemer who binds together all our capacity for love and dedication. The Spirit, who makes us Christians and raises us to supernatural life, is the true and deep root principle both of our interior life and of our external apostolic activity.

### The Interior Life

And if we follow this unmistakable orientation, where are we directed? Where are we led? To the interior life; to that life of recollection, silence, meditation, absorbing of God's word and spiritual exercises which (we say this with sorrow and amazement) seems to annoy some people, some beloved sons of the Church. They act as if the interior life were an outgrown phase, a pedagogy no longer needed for a Christian life. They would have the latter projected outward, into the secular and naturalistic experience offered by the world, as if, relying on this alone and deprived of the protective and strengthening force of interior grace, we could succeed in mastering and redeeming it with our own poor forces.

No, if we want to be wise and give the Church what it needs most of all, the Holy Spirit, then we must be prompt and faithful in keeping the appointment fixed for a vivifying encounter with him, namely, the interior life.

NOTE—October 12, 1966

1. Vatican II, *The Church,* #4. (This text is cited in full at May 18, 1967—Editor.)

# Our Relationships with the Spirit and with the Church*

How have you celebrated the feast of Pentecost? Have you tried to meditate on how the wonderful event narrated in the Acts of the Apostles stands at the origin of the Church not only as an important historical fact, but as a vital principle? It is the beginning of the Church's supernatural animation, the source of a permanent miracle, that of the infusion of the Holy Spirit into the Apostles and believers in order to form Christ in their individual lives and in the entire community. This community, united but internally differentiated and hierarchical, is what we call the Church. Have you considered that this fact continues, develops in time, and spreads over the earth, wherever faith and grace reach, and that it profoundly concerns each of you? Have you reflected that the outpouring of the Holy Spirit has reached each of your souls, penetrated the inmost sphere of your psychology, and enkindled the divine life in you?

## The Work of the Holy Spirit

One of the most mysterious and wonderful pages of our catechism is that which concerns the communication of the Holy Spirit to the faithful. He produces in them a new state, the state of grace, with its whole accompaniment of operative attitudes: the infused virtues, spiritual gifts and fruits. This is how the divine animation enriches the souls that have the inestimable happiness of being invaded by vivifying and sanctifying Love. It is a difficult page, because it speaks of truths which exceed our human knowledge and are not ordinarily perceptible to our experience, except by some interior reflection. (We are urged to make such reflection by our conscience, which speaks more or less plainly, but always with inward joy and the characteristic breath of peace, the "peace of the Christian conscience.") Nevertheless it is necessary to know this page, which the Council has repeatedly emphasized. The Holy Spirit had a place of honor in the documents of the Council, as is his due; a single citation is enough for us here:

> When the work which the Father gave the Son to do on earth (cf. Jn 17:4) was accomplished, the Holy Spirit was sent on the day of Pentecost to sanctify the Church perpetually. Thus all who believe through Christ would have access to the Father in one Spirit (cf. Eph 2:18). He is the Spirit of life, and the fountain of water springing up to eternal life (cf. Jn 4:14; 7:38–39). Through him the Father gives life to men dead in sin until the day when he will bring their mortal bodies to life in Christ (cf. Rom 8:10–11).
> The Spirit dwells in the Church and in the hearts of the faithful as in a temple (cf. 1 Cor 3:16; 6:19). He prays in them, bearing witness to the fact that they are adopted sons (cf. Gal 4:6; Rom 8:15–16, 26). He guides the Church in the way of all truth (cf. Jn 16:13), unifies it in communion and ministry, equips and directs it with various hierarchical

*Address at a General Audience on the Wednesday during the octave of Pentecost (*OR*, May 18, 1967). Translation by Thomas Bonaiuto.

and charismatic gifts, and adorns it with his fruits (cf. Eph 4:11–12; 1 Cor 12:4; Gal 5:22). By the power of the Gospel he maintains the Church in the freshness of youth, constantly renewing it and leading it to complete union with its Bridegroom. Both the Spirit and the Bride say "Come!" to the Lord Jesus (cf. Apoc 22:17).

Thus, the Church shines forth as "a people made one with the unity of the Father, the Son, and the Holy Spirit."[1]

### Our Relationship with the Holy Spirit

From this wonderful doctrinal synthesis we will draw two simple but important conclusions. The first concerns the relationship of our souls with the Holy Spirit, that is the worship of this ineffable *dulcis hospes animae,* "sweet guest of the soul," which we ought to nourish both in the secret of our heart and in the utterance of prayer. This worship begins with the inner sense of sacredness which every Christian ought to have in regard to himself, since Baptism has made him a temple of the Holy Spirit. It involves a refined conscience for which "a small fault has a bitter sting,"[2] and for which one thing is important above all: to be in the grace of God, to be vigilant in love for and fidelity to the ever-present God. This worship learns to recognize in the Holy Spirit the very root-principle of prayer from whom we receive the blessed possibility of uttering the name of Jesus, as well as the mystic source of the most deeply touched orison. It attributes the liturgical renewal of our times to him, to his passing over his Church. The first of all our devotions should be to the Holy Spirit.

### Our Relationship with the Visible Church

The second conclusion concerns our relationship with the Church, understood as a society that is visible, i.e., hierarchical, dogmatic, sacramental and canonical. Some have tried to regard this exterior ecclesial relationship as alien, superfluous, contrary, and almost abusive in comparison with the intimate and "charismatic" relationship of the soul with the Holy Spirit. Let us be careful, dearest children, with respect to this problem, and let us try to resolve it as we ought: the Church as the mystical Body of Christ, is not to be distinguished from the socially organized Church, which gives us our title of Catholics. This is the Church which gives to souls sanctified by grace the very form of the new Christian life; it is the indispensable instrument through which we have the doctrine, sacraments, and guidance which bring us into communion with the Holy Spirit and keep us there. Let our soul indeed open its sails to the wind of the Spirit of Jesus, which blows, free and mysterious, wherever it wishes; but let us not abandon the helm of our boat, the helm of the apostolic Fisherman, which steers us to a good end.

NOTES—May 18, 1967

1. Vatican II, *The Church,* #4.
2. Dante, *Purgatorio,* III, 9.

# Hope for Reunion with Orthodox*

... Before giving expression to our deepest sentiments, we should begin by proclaiming that "every good gift and every perfect gift is from above, coming down from the Father of Lights" (see Jas 1:17), and in giving glory to him we should open ourselves to the enlightenment of his Spirit, who alone can guide us in understanding his mysterious ways.

### The Impulse of the Holy Spirit

... In fact, on both sides we are impelled, by the single desire of purifying our souls in obedience to truth, to love one another sincerely as brothers, loving one another earnestly from the heart.[1] The honorableness of our intentions and the sincerity of our plans are surely a marvelous sign of the Holy Spirit's powerful action of renewing men and deepening their understanding, not only in the Church but also in individual Christian believers.

We are pleased to repeat this and to reflect on it with you during this Year of Faith, at the beginning of which we desired to visit you in your noble country. In visiting Smyrna and Ephesus we heard echoing in our heart the message addressed by the Spirit through John to the churches of Asia Minor: "He who has an ear, let him hear what the Spirit says to the churches."[2] The Spirit gives us to know Christ,[3] to guard the truths entrusted to the Church,[4] and to penetrate the mystery of God[5] and his truth,[6] for he is life[7] and inner transformation.[8] And he is demanding with greater insistence than ever that we be one so that the world may believe.[9]

### Reward in the Two Churches

This request of the Holy Spirit we see manifested first of all in the movement of renewal that he is bringing about everywhere in the Church. This renewal, the desire to be more attentive and receptive in our faithfulness, is in fact the most fundamental prerequisite for our drawing closer to one another.[10]

The Second Vatican Council of the Catholic Church was one of the stages in this journey. The Council's decisions are being carried out with prudence and determination on every level of Church life. The Synod of Bishops gathered here is a sign of it; today, when problems are on a world scale, it guarantees in new forms a better cooperation between local churches and the Church of Rome, which presides in charity.[11]

We have also undertaken the revision of our Canon Law, and without waiting for its completion have already promulgated new directives with a view to removing certain obstacles to development in the daily life of the Church and of the brotherhood we are increasingly rediscovering between the Orthodox Church and the Catholic Church.

*Address to Orthodox Patriarch Athenagoras of Constantinople (*OR*, Oct. 27, 1967; *The Pope Speaks*, v. 12, pp. 342–346).

We know that a like effort for renewal is in progress in the Orthodox Church, and we are following its development with love and attention. You too are experiencing the need we have mentioned of securing a better cooperation between local churches.

The first Pan-Orthodox Conference at Rhodes, the fruit in great measure of the patient and persevering efforts of Your Holiness, marked an important stage on this path, and it is significant that the program it set itself, although worked out previously and independently, bears in essentials a striking resemblance to that of the Second Vatican Council. Is that not a further sign of the Spirit's action, urging our churches to active preparation so as to make possible the reestablishment of their full communion with one another?

### Continued Cooperation and Efforts

We should on both sides take courage and follow up this effort, developing it as much as we possibly can by contacts and by a cooperation the forms of which we should work out together. It is in a positive collaboration toward responding to what the Spirit asks of the Church today that we shall eventually surmount the obstacles still separating us, far more than by a discussion of the past.

If in our efforts for renewal we see a sign of the action of the Spirit urging us on to reestablish full communion with one another and preparing us for it, does not the contemporary world—filled with unbelief in many forms—also give us a peremptory reminder of our need for unity with one another?

### The Spirit Calls us to Deeper Faith

If the unity of Christ's disciples was given as the great sign that was to call forth the faith of the world, is not the unbelief of many of our contemporaries also a way whereby the Spirit speaks to the churches, causing a fresh awareness in them of the urgency there is to fulfill this precept of Christ, who died "that he might gather into one the children of God who were scattered abroad" (Jn 11:52)? This common witness—one, varied, decided and persuasive—of a faith that is humbly self-confident, breaking forth in love and radiating hope, is without doubt the foremost demand that the Spirit makes of churches today.

. . .

There are so many ways which the Holy Spirit uses to bring us with our whole being toward the fulness of this communion which, already so rich but still incomplete, unites us in the mystery of the Church.

### The Spirit Calls Us to Holiness

We spoke earlier of the action of the Spirit in each member of the Christian faithful, producing the fruits of holiness and generosity. Another aspect of this action, constituting another fundamental prerequisite for our drawing closer to one another, is change of heart.[12] This enables us to hear and carry out with ever greater docility in our personal life, the bidding of the Spirit. There can be no true lasting brotherhood without an unceasing effort to be faithful to the Holy Spirit, who transforms us into the likeness of the Son.[13]

It is only by becoming truly sons in the Son (1 Jn 3:1-2), that we also truly become, in a mysterious manner, brothers of one another. "For the closer their communion with the Father, the Word and the Spirit, the easier it will be for them to grow more deeply in mutual brotherly love."[14] Besides, this effort for holiness sets to work the entire common heritage we have just mentioned and which the Second Vatican Council saw fit to explain at length.[15]

. . .

United in a fraternal love that nothing must be allowed to lessen, and inspired only by the desire to carry out what the Spirit asks of the Church, we shall, in a hope stronger than all obstacles, go forward in the name of the Lord.

### NOTES—October 26, 1967

1. Cf. 1 Pt 1:22: "Having purified your souls by your obedience to the truth for a sincere love of the brethren, love one another earnestly from the heart."
2. Cf. Apoc 2:7, 11, 17, 29; 3:6, 13, 22.
3. Cf. 1 Cor 12:3: "Therefore I want you to understand that no one speaking by the Spirit of God ever says, 'Jesus be cursed' and no one ever can say 'Jesus is Lord' except by the Holy Spirit."
4. Cf. 2 Tim 1:14: ". . .guard the truth that has been entrusted to you by the Holy Spirit who dwells within us."
5. Cf. 1 Cor 2:11: "For what person knows a man's thoughts except the spirit of the man which is in him? So also no one comprehends the thoughts of God except the Spirit of God."
6. Cf. Jn 16:13: "When the Spirit of truth comes, he will guide you into all the truth; for he will not speak on his own authority, but whatever he hears he will speak, and he will declare to them the things that are to come."
7. Cf. Gal 5:25: "If we live by the Spirit, let us also walk by the Spirit."
8. Cf. Rom 8:9, 13: "But you are not in the flesh, you are in the Spirit, if the Spirit of God really dwells in you. Anyone who does not have the Spirit of Christ does not belong to him. . . . for if you live according to the flesh you will die, but if by the Spirit you put to death the deeds of the body you will live."
9. Cf. Jn 17:21: ". . .that they may all be one; even as thou, Father, art in me, and I in thee, that they also may be in us, so that the world may believe that thou hast sent me."
10. Vatican II, *Ecumenism,* #6.
11. St. Ignatius of Antioch, *Letter to the Romans,* salutation.
12. *Ibid., #7.*
13. Cf. 2 Cor 3:18: ". . .and we all, with unveiled face, beholding the glory of the Lord, are being changed into his likeness from one degree of glory to another; for this comes from the Lord, who is the Spirit."
14. Vatican II, *Ecumenism,* #7.
15. *Ibid., #13–18.*

# Faith and Witness*

...As you know, the passage just read belongs to the lengthy discourse, that Jesus Christ, on the last night of his earthly life, and before yielding himself to the agony of the Passion, wished to leave as a spiritual inheritance to the eleven disciples who remained after the traitor Judas left the table. In the Last Supper discourse, Jesus allows his heart to open in incomparable revelations on a marvelous theme.[1]

First of all, note the fact: the Lord is leaving his disciples. How is he going to leave them? Alone, orphans, poor, and without means of communication with him? Will he never be in their midst again? Will he never speak again or have any influence on their souls?

No, the Divine Master reveals a new way of communicating with his chosen ones, or rather, a new mystery of the divine presence among men. He announces the sending of the Paraclete: the Helper, the Comforter, the Advocate—the Holy Spirit, the third person of the Blessed Trinity. The Holy Spirit will be sent by the Father and the Son—"who proceeds from the Father and the Son," as we are about to sing in the Creed. Jesus will send him to maintain not only the memory of our Lord, but his presence, his action and his grace in the disciples. Grace is the new life that Jesus infuses into those faithful men who are to be his Apostles, and, after them, into the vast array of believing humanity throughout all the centuries which follow that sublime event.

We ourselves are recipients of the Lord's promise. He repeats it: "I will send you the Holy Spirit, the Comforter; he will bear witness to me." Note these words well: "then you, in your turn, will offer the same witness to others."[2]

### Witness

What does witness mean? It means the transmission of a truth to one who, on receiving it, cannot directly examine and know it. He must accept it on trust, by faith. As the catechism tells us: we must believe. Our religious life is established on faith, that is, on the acceptance of testimony.

In the extract of the Gospel read today, the Lord shows us two principal applications of this word, which has various meanings. The first is the inner witness which the disciples, the followers, the faithful (among whom we ourselves by divine election are numbered) may receive in a way that is imponderable but real and, in certain aspects, tangible. This first witness declares that Christ was and is truly God's messenger, God's Son. Therefore we know we can trust Christ, his Gospels, his work, his precepts, and everything resulting from his appearance in the world.

Can we perhaps attain this interior certainty by ourselves, through studying the Gospels, religion or the catechism, or by listening to lectures, as so many scholars and lecturers do for the human sciences? No, we cannot. In spite of knowing a thousand

*Homily at Mass for the "Volunteers of Suffering," May 26, 1968 (*OR*, May 29, 1968; *ORe*, June 6, 1968).

150

things about Jesus, his life, his appearance in history, the episodes and circumstances of his earthly journey, well-known scientific experts have written voluminous works and yet have remained blind, deaf and inert before this extraordinary figure, who is unique—as they themselves admit—and superior to all human manifestations. What is the explanation of this negative phenomenon? It is that they do not possess that vital adherence which we call faith, and which brings Christ himself into our spirit: *"Christum habitare per fidem in cordibus vestris"* (Eph 3:17), as St. Paul writes: Christ dwells in our hearts through faith.

This witness of the Spirit, the grace of faith, is therefore necessary. The Lord must instill into our souls a new light, a capacity of thought, a disposition of soul, an ineffable certainty, a joy in accepting his message, in such a way that we are made sure, blessed and completely his. This goes to such a point that we can in a way foresee how we shall one day possess him; foresee the meeting with God that will be full and visible in the sublime and vital relationship uniting us to him. Meanwhile—it is well to repeat it—the grace of our Lord must ever nourish in us the authentic happiness of faith. Blessed are those who have believed!

### Our Witness

Besides this first kind of witness there is another, not equal but analogous to it: the transmission by us to others of the truth of the faith which the Lord in his grace and goodness has given to us. This communication, which is carried out in various ways, in accord with the inexhaustible activity of the Church, such as the apostolate and missions, is defined by Christ himself as a witness we give for the benefit of our neighbors. The first witness is interior, the second social. We must propagate it to all our brethren in the world around us, to all who expect comfort from our words we must convey it, particularly to those who watch us, wondering whether we know how to spread the truth, and whether we succeed in living it.

As we consider these two different but related witnesses, the question arises: how can we put them into practice? How can we acquire this gift which transcends all the instruments of science, study and intellectual research? How can we obtain from heaven the light that increases our understanding and makes us sure in our belief, without being supported by clear, visible, and tangible arguments of ordinary natural knowledge?

### The Promise of the Spirit

Here the Lord meets us with his promise: I will send you the Holy Spirit, the Comforter, the one who speaks to you within your soul. I will send you the Holy Spirit. Here it is obvious that there is an unfathomable mystery. It is enough for us to know that it is real and is at work in our salvation and sanctification.

My very dear sons and daughters, you possess an enormous treasure. If we ask, "Do you believe in Jesus Christ?" we are sure that you would answer with one voice, "Yes." Well, who makes this affirmation possible? Who gives you the interior strength to adhere to the truth that was announced 20 centuries ago, and which we accept today as if it were presented in our times and in the circumstances of modern life? It is the breath of God, which comes to breathe in us. It is the Holy Spirit who comforts us, enlightens us with a clarity which is not rash, and dispels our doubt. He saves us from the danger of building our personality on unstable or inadequate bases, giving instead a certainty that makes us tranquil, joyful, and sure. I believe in you, O Lord! With St. Peter, over whose glorious tomb we stand we can add, "You alone, O

Lord, have the words of eternal life. I believe that you are the Christ, the Son of the living God!''

Let us feel this faith vividly; then we can communicate it. As a practical consequence, confronted by a reality that is essential for us, what are we to do? Above all, we must worship the Holy Spirit. We must be less unworthy to receive him when and where his light and his divine word—interior, soft, persuasive—makes itself present within us. For this reason our souls must always be open and receptive.

Let us make a comparison with the profane world. In the mechanized life of today we are surrounded by myriads of voices from the radio stations that broadcast their programs all around us. Who is it that succeeds in turning on the one he wants to hear? It is the person who has a suitable apparatus, and adjusts it to select the one voice among the many others that differ and often conflict with one another.

It is the same with our souls: we must put them on the right wavelength to hear the Holy Spirit perfectly. We must be rightly adapted and prepared to pick up the voice of God which wants to speak within us. The first condition for accomplishing this is to keep our spirit pure, always ready to understand the divine voice. A very intelligent university professor gave this advice to a student at the start of his higher studies, "Take care, my son, to be pure, attentive and good at every moment so that if, one day, the Lord wishes to call and speak to you, you will be able to receive and take into yourself the voice of the Divine Master who knocks at the door of your heart."

It is evident that, if we are honest, pure and faithful, the Lord will make himself felt, even if it is only by giving us the gracious fortune—which we shall never appreciate at its true worth—of professing the faith, of possessing that heavenly universe that is given to us through the word of Christ when it has become persuasive, vibrant and conquering in us.

Let us worship the Holy Spirit! Right now we are celebrating the novena which prepares us for the feast of Pentecost. Let us try to be less unworthy to receive the voice of the Lord.

To the dear ones who are sick, and to those who take care of them, as well as to all who are listening: of all the experiences afforded by human life, the finest, the most joyful, the richest in promise and consolation is that of possessing the Spirit of God, his grace, the infusion of that vital energy of his which does not die with our mortal body, but gives us here and now the guarantee that we will possess the reality and the glory of God forever in the light of clear vision.

Our parting word to you is this: be devoted to the Holy Spirit; receive his testimony so that you can communicate it to your brothers, as he has instructed us. We implore Almighty God that our meeting here today may fill you with consolation and with a strength that cannot fail.

NOTES—May 26, 1968

1. This homily was preached at the Mass for the Sunday within the octave of the Ascension. The Gospel for that Sunday, prior to the publication of the new Lectionary, was from Jn 15:26–27, and 16:1–4. (Editor's note.)
2. Cf. Jn 15:16. (Editor's note.)

# True and False Concepts of the Charismatic*

A treatise on the Holy Spirit, as he was exalted and proclaimed to us by the whole Council, would be very long. Among other things, it would oblige us to rectify certain opinions which some people form about his charismatic action. They suppose that anyone can claim to be favored with this action in such a way as to be released from obedience to hierarchical authority, or that one could appeal to a charismatic Church as opposed to one that is institutional and juridical.[1] They act as if authentic charisms of the Holy Spirit were not benefits granted for the utility of the ecclesial community in the building up of the Mystical Body of Christ,[2] as if they were not granted by preference to those who have special directive functions within his community,[3] and as if the charisms were not subject to the authority of the hierarchy.[4]

But for anyone who wishes to live with and by the Church, the mystery of the Church's animation by virtue of the Holy Spirit, which the Council has enormously extolled, still remains. It obliges us to appreciate him there where he is present and active: in our prayer and meditation, in our contemplation of Christ's presence in us (Eph 3:17), in our setting of the highest value in charity, the great and the first charism (1 Cor 12:31), in our jealous guarding of the state of grace. Grace is the communion of the divine life in us: why is it so little spoken of today? Why do so many seem to take no note of it? They seem more eager to delude themselves about the lawfulness of every forbidden experience, and to blot out of themselves the sense of sin, than they are to protect the inner witness of the Holy Spirit (Jn 15:26) in their own consciences.

We exhort you, dearest children, to a spirituality that is not purely subjective, which does not preclude sensitivity to the needs of others, nor inhibit cultural and exterior life with all its demands: the spirituality of Love, which is God, into which Christ has initiated us and which the Holy Spirit completes with his seven gifts of Christian maturity.

## NOTES—March 26, 1969

1. Cf. the encyclical, *Mystici Corporis,* of 1943, n. 62 ff. (See the citations from this passage in chapter 2 at notes 21 and 22—Editor's note.)
2. Cf. 1 Pt 4:10: "As each has received a gift, employ it for one another, as good stewards of God's varied grace. . . ."
3. Cf. 1 Cor 12:28: "God has appointed in the Church first apostles, second prophets, third teachers, then workers of miracles, then healers, helpers, administrators, speakers in various kinds of tongues."
4. Cf. Vatican II, *The Church,* #7; *The Apostolate of the Laity,* #3.

*From an address at a General Audience (*OR,* March 27, 1969). Translated by Thomas Bonaiuto.

# The Outpouring of the Spirit*

... Let us rejoice! Today is our feast, the Church's feast, the feast of the continuation of Christ's work, the feast of the spread of the Messianic plan of salvation in time and in the world, the feast of Christ's Mystical Body, to which we all have the greatest of good fortune to belong, the feast of a twofold and indescribable communion: communion with Christ and communion among ourselves. It is the feast of the Holy Spirit.

Yes, let us rejoice! Let our hearts be filled this once with the enthusiasm and inebriation of peace and joy proper to us whose lot it is to believe and to live by the animating influence of the Holy Spirit. Please God that today (and also tomorrow, as we remember this blessed day) we may have some inner experience of them, some spiritual fullness, some stirring of that inner witness which assures us that we are God's adopted children,[1] and speaks to us interiorly so as to enable us also to give witness to Christ.[2]

### The First Pentecost

The Holy Spirit's feast is the Church's feast. Pentecost rouses a whirlwind of thoughts in those who meditate on it and relive it. But let us just fix our minds for a while on two aspects of the blessed mystery. The mystery is actually only one: ... the mystery of Jesus Christ's continued presence on earth, in the human race, in history, in our temporal reality, after his departure from this world. We are told that "he showed himself alive after his passion by many proofs" (Acts 1:3), and was then "lifted up before their eyes" into heaven, "after he had given commandments through the Holy Spirit to the apostles whom he had chosen," and had told them that "you shall receive power when the Holy Spirit comes upon you, and you shall be my witnesses in Jerusalem and in all Judea and Samaria and to the ends of the earth" (Acts 1:2–8).

Jesus, though absent, would be present, as he promised, through "another Paraclete" (that is, another defender), "to be with you forever, even the Spirit of truth, whom the world cannot receive, because it neither sees him nor knows him. But you shall know him, because he dwells with you and will be in you. I will not leave you orphans...." (Jn 14:16–18).

### The Outpouring of the Holy Spirit

But how will Jesus be present with us here on earth while he is still in heaven? How will he carry out his redeeming mission? How will he "build his Church," as he foretold? (cf. Mt 16:18). By the outpouring of his Spirit. "Although Jesus Christ made himself invisible to our eyes after his resurrection, we nevertheless feel that he is still

*From a homily on Pentecost Sunday, at which 24 newly ordained priests of various nationalities concelebrated with the Pope (*OR*, May 26–27, 1969; *ORe*, June 5, 1969).

living with us, because we are aware of his breath. By his breath I mean the outpouring of the Holy Spirit."[3]

Where does this enlivening flood spread to? You know the answer. It spreads into two distinct fields which are animated by the same Spirit. It produces in both of them, in differing ways but with a single aim, the life of Christ, so that the words of St. Paul may properly be applied to both of them: "I live, now not I, but Christ lives in me" (Gal 2:20).[4]

### The Spirit and the Individual Soul

The first is the field of the individual soul, our interior life, our spiritual being, our person, which is also our own "ego," that profound cell of our own existence which is mysterious even to our own minds. The Holy Spirit's breath enters there, and spreads in the soul with that first and supreme charism which we call grace, and which is like a new life. This immediately makes the soul capable of acts that surpass its natural abilities; that is to say, it confers supernatural powers or virtues upon it. Grace spreads through the network of human psychology with impulses which we call gifts, leading us to act with ease and strength. Grace fills the soul with wonderful spiritual effects which we call Fruits of the Spirit, the first of which are joy and peace. It is normal for the soul filled with grace to experience them (Gal 5:22). In brief, our human being, including the body, becomes God's abode (Jn 14:23), his temple.[5]

How much could be said about this "discernment of the Spirit!" What a study could be made of this experience of the Holy Spirit's presence in the Christian soul![6] But you have already heard about it in your theology classes, and perhaps have had some experience of it in your own religious and moral lives. It is a field to be explored and cultivated throughout the years of your ministry, for your own and others' edification. This part of Catholic doctrine contains the secret and the fount of the living mystery of Christ's presence and action in us: "*per Spiritum Sanctum, qui datus est nobis*" (through the Holy Spirit who has been given to us).[7] We will say no more about this now, but, beloved sons and brethren, we recommend above all that you give the greatest importance to the reality of this mystery of the Holy Spirit dwelling in us, inspiring, enlivening and sanctifying us. Our final salvation depends on having personal possession of this mystery. Likewise, the effective mystical value of our ministry, as well as its beneficial and fruitful exercise, derive in no small measure from this interior source, which is the state of grace. (We prescind of course here from the intrinsic and autonomous effectiveness of the sacraments.) Always have before your mind how this is to be attained, preserved and nourished. Concern yourselves with the cultivation of a pure conscience, of that inner silence which knows how to hear "*quid Spiritus dicat*" . . . (what the Spirit says—Apoc 2:7), of interior life, in a word, of the whole contemplative enterprise. This is the mark of anyone who wishes to be led by the Spirit (as we hear so often these days) and to benefit from charismatic inspiration.

### The Spirit and the Visible Institution

Our line of thought now brings us to the second field in which the power of Pentecost is poured out: the Apostles and the followers of the Lord Jesus, that is to say, the visible body of the Church, which the Holy Spirit transforms into the mystical Body of Christ. We are reminded of the words of St. Augustine:

Only the Body of Christ lives by the Spirit of Christ. . . . Do you wish to live by the Spirit of Christ? Then be incorporated in the Body of

Christ. . . . Let us love unity and fear separation. The Christian should fear nothing more than to be separated from the Body of Christ. For if he is separated from the Body of Christ, he is not a member of that Body; if he is not a member of Christ, he is not quickened by his Spirit.[8]

The outpouring of the Holy Spirit takes place within certain ordinary, well-defined limits, so far as we believers are concerned. These limits are constituted by the ecclesial institution. No doubt, "the Spirit blows where he wills" (Jn 3:8), but in the arrangements laid down by Christ, the Spirit comes through the channel of the apostolic ministry. "God created the hierarchy, the ministerial priesthood,[9] and thus more than sufficiently provided for the Church's needs until the end of the world."[10]

Our thoughts must be directed today to this apostolic ministry, in order to appreciate the mystery of Pentecost, to marvel at it in profound humility and exalting blessedness. We must consider this apostolic ministry today, contemplating it in our own selves, endowed as we are with that special power of the Holy Spirit, which enables us to bring him to the faithful in our preaching, in guiding the People of God, and in distributing the sacraments, which are the very source of grace, that is, of the sanctifying action of the Paraclete. There can be no more devoted service, but also no higher power.

Thus the Church is both hierarchical and a community; it is apostolic, holy, one and universal. Today is the feast of the Church, the feast of the Spirit; it is the feast of God who is Love. Let us invoke him, bless him, live him and pour him out upon others. Amen.

## NOTES—May 25, 1969

1. Cf. Rom 8:16: ". . .it is the Spirit himself bearing witness with our spirit that we are children of God."
2. Cf. Jn 15:26–27: "But when the Paraclete comes, whom I shall send to you from the Father, even the Spirit of truth, who proceeds from the Father, he will bear witness to me; and you also are witnesses because you have been with me from the beginning."
3. Formari, *Vita di Gesu Cristo,* III, 3.
4. Cf. S. Tromp, *De Spiritu Sancto anima Corporis mystici* I & II (Rome, Gregoriana, 1948–1952).
5. Cf. 1 Cor 3:16–17: "Do you not know that you are God's temple and that God's Spirit dwells in you? If anyone destroys God's temple, God will destroy him. For God's temple is holy, and that temple you are." See also 6:19; 2 Corinthians 6:16.
6. Cf. Jean Mouroux, *The Christian Experience.* New York, Sheed and Ward, 1954.
7. Cf. Yves Congar, O.P., *The Mystery of the Church,* revised ed. (Baltimore, Helicon, 1965), p. 109.
8. Augustine, *Homilies on the Gospel of John,* 26 and 27 (*NPNF,* First Series, vol. 7; *PL* 35:1612–1613; 1618).
9. Cf. Vatican II, *The Church,* #10.
10. Johann-Adam Moehler, *Theologische Quartalshrift,* 1834; quoted by Y. Congar in *Esquisses du mystère de l'Eglise,* Paris, Cerf. p. 176 (omitted from the English translation).

# Alleluia Joy*

...The Easter season puts the exclamation, *Alleluia,* on the lips of the Church, as all of you know. We will therefore say *Alleluia* to you, too, dear visitors, inviting you all to repeat it with us in your hearts. It is a cry of joy which expresses the feeling that overflows in the hearts of believers when they celebrate the feast of Christ's resurrection. This feeling, simple but full and rich, is theirs at the memory of the real, historical fact which concludes the Gospel narrative, and at the exultant, dazzling understanding of the mystery of redemption and of the new life communicated from Christ to Christians.

*Alleluia* means "Praise the Lord!" It expresses the joy and enthusiasm which, like a song, sustain and accompany our now safe pilgrimage toward the fullness of eternal life.[1]

. . .

Religion, faith and grace have these moments of inner exultation, these surprises of the Spirit, these sweet, impetuous preludes of God's life in us. Yes, Alleluia! in Christ and in the Church. "Joy, joy, tears of joy" (Pascal).

We also have a pastoral intention in repeating this cry of exuberant gladness. It is not enough to have joy at a moment of sensible and spiritual fullness; joy must be perennial, even if at a less intense degree. The believer, the person who has succeeded in meeting the risen Christ, even though in the incognito of our earthly pilgrimage,[2] should always have the charism of joy within himself. Joy, together with peace, is the first fruit of the Spirit (Gal 5:22). And in the divine plan of salvation, there is, as we know, a relationship between the Spirit and the Church. We will not specify it here; let us merely repeat the vivid saying of St. Augustine: *Quantum quisque amat Ecclesiam, tantum habet Spiritum Sanctum*—"in the measure that you love the Church, you have the Holy Spirit."[3] To have the joyous charism of the Spirit, it is necessary to love the Church.

People speak of the "sense of the Church." We would like to go even farther with this interior phenomenon, and exhort you to have "delight in the Church." This seems unfortunately to be lacking in so many people, even among those who set themselves up as reformers of the Church. They take delight in contention, criticism, emancipation, arbitrary views, and often in the disintegration and demolition of the Church. No, they cannot have "delight in the Church," and perhaps not even love. We do not see how these restless sons can really experience within themselves a true understanding of what is and what must be.[4]

Brothers and sons, we hope that, in thinking of the Church, its history, its glories, its weaknesses, its needs and its real postconciliar rebirth, you will always have on your lips and in your hearts the paschal cry, Alleluia!

*From an address at a General Audience (held, by exception, on a Saturday). *OR,* April 26, 1970; *ORe,* May 7, 1970.

157

NOTES—April 25, 1970

1. Cf. St. Augustine, Sermon 255 (*PL* 38:1186; *Fathers of the Church,* vol. 28, pp. 349–357.
2. Cf. the appearance of Christ to the disciples on the way to Emmaus, Luke 24:32.
3. St. Augustine, *Homilies on the Gospel of John* tr. 32:8 (*PL* 35:1645–1646; *NPNF* vol. vii, first series, pp. 195–196).
4. Cf. St. Augustine, *On the Morals of the Catholic Church* I, 30 (*PL* 32, 32:1336; *NPNF* vol. iv, first series, p. 58).

# The Spirit and the Priest*

Today is Pentecost, the commemoration of the fact and the mystery that gave life to the Church as Christ's mystical Body. For Christ sent the Church his Spirit, as he had promised,[1] and that divine Paraclete continues to give the Church life and breath. Thus Pentecost bursts in upon our minds, not only as a recollection of that event, but also as a reliving of it.

### The Experience of Pentecost

It is as if our customary invocation, "Come, Holy Spirit," were met by the reality of his response and his presence, infusing into us some slight yet living experience of his beatifying coming. It is as if that indescribable current of undying history—the history of supernatural life, were passing into our mortal limbs. Meanwhile, the echo of the first sermon delivered to the newborn Church, the prophetic sermon of St. Peter, resounds in our ears. . . .[2]

Pentecost grips us all; it moves us all and makes us think. At the same time, there shines in our souls a ray of new brightness, that "light of hearts" which is full of love and truth. This is the feast of the Holy Spirit, the feast of the nascent and imperishable Church, of souls alight with the divine inward presence. It is the feast of wisdom and charity, of consolation and joy, hope and holiness. It is the beginning of Christian culture. It is Pentecost.

. . .

### Priestly Ordination

But another, truly Pentecostal event enhances the reality and splendor of this festive celebration—the ordination of these deacons to the priesthood. . . . We will try to summarize in a single word everything that can be thought and said of the event which is about to occur for you. That word is transmission—transmission of a divine power, of a miraculous capacity for an action which of itself belongs only to Christ. It is the *traditio potestatis*.[3]

Through the imposition of our hands and the meaningful words that confer sacramental power on this action, Christ sends down from on high and pours into you his Spirit, the Holy Spirit, the vivifying, powerful Spirit. He comes to you not only to dwell in you, as in the other sacraments, but also to enable you to perform certain definite actions characteristic of Christ's priesthood, and to make you his efficacious ministers, vehicles of the word and of grace. In this way he modifies your very persons in such a way that they not only represent Christ, but also act in a certain way like him. This occurs through a delegation which stamps an indelible "character" on your souls and conforms each of you to him as another Christ.

*Homily at an ordination ceremony on Pentecost (*OR*, May 18–19, 1970; *ORe*, May 28, 1970).

### At the Service of Others

Never forget that this marvel happens in you, but not for you. It is for others, it is for the Church—which is to say, it is for the world that is to be saved. Your power is one of function, like the power of a special organ working for the benefit of the whole body. You become instruments, ministers at the service of the brethren.

. . .

### A Prayer for New Priests

This is how we will pray for you today:

Come, Holy Spirit, and give a new heart to these ministers, dispensers of the mysteries of God, renewing in them all the education and training they have received. Make them perceive the sacrament they have received as a surprising revelation. Make them respond always with new freshness, as they do today, to the unceasing duties of their ministry to your Eucharistic Body and to your Mystical Body. Give them a new heart, always young and cheerful.

Come, Holy Spirit, and give these ministers, disciples and apostles of Christ the Lord, a pure heart, trained to love him alone who is God with you and the Father; to love with the fullness, joy and depth which he alone can infuse, when he is the supreme and total object of the love of a man living in your grace. Give them a pure heart, which knows evil only in order to define it, combat it and put it to flight; a pure heart like that of a child, capable of enthusiasm and awe.

Come, Holy Spirit, and give these ministers of the People of God a great heart, open to your inspiring word, silent and powerful, but closed to every mean ambition; a stranger to every kind of miserable human competition, but totally imbued with feeling for our Holy Church. Give them a great heart that yearns to be like that of the Lord Jesus, wide enough to embrace the dimensions of the Church and of the world; a heart great and strong in loving all, serving all, and suffering for all; a heart great and strong in bearing up under all temptations, trials and weariness, as well as every annoyance, every disappointment, every offense. Give them a heart that is great, strong and constant when sacrifice must be made, a heart that is happy only to beat with the heart of Christ and to carry out the divine will humbly, faithfully and manfully. . . .

### NOTES—May 17, 1970

1. Cf. Jn 15:26 and 16:7.
2. Acts 2:17; cf. Jl 2:28.
3. "Transmission of power"—a technical term in scholastic theology for the imparting of priestly power in Holy Orders.

# The Interior Manifestation of Jesus*

But there is still another form, another step toward mystical contact with God, perhaps less rare than we might think. It is that of grace jealously guarded in the soul; it is the interior manifestation of Jesus, promised to the one who really loves him: "I will manifest myself to him," he said (Jn 14:21). It is that "light of hearts" which makes faith a light and a security. It is the inspiration of the Holy Spirit, that guidance which God, in the economy of grace, exerts over faithful souls, especially those devoted to interior silence, prayer and contemplation. It is a gift or fruit of the Spirit,[1] a charism infusing into the heart an unmistakeable pull toward the God who is real, living and present.

NOTE—September 9, 1970

1. Cf. Gal 5:22 and Eph 5:9.

*From an address at a General Audience at Castel Gondolfo (*OR,* Sept. 10, 1970; *ORe,* Sept. 17, 1970).

# Church Authority and the Charisms*

... Some people today stress the "service" character of Church authority to such a degree that two dangerous consequences in our concept of the Church's constitution could result. The first is the assigning of priority to the community, thereby according to it effective "charismatic" power proper to itself. The second consists in ignoring the fact of power in the Church, with a marked discrediting of the canonical functions in the ecclesial society. This leads to the idea of indiscriminate liberty and autonomous pluralism, while tradition and the normative function of the hierarchy are attacked as "juridicism."

Confronted with these interpretations which are fundamentally at variance with the mind of Christ and of the Church, we would like to repeat once again today that authority, that is, the power or ordering the means suitable for attaining the end of the ecclesial society, is not opposed to the outpouring of the Spirit in the People of God; rather it is the vehicle and guardian thereof. That authority was granted by Christ to Peter and the Apostles with their legitimate successors: "All power in heaven and on earth has been given to me. Go therefore and make disciples of all nations . . . teaching them to observe all that I have commanded you" (Mt 28:18–19); "Whatever you bind on earth shall be bound in heaven, and whatever you loose on earth shall be loosed in heaven" (Mt 18:18); "He who hears you hears me, and he who rejects you rejects me, and he who rejects me rejects him who sent me" (Lk 10:16).

. . .

St. Paul, who is acclaimed by some as the supporter of charisms in opposition to institutionalism in the Church, provides us with striking examples of the exercise of judicial and coercive[1] power. For him, it is a matter of principle that judicial power is reserved to the "saints," that is, to those who belong to the Christian community, with all the more reason since it pertains to them to judge the world (I Cor 6). On his own part, St. Paul forcefully exercises the power to judge and to punish. We do not wish to recall here his judgment and condemnation of one of the faithful of Corinth who was guilty of incest (1 Cor 5). Read the Second Epistle to the Corinthians and the Epistle to the Galatians, written immediately afterwards; that will suffice to show how the Apostle of the Gentiles, he who was inspired to sing the praises of charity (1 Cor 13), exercised the power which he felt had been granted to him by Christ.

Examples could be multiplied; but it is worthwhile to see how the Apostle Paul exercises his judicial power in regard to charisms and charismatics. It is very true that the Spirit is completely free in what he does, and St. Paul, taking his stand in regard to the Thessalonians, counsels them not to quench the Spirit (1 Thes 5:19). But it is also true that charisms are for the benefit of the community, and all do not possess the same charisms. Moreover, as a result of human frailty, charisms may be confused at times with one's own disordered ideas and inclinations.

Hence it is necessary to judge and discern charisms in order to check their

*From an address to the Judges and Officials of the Tribunal of the Sacred Roman Rota (*OR*, Jan. 29, 1971; *ORe*, Feb. 11, 1971).

162

authenticity, and to correlate them with criteria derived from the teaching of Christ, and with the order which should be observed in the ecclesial community. Such an office pertains to the sacred hierarchy, which is itself established by a singular charism. So true is this, indeed, that St. Paul does not recognize as valid any charism that is not subject to his apostolic office.[2]

NOTES—January 28, 1970

1. Theologians generally distinguish three aspects of the Church's jurisdictional authority: legislative (the power to make laws), judicial (the power to judge its members according to those laws), and coercive (the power, for instance, to punish delinquents). The latter two especially are often challenged on the grounds that the Church ought to limit itself to purely persuasive means (cf. Denzinger-Schönmetzer's *Enchiridion*, #2605). Hence Pope Paul is here showing how even the latter two functions, distasteful as they may be, are a necessary part of the Church's activity in this world. (Editor's note.)

2. Cf. 1 Cor 4:21; 12:4 f.; Gal 1:8; Col 2:1-23.

# The Spirit, Mary and the Hierarchy*

One of the most important, most characteristic and most fruitful teachings that Vatican II left the Church is that of the very mystery of the Church itself, which consists in the life it lives as the Mystical Body of Christ. This life or animation derives from the outpouring of the Holy Spirit, the Spirit of Christ. This has always been known, from Pentecost, from the doctrine of the Fathers (let us cite, for the Eastern Church, St. Athanasius, St. Basil and St. Gregory of Nyssa; and St. Hilary, St. Ambrose, St. Leo the Great for the Western Church), from recent pontifical documents (of Leo XIII,[1] Pius XII[2]), and from the outstanding theological studies (such as those of Johann Moehler,[3] Cardinal Journet,[4] Father Congar[5] . . .). But ordinary catechesis rather tended to consider the Church in her visible and social aspect, which was stressed particularly by the Council of Trent against certain heresies of the Reformation. Without denying this aspect, but rather elevating it and considering it as a sign and instrument of salvation, the recent Council[6] fixed attention on the spiritual, mysterious, divine aspect of the Church—its "pneumatology."

If we wish to be faithful followers of the teaching of the Council, we must deepen our knowledge of the Holy Spirit. There exists a vast new literature on this magnificent and fruitful subject.[7]

### Titles of the Holy Spirit

This literature dwells not so much on theological research on the Holy Spirit in himself as on the relations that the third Person of the Holy Trinity has with the Church and with individual souls. Thus we are reminded of the titles that denote the operations of the Holy Spirit with regard to humanity, redeemed and to be redeemed through Christ. The Spirit is called *par excellence* Holy and the sanctifier; he is the Paraclete, or our patron and comforter; he is the bringer of life; the liberator; he is Love. He is the Spirit of God, the Spirit of Christ, the Uncreated Grace that dwells in us as the source of created grace, and of the efficacy of the sacraments. He is the Spirit of truth, and unity, that is, the principle of communion, and therefore the leaven of ecumenism. He is the joy of the possession of God. He is the giver of the Seven Gifts and the charisms; he is the driving force of the apostolate; the support of martyrs; the inner inspiration of teachers; he is the leading voice of the Magisterium and the superior authority of the hierarchy. Finally he is the source of our spirituality: "*fons vivus, ignis, caritas, et spiritualis unctio*" (living fountain, fire, charity, and spiritual anointing).[8]

### Dispositions to Receive the Spirit

Why do we speak to you today of this immense and ineffable subject? Because we are in the well-known "novena" in preparation for the feast of Pentecost. And so we should dwell upon the dispositions of spirit which enable us to celebrate better this

---

*Address at a General Audience (*OR*, May 27, 1971; *ORe*, June 3, 1971).

central feast of our Catholic worship, *metropolim festorum,* as St. John Chrysostom says;[9] and to be not unworthy to receive the Gift par excellence, which is the Holy Spirit himself (a gift being the effect and sign of love).[10]

How are we to receive this Gift, which is God himself in the act of communicating himself? The best preparation is indicated to us by the Apostles together with Mary and the disciples who waited in the upper room for the fulfillment of Christ's last promise, before his Ascension. They must wait, he told them, to be baptized in the Holy Spirit, in a few days' time (cf. Acts 1:5). They waited, trusting in the word of the Lord, in meditation and prayer, all together. It is necessary to have souls that are open, that is, purified by repentance[11] and faith; filled with the sense of time, i.e., of God's hour; in silence, yet at the same time in loving communion with their brothers, in the company of Mary, the blessed Mother of Jesus. We may say that devotion to the Blessed Virgin began at that moment when the mystical Body of her divine Son, whose physical body she begot, was about to be born. A triple motif of central interest is offered to our spirituality: the Spirit, the Virgin Mary and the Church.

### The Spirit, Mary, and the Hierarchy

We cannot refrain from making a recommendation. Do not separate these elements, which are very diverse, yet complementary, forming a marvelous synthesis prepared by the divine plan. At the summit of your worship, particularly your interior worship, you should have the Holy Spirit. This worship will be expressed mainly in the watchful and anxious care to possess and shelter this "dulcis hospes animae" (sweet guest of the soul). In catechetical and realistic terms: take care that you are always, always in a state of grace.[12] Do not follow those who, on the pretext of ridding the conscience of useless anxieties and troublesome scruples, try to persuade you that there is no need to be in a state of grace before receiving Holy Communion, or in order to live as respectable Christians!

Secondly, do not let your devotion to Mary abate. Mary had the privilege of bringing Christ into the world, and she became the spiritual Mother of the Church in the upper room!

Finally, do not separate the Spirit from the hierarchy, from the institutional structure of the Church, as if they were two antagonistic expressions of Christianity, or as if we could obtain the one, the Spirit, without the ministry of the other, the Church, which is the qualified instrument of truth and grace. It is true that the Spirit "blows where he wills" (Jn 3:8), but we cannot presume that he will come to us, if we are deliberately absent from the vehicle chosen by Christ to communicate him to us. He who does not adhere to the body of Christ, we will repeat with St. Augustine, leaves the sphere animated by the Spirit of Christ.[13]

### NOTES—May 26, 1971

1. Leo XIII, *The Holy Spirit (Divinum illud),* in *The Great Encyclical Letters of Pope Leo XIII,* New York, Benziger, 1903 (*ASS* 29, 1896–1897, 644–658).
2. Pius XII, *The Mystical Body of Christ (Mystici Corporis),* Washington, D.C., National Catholic Welfare Conference (*AAS* 35, 1943, 193–248).
3. Johann-Adam Moehler, *Die Einheit in der Kirche,* Tübingen, Laupp, 1825.
4. Charles Journet, *The Church of the Word Incarnate,* vol. I, New York, Sheed and Ward, 1955. (Volumes II and III of *L'Eglise du Verbe Incarné,* published in French by Desclée de Brouwer, 1955 ff. have not appeared in English.

5. Yves Congar, O.P., *The Mystery of the Church,* Baltimore, Helicon, 1960.

6. Cf. Vatican II, *The Church,* #1, 48; *The Liturgy,* #26; *The Church Today,* #5, 45.

7. For the use of experts, as well as the guidance of the faithful, we will cite the article on the Holy Spirit in the *Dizionario del Concilio Ecumenico Vaticano II,* by Prof. T. Federici, Unione Editoriale, 1969; the volume, *Ecclesia a Spiritu Sancto edocta; Mélanges théologiques: "Hommages à Mgr. Gerard Philips"* (*Lumen Gentium,* 53). (Bibliothèque Ephemerides Theologicae Lovanienses 27), Gembloux, Duculot, 1970; G. Philips, *L'Eglise et son mystère au II<sup>e</sup> Concile du Vatican,* I, Paris, Desclée, 1967; etc.

8. From the Sequence for the Mass of Pentecost.

9. St. John Chrysostom, *De Sancta Pentecosta,* Homilia II, (*PG* 50:463).

10. Cf. St. Thomas Aquinas, *Summa Theologiae* I, 38, 2.

11. Cf. Acts 2:38: "Peter said to them, 'Repent, and be baptized every one of you in the name of Jesus Christ for the forgiveness of your sins; and you shall receive the gift of the Holy Spirit.' "

12. Cf. 1 Cor 11:29: "Let a man examine himself, and so eat of the bread and drink of the cup." See also Dante, *Purgatorio,* 2, 3, 9.

13. Cf. St. Augustine, *Homilies on the Gospel of John,* 27 #6 (*NPNF,* new series, vol. 7, p. 176; *PL* 35:1618).

# Living by the Spirit*

*(The Pope has been speaking of the many people today, especially among the young, who, in aspiring to be authentic Christians, become sharply critical of the society around them. They do not share the more general tendency of modern man, of refusing to relate human actions to God as the supreme criterion of good and evil.)*

...Those who seek authenticity in the Christian life... often refer today to another order of considerations, which is absolutely true, provided it is integrated into the context of full Christian reality. These gifted inquirers say, "We must live according to the Spirit." We have already spoken of this on another occasion,[1] but it is useful to complete the examination of St. Paul's words, "Let us live by the Spirit" (Gal 5:25), because this great principle may lead to wrong conclusions. One such inadmissible conclusion is that by which they are supposedly freed from the guidance of the ecclesiastical Magisterium in the interpretation of Holy Scripture (the so-called "free examination"). The same principle is also taken to justify rejection of obedience to the pastoral government of the Church, and of conformity with the lived communion of ecclesial society.

Let us admit, therefore, that our Christian life must be modeled and inspired by something great and new—grace, that is, the action of the Holy Spirit in the souls united with Christ's life. This is the essential and characteristic aspect of the "New Law," that of the Gospel, which reigns in the Church. Listen to the following words of St. Thomas, which will seem surprising on the lips of the great scholastic Doctor: "The New Law consists mainly in the grace of the Holy Spirit written in the hearts of the faithful.... The Law of the Gospel... is the very grace of the Holy Spirit...."[2]

Just think what newness, what freedom, what inner life and spirituality define the authenticity of the Christian life. Our first and, in a certain sense, only duty is to live in God's grace. This can be further reduced to the supreme and summary precept of Christ: to live in love of God and of neighbor (Mt 22:37). Just think, living here does not mean only being, but also acting. Our art of living should spring from this real and conscious animation, that of God's mysterious presence, blessed and operative, in us,[3] a presence to which the faithful and authentic Christian listens, and to which he directs his questions. He can deduce the illuminating and formative answer from the words of divine revelation on which he meditates.[4]

What inner riches, what energy! And these gifts are not reserved solely for contemplative souls, privileged though they are at the banquet of the Lord's word,[5] but are accessible to every Christian in search of authenticity.

Are we perhaps to align ourselves with those charismatic contemporaries of ours who claim to draw the inspiration of their activity from some inner religious experience of theirs? We say: prudence. Here opens one of the most difficult and complex chapters of the spiritual life, that of the "discernment of spirits." Misunderstandings are very easy in this field; illusion no less so. So many masters have spoken about it.[6] We can be content to reread chapter 54, book III of the ever-wise *Imitation of Christ*, and thus learn humbly to discern the language of grace speaking within us.

*From an address given at a General Audience (*OR*, June 24, 1971; *ORe*, July 1, 1971. *Teachings*, 1971, pp. 92 ff.).

167

NOTES—June 23, 1971

1. At the General Audience of June 16, 1971 (*OR,* June 17, 1971; *ORe,* June 24, 1970).
2. Thomas Aquinas, *Summa Theologiae* I–II, 106, 1 and 2.
3. Cf. Jn 14:23: "Jesus answered him, 'If a man loves me, he will keep my word, and my Father will love him, and we will come to him and make our home with him.' "
4. Vatican II, *Revelation,* #7.
5. Cf. Lk 10:39: "And she had a sister called Mary, who sat at the Lord's feet and listened to his teaching."
6. E.g., St. Ignatius, Scaramelli, Cardinal Bona, etc. Cf. the article, *"Discernment des esprits,"* by A. Chollet in the *Dictionnaire de Théologie Catholique,* IV, col. 1375–1415.

# The Fruitfulness of Prayer*

The discovery of intimacy with God, of the necessity of adoration and the need for intercession, in short, the experience of Christian holiness, shows us the fruitfulness of prayer. In it God reveals himself to the spirit and heart of his servants. The Lord gives us this knowledge of himself in the fervor of love. The gifts of the Spirit are many, but they always grant us a taste of that true and intimate knowledge of the Lord. Without it we shall not succeed either in understanding the value of the Christian and religious life or in gaining the strength to advance in it with the joy of a hope that does not deceive.

The Holy Spirit also gives you the grace to discover the image of the Lord in the hearts of men, and teaches you to love them as brothers and sisters. Again, he helps you to see the manifestations of his love in events. If we are humbly attentive to men and things, the Spirit of Jesus enlightens us and enriches us with his wisdom, provided that we are imbued with the spirit of prayer.

*From the Apostolic Exhortation, *The Renewal of the Religious Life According to the Teaching of Vatican II*, # 43 & 44 (*OR*, July 2, 1971; *ORe*, July 15, 1971).

# The Holy Spirit in the Sacrament of Confirmation*

*(In compliance with Vatican II's Constitution on the Sacred Liturgy, #71, a new order for the sacrament of Confirmation was drawn up by the Congregation for Sacred Rites. In the Constitution which promulgated the new rite, Pope Paul gave an explanation of the rationale behind it, from which the following is taken.)*

... it has been our wish also to include in this revision that which concerns the very essence of the rite of Confirmation, through which the faithful receive the Holy Spirit as a gift.

The New Testament shows how the Holy Spirit assisted Christ in fulfilling his messianic mission. On receiving the baptism of John, Jesus saw the Spirit descending on him (Mk 1:10) and remaining with him (Jn 1:32). He was impelled by the Spirit to undertake his public ministry as the Messiah, relying on the Spirit's presence and assistance. Teaching the people of Nazareth, he implied by what he said that the word of Isaiah, "The Spirit of the Lord is upon me," referred to himself (Lk 4:17–21).

Later, he promised his disciples that the Holy Spirit would help them also to bear fearless witness to their faith, even in the face of persecution (cf. Lk 12:12). The day before he suffered, he assured his Apostles that he would send the Spirit of truth from his Father (Jn 15:26) to stay with them "forever" (Jn 14:16) and help them to be his witnesses (Jn 15:26). Finally, after his resurrection, Christ promised the descent of the Holy Spirit: "You shall receive power when the Holy Spirit comes upon you, and you shall be witnesses for me" (Acts 1:8; cf. Lk 24:49).

In fact, on the feast of Pentecost, the Holy Spirit descended upon the Apostles in an extraordinary way, as they were gathered together with Mary, the Mother of Jesus, and the group of disciples. They were then so "filled with the Holy Spirit" (Acts 2:4) that by divine inspiration they began to proclaim "the mighty works of God." Peter regarded the Spirit who had thus come down upon the Apostles as the gift of the messianic age (Acts 2:17–18). Those who believed the Apostles' preaching were then baptized, and they too received "the gift of the Holy Spirit" (Acts 2:38). From then on the Apostles, in fulfillment of Christ's wish, imparted the gift of the Spirit to the neophytes by the laying on of hands, thereby completing the grace of Baptism. Hence the Epistle to the Hebrews lists among the elements of basic Christian instruction the teaching about Baptism and the laying on of hands (Heb 6:2). This laying on of hands is rightly recognized by Catholic tradition as the beginning of the sacrament of Confirmation, which in a certain way perpetuates the grace of Pentecost within the Church.

This makes clear the specific importance of Confirmation for the sacramental initiation whereby the faithful "as members of the living Christ, are incorporated into him and made like to him through Baptism, Confirmation and the Eucharist."[1] In Baptism, neophytes receive forgiveness of sins, adoption as sons of God and the character of Christ, whereby they are made members of the Church and given a first sharing in the priesthood of their Savior (1 Pt 2:5 and 9). Through the sacrament of Confirmation, those who have been born anew in Baptism receive the inexpressible

*From the Apostolic Constitution, *Divinae Consortium Naturae,* promulgating the revised order for the sacrament of Confirmation. *AAS* LXIII (Sept. 30, 1971), 657–664; *OR,* Sept. 13–14, 1971; *ORe,* Sept. 23, 1971.

gift, the Holy Spirit himself, by which they are endowed with special strength."[2] Moreover, having received the character of this sacrament, they are "linked more perfectly to the Church"[3] and are "more strictly obliged to spread and defend the faith in word and deed, as true witnesses to Christ."[4] Finally, Confirmation is so closely linked with the Holy Eucharist[5] that the faithful, after being signed by holy Baptism and Confirmation, are incorporated fully into the Body of Christ by participation in the Eucharist.[6]

## NOTES—September 30, 1971

1. Vatican II, *The Missionary Activity of the Church,* #36.
2. Vatican II, *The Church,* #11.
3. *Ibid.*
4. *Ibid.* See also *The Missionary Activity of the Church,* #11.
5. Vatican II, *Priestly Ministry and Life,* #5.
6. *Ibid.*

# The Holy Spirit and Church Structure*

. . . today a controversy (not without historical precedents) has arisen within the Church itself, and public opinion has taken an interest in it. Starting from the claim to restore the Church to its original form, or to its authentic spiritual values, it sees in it two constituent principles: structures and the Spirit; we might call them the Church's organic human body and divine animation. Up to this point, we have no objections to make. Difficulties arise when the first principle, that of the structures, is accused of being unauthorized, deformed, impermanent and harmful; in other words, of being now either useless or so much in need of and liable to change that every criticism of it is to be considered justified, and every hypothesis about its dissolution or radical transformation, well-founded.

In this view, structure is an illegitimate, or at least unnecessary deviation from the authentic form of the apostolic Church. It is authoritarian, juridical, formalistic and contaminated by an inclination toward power and riches; it tends to traditionalist immobilism and separation from the world. In a word, it is antievangelical and antihistorical. The Spirit, on the other hand, is said to be charismatic, prophetic, free and liberating.

Certainly we can only rejoice at the preeminence which this summary picture accords to the Holy Spirit as the one who illuminates, guides and sanctifies the Church by his grace. In this day when materialism is stupifying minds and estranging them from spiritual realities, this precedence given to the charisms of the Spirit is worthy of favorable consideration. From this point of view, the Church stands out as a religious fact *par excellence:* personal, interior, free and happy on the subjective side, yet at the same time a fact stemming from an objective, transcendent and mysterious communication with the true and life-bringing divine Spirit. But this very fact, if it is not to be confused with religious pathology, superstition, spiritual subjectivism or collective excitement, must be put back in the sphere of the community of faith, from which it is derived and which it must help to build up. It cannot disregard the divine plan, which destines the polyvalent gift of the Spirit for the Church as the organic community of believers, and which effects its ordinary outpouring through a complex and qualified ministry.[1] That is, it is impossible to isolate the economy of the Spirit (even if the latter does, as the Lord said, blow where he pleases [Jn 3:8]) from the ministerial and sacramental structures, as they are called. The latter have been instituted by Christ, and have sprung from his word like a plant from the seed, with vital continuity.

## Relationship Between the Spirit and the Structure

One of the problems over which the most lively discussions take place today is precisely the attempt to find the right relationship between the visible, human, sacramental structure of the Church, and the mystery of the Spirit, of which the structure is a

*From an address at a General Audience, November 24, 1971 (*OR,* Nov. 25, 1971; *ORe,* Dec. 2, 1971).

sign and instrument, and from which our Christian life is derived. It is evident that this relationship bears upon the very plan of the Incarnation and the Redemption. It confers a sacred character on every Christian—a royal priesthood, common to all. It also creates a ministerial priesthood, by which the community of the People of God is made organic, united and unmistakable. This priesthood is refulgent with an incomparable, Christ-like dignity. (St. John Chrysostom's famous dialogue on the priesthood especially highlights this sublime and tremendous aspect.) It is a priesthood endowed with transcendent pastoral powers of teaching,[2] sanctification,[3] guidance and government.[4] It is so ordained to charity that it is to be called a service (Mt 20:18)—an authoritative service[5] but one so generous, human, fatherly and brotherly as to conform to that of Christ, the good Shepherd *par excellence,* who lays down his life for his flock (Jn 10:11–12).

Fortunately for us, this study on the relationship between the structures of the Church and the Spirit of Christ has been the object of deep study by thoughtful and faithful theologians, and especially by our Theological Commission.[6] Then, as regards the priesthood in particular, it has been illuminated at a high level by documents of the Bishops and of the whole Council, and most recently by the Synod of Bishops in a synthesis that will be published shortly[7] and which we trust will edify the whole Church, and in the first place our venerated and beloved priests.

Once again (may God grant this for our common consolation) we will see what this Church of ours *in fieri* is: a pilgrim toward the one Church that will be dominated wholly and solely by the "hierarchy of holiness." It is the manifestation both of the human apostolate, in its hierarchized structures which range throughout the entire People of God, and of the Pentecostal Spirit, bearing joint witness to Christ. In other words, it is the epiphany of the mystical Body, both apostolically structured and spiritually animated.[8]

## NOTES—November 24, 1971

1. Cf. 1 Cor 4:1; 12:1 ff.; 14:37–40: 1 Pt 4:10 ff.
2. Cf. Lk 10:16; Jn 15:26–27; 16:13; Mt 28:19; etc.
3. Cf. 1 Cor 11:24; Jn 20:23.
4. Cf. Mt 16:8; John 21:15; 1 Pt 5:2; etc.
5. Cf. I Cor 4:21; 1 Pt 4:11.
6. *Le ministère sacerdotal.* Paris, Cerf, 1971.
7. *De Sacerdotio ministeriali, AAS* 63 (1971), 898–922. English tr.: *The Ministerial Priesthood,* United States Catholic Conference, Washington, D. C. (Editor's note.)
8. Cf. *Yves Congar, The Mystery of the Church,* 2nd ed. (Baltimore, Helicon, 1965), ch. 5.

# The Charism of Bishops*

... another mysterious voice is heard, which is closely linked with our earlier reflections. It has to do with the charism of pastoral power conferred upon the bishops of the Church of God according to the precise will of Christ and the disposition of the Holy Spirit (Acts 20:28). The bishop's interior and exterior charism consists therefore in his being called to leadership of that part of the flock which has been entrusted to him, and which belongs to the one Church. It unfolds in the exercise of the triple pastoral function of teaching, ministry and government.

We are aware that some have recently ventured to place the charismatic and the hierarchical Church in opposition, as though it were a matter of two distinct—indeed, contrasting and opposed—bodies. On the contrary, in this pastoral power, charism and authority are one and the same thing. We receive the Holy Spirit who manifests himself in the episcopal mission through the vital combination of *teaching,* on which the Paraclete sheds his light; *ministry,* which sanctifies through his grace; and *governing,* which is exercised through the charity of service. These are all powers of the bishop and also gifts of the Spirit. St. Paul himself reminds us of this and confirms it: "Now there are varieties of gifts, but the same Spirit; and there are varieties of ministries, but the same Lord; and there are varieties of workings, but the same God, who works all things in all" (1 Cor 12:4–6).

From the one Triune God comes the one Church, for which the bishops have primary responsibility, sharing as they do both charismatic gifts and hierarchical offices in a unique way. Certainly the particular charisms of the faithful are not denied—quite the contrary. The same passage from the First Letter to the Corinthians presupposes and recognizes these charisms, for the Church is a living body animated by the very life of God—a life which is mysterious and manifold, ever moving, never predictable, a life which sanctifies and transforms. But as Paul also emphasizes (1 Cor 14:26–33, 40) the charisms granted to the faithful are subject to discipline, which only the charism of pastoral power, acting in charity, can maintain.

This mission which has been conferred upon the College of Bishops obliges us to reflect upon the Church and likewise upon the world, at whose service God has placed us. In the Church we are the instrument for bringing life to the family of God, and we are called, like Christ and in imitation and following of him (Jn 15:16), to give service and sacrifice in daily immolation for the flock, at the same time ensuring for it security, communion, joy and all the gifts of the Spirit (Gal 5:22–23). This is a wonderful, tremendous, exhilarating vision of our office in the Church; we must preserve the Church's unity through the obedience and love of our dear sons and daughters! To be able to do this, we must remember that in a certain way we have been set apart, selected: "set apart for the gospel of God" (Rom 1:1).

*From a homily at the ordination of 19 bishops (*OR,* Feb. 14–15, 1972; *ORe,* Feb. 17, 1972).

*For the Good of Mankind*

The demands of our ministry require a total gift of self and sever us from every binding or ambiguous tie with the world. At the same time they make us realize that we have been appointed for the world—to elevate and sanctify it, to inspire and consecrate it. Woe to the shepherd who would forget even one sheep, for he will be called to give an account of all: the biblical tradition of the prophets and the Gospels reminds us of this with frightening severity. Christ's love, which has conferred upon us the charism of pastoral authority, has granted us this charism for the sake of all men, especially "those who have strayed in any way from the path of truth or who are ignorant of the Gospel of Christ and his saving mercy."[1]

NOTE—February 13, 1972

1. Cf. Vatican II, *The Pastoral Office of Bishops in the Church,* #11.

# On Preparing for the Coming of the Spirit by Interior Life*

We are near the feast of Pentecost. It commemorates and, God willing, renews in a certain measure the event of the descent of the Holy Spirit on the Apostles, gathered in the upper room in Jerusalem with the first community of the followers of Jesus, the Master, the Messiah, who had died on the cross, risen again, and had now disappeared, ascending into heaven. The group of faithful who remained amounted to about 120 persons, including the pious women and Mary, the Mother of Jesus.

It is not easy to say what that mystery-event was, although it took place with very striking external signs: a sudden rumbling noise in the heavens, the rush of a mighty wind filling the whole house, and the appearance of bright flames, like tongues of fire, above each of those present. They felt intoxicated with energy, joy and a great desire to cry out ardent and wise praises to God, springing like prophetic poetry from the bottom of their hearts. It was the Holy Spirit, that is, living Love, proceeding from God the Father and from God the Son, the Word, himself being God, the third Person of the Blessed Trinity. He is the one God revealing himself in this way in the mystery of his intimate life, infinite and unfathomable, made accessible to men in a certain way (always minimal and analogical in comparison with the infinite reality of God who is One and Three) but overflowing with light, joy and mystery in comparison with the limited capacity of the human mind (Rom 11:33-36).

## The Work of the Spirit Determinant for Christianity

The fact is that the Church was born at that moment. Its body, composed of men of this world, received its supernatural animation which penetrated it entirely, infusing new unity into that assembly that was called the Church, and at once conferring various and distinct functions on this or that member of the ecclesial assembly, as on a special organ for the benefit of the whole organism. The Church was born, from that first seminal hour, hierarchical and communitarian, constitutionally one, organized and united (cf. I Cor 12:4 ff).

If this event is true and real, as in fact it was and still is, no one will fail to see its supreme importance. The work of the Holy Spirit is determinant for the Christian religion; it transfigures that privileged part of humanity which enters within the range of its influence; it is decisive for our salvation. This does not prevent it from being mysterious, that is, from exceeding our normal capacity of knowledge, and even being wrongly interpreted, or confused with equivocal forms of spiritualism and spirituality, as a utopia, a fantasy, a work of folly, and even an act of the devil. Not for nothing did the evangelist John write in his First Epistle: "Beloved, do not believe every spirit, but

*Address at a General Audience (*OR*, May 18, 1972; *ORe*, May 25, 1972).

176

test the spirits to see whether they are of God; for many false prophets have gone out into the world'' (4:1). And St. Paul to the Thessalonians: ''Do not quench the Spirit, do not despise prophesying, but test everything; hold fast what is good'' (1 Thes 5:19–20).

### The Psychology of the Spirit Unexplored

With all that has been said in our times about idealism, psychoanalysis, psychiatry, magic, etc., we have not yet, perhaps, studied properly the theology of the Holy Spirit, and the realities that derive from his action on the human soul. These are, in the first place, grace, and then his gifts[1] and his fruits,[2] as well as the ways though which the Holy Spirit is normally conferred on us, prayer[3] and especially the sacraments, the vehicles of grace, that is, of the Holy Spirit's action in us.[4]

This is just the catechism; but it is fundamental in order to have a correct conception of the Christian life, particularly on some points which it seems useful and necessary to recall today. Let me mention them.

### Interior Life Needed to Receive the Spirit

''The Spirit blows where he wills,'' Jesus says in his famous talk with Nicodemus (Jn 3:8). We cannot, therefore, draw up exclusive doctrinal and practical norms about the interventions of the Spirit in the lives of men. He can manifest himself in the most free and unlikely forms; he ''rejoices in his world'' (Prv 8:31). Hagiography tells us so many curious and stupendous adventures of holiness; every spiritual director knows something of this. But there is one rule: an ordinary requirement is called for from anyone who wishes to pick up the supernatural waves of the Holy Spirit; it is interior life. The appointment for the meeting with the ineffable Guest is fixed inside the soul. *''Dulcis hospes animae''* (sweet guest of the soul), the admirable liturgical hymn of Pentecost says. Man is made the ''temple'' of the Holy Spirit, St. Paul repeats to us.[5] However much modern man, and often also Christians and consecrated persons, tend to become secularized, they cannot, they must not ever forget this fundamental rule of life, if the latter is to remain Christian and animated by the Holy Spirit, namely cultivation of interior life.

Pentecost has had its novena of meditation and prayer. Inner silence is necessary to listen to the word of God, to experience his presence, to hear God's call. Today our psychology is turned outwards too much. The exterior scene is so absorbing that our attention is mainly directed outside; we are nearly always absent from our personal abode. We are unable to meditate, unable to pray. We cannot silence the hubbub inside, due to outside interest, images, passions. There is no quiet, holy space in the heart for the flame of Pentecost. We pretend, perhaps, to have special ''charisms'' in order to claim blind autonomy for the spiritual caprices of our instincts, and we do not try to bring back our feelings and thoughts to the authentic phase of divine inspiration. The conclusion follows automatically: we must give inner life its place in the program of our busy existence; a primary place, a silent place, a pure place. We must find ourselves again in order to be fit to have the life-bringing and sanctifying Spirit in us. If not, how can we listen to his witness?[6]

### The Voice of the Spirit and the Voice of Conscience

There would be other points to consider regarding this great phenomenon of the welcoming of the Holy Spirit in us. What may be the connection, for example, between this voice of the Spirit, the voice of the heart inhabited by the Paraclete, our defender, advocate and inner teacher, and the natural, though also delicate and noble voice, of our human conscience? Socrates had a "demon," which inspired him in the depths of his conscience like a divine voice;[7] Gandhi obeyed a "still small voice" which he heard within him at certain moments.[8] But without drawing upon extraordinary examples, every true man has an intuitive and normative source within him. The question arises is: is this voice contrary to, distinct from, or coincident with the supernaturally inspired voice of the divine Paraclete? We will leave the question, which is mainly one of fact, to the analysis of scholars, contenting ourselves for the present with pointing out what interesting avenues are opened up by the contact of the theology of the Holy Spirit with the psychology of man.

Another question is the old one, but very much in fashion today, which contrasts the religion of authority with the religion of the spirit.[9] The latter is preferred by adversaries of the institutional, hierarchical Church, who claim the freedom of a democratic Church, living in the spirit expressed by the religious sense of the community. We all know in some way how this criticism expresses itself. We think that the question, if raised within the Catholic Church, is an attack on the very existence of the Church and leads to extinguishing the real flame of Pentecost, disregarding the thought of Christ and of the whole of Tradition.[10]

Let us rather make an effort to celebrate Pentecost well, as the fusion of the Holy Spirit with his Church.

### NOTES—May 17, 1972

1. Cf. Is 11:2: "And the Spirit of the Lord shall rest upon him, the spirit of wisdom and understanding, the spirit of counsel and might, the spirit of knowledge and the fear of the Lord."
2. Cf. Gal 5:22: "But the fruit of the Spirit is love, joy, peace, patience, kindness, goodness, faithfulness, gentleness, self-control."
3. Cf. Lk 11:13: "If you then, who are evil, know how to give good gifts to your children, how much more will the heavenly Father give the Holy Spirit to those who ask him."
4. Cf. Rom 5:5; 1 Cor 3:16; etc.
5. Cf. 1 Cor 3:16–17; 6:19; 2 Cor 6:16; Eph 2:22.
6. Cf. Jn 15:26: "When the Paraclete comes, whom I shall send to you from the Father, even the Spirit of truth, who proceeds from the Father, he will bear witness to me"; Rom 8:7: "For the mind that is set on the flesh is hostile to God; it does not submit to God's law, indeed it cannot."
7. Cf. Plato, *Apology,* 29–30.
8. Cf. C. Fusero, *Gandhi,* Milano, Dall Oglio, 1968, p. 511.
9. Cf. Auguste Sabatier, *The Religions of Authority and the Religion of the Spirit,* London and New York, 1904.
10. Cf. Yves Congar, O.P., *The Mystery of the Church* 2nd ed. (Baltimore, Helicon, 1965) pp. 119 ff.

# Pentecost Is Forever and for All*

. . . What is Pentecost in the divine plan of man's salvation? It is the descent of the Holy Spirit on the first disciples who remained faithful to Jesus after the tragic drama of his death and the triumph of his mysterious resurrection. The Holy Spirit came while they waited and prayed in the Cenacle with Mary, the Mother of Jesus. We shall not dwell here on the description of the event. Let us remember only that it is God's Spirit of love who instills a new awareness, an insuperable energy and a lively joy into each and every one of the 120 people gathered in the Cenacle. The Church is born in that moment of wind and fire. Life is breathed into the mystical Body of Christ, and his promise of perennial consolation is fulfilled. What a stupendous truth, and what a stupendous event! Man becomes the temple of the Holy Spirit.

### The Fire of the Holy Spirit Not Quenched

But from the depth's of man's heart comes the searching question: did this event take place only then? Is it over and done with, like all the other events of human history? No! The fire of the Holy Spirit will never again be quenched in the living Church of Christ, even if it no longer appears with the same impact as it did on that occasion. If, in certain moments of crisis and times of trial, it remains hidden beneath the ashes of human frailty, it is not thereby extinct. It still burns and, in every sacramental act, in every humble prayer, the "good Spirit" is present and operative.

Will it not be so for us too, brethren, in this privileged hour?

What meaning does this hour have for us if not that of an extraordinary "epiclesis," an extraordinary prayer to the Holy Spirit to descend on us and on those around us? And if our lips are hesitant in prayer, does not this holy place, so near the tomb of Peter, pray for us? Does not this very house pray for us—this house which is a Cenacle of faithful disciples and exemplary missionaries of Christianity? And our liturgy! By the very fact that we are gathered here together in the name of Jesus, does not our liturgy have the power to make present Jesus himself, who will not leave his chosen ones orphans but promises to send the Holy Spirit upon them?[1]

### The Spirit Does Not Forsake His Church

Is Pentecost, then, present here? Furthermore, is Pentecost a permanent reality? Yes, it is permanent and present. We wish you to keep this truth ever before your minds, in every moment of your lives, in every happening, however adverse or unfamiliar. The Holy Spirit does not forsake his Church, does not forsake his chosen ones. Faced with the realities of this life—the opposition of culture, the antagonism of the world, the spread of evil, we may feel our souls disturbed and our faith shaken, but we must never forget that we are not on our own. The Paraclete, that is to say the Consoler and Defender, is nearby. He is watching within us.

*Excerpt from the homily at the Mass of Pentecost (*OR,* May 22–23, 1972; *ORe,* June 1, 1972).

### For the Whole World

This revelation, which makes us possessors of the Spirit of Christ, awakens in us a further question—a compelling question, yet one which is a cause of joy, because we are certain that the reply is victorious. The question is this: is the economy of grace, which although imperfectly known to us is nevertheless the greatest good fortune for man, reserved to a few chosen souls or is it accessible to all? Is it restricted to some more fortunate individuals or is it granted to all who accept and desire it? Is it destined for a separate caste or is it open to everyone? What a wonderful revelation is contained in the reply to our questioning! "I shall pour forth my Spirit," says the message of Pentecost, "on every living thing" (Acts 2:17). The message is for all the world. It has no limitations, whether geographical, historical, ethnic or social.

Our human way of thinking, which is naturally egotistic and tends to think of precious things as limited and rare, would be inclined to think of the kingdom of grace as being for a privileged few. But in fact the religious and historical reality inaugurated at Pentecost, is different: it is open and universal. A well-known miracle immediately made it clear. The message of Pentecost has in itself the charism of being understood by all. It is a call to all peoples, however diverse they may be. It is the first dialogue with the whole of humanity. It was the first miracle of Christianity as it shone forth among the nations divided from one another by language, which ought to be a means of uniting them.

### One and All

Listen again to these words from the first page of the Church's history: "They were all filled with the Holy Spirit and began to speak in other tongues, as the Spirit gave them utterance ... the multitude came together, and they were bewildered, because each one heard them speaking in his own tongue" (Acts 2:4, 6). This is the miracle of tongues: each one keeps his own language, but all converge, in expression and understanding, on the same truth. The most diverse peoples, through the power of the Gospel, come together in a harmonious and fraternal unity. You should respect one another in love, St. Paul says, "eager to maintain the unity of the Spirit in the bond of peace. There is one body and one Spirit, just as you were called to the one hope that belongs to your call, one Lord, one faith, one baptism, one God and Father of us all" (Eph 4:2–6). One and all: these are the two hinges of this new conception of man's spiritual and social life, polarized in Christ.

Is it not this that brings us together here to celebrate the perennial mystery of Pentecost, presenting it to us as realized here today in symbolic manner and in actual fact? One and all! The Church, the Mystical Body of Christ, which, in his Spirit, we are, is one, and we are all called to announce the Gospel, to celebrate the glory of God. *"Laudate Dominum, omnes Gentes!"* ("Praise the Lord, all you nations!" Ps 117:1). We see in you, brothers and dear sons, candidates for the ministry of evangelization,[2] a symbol of the chorus of all peoples, present and future, who, in unison and yet each in his own tongue, will tell of man's salvation in Christ our Lord. We may take on our own lips here the words of the prophet Joel, quoted by St. Peter on the morning of the first Pentecost: "And in the last days it shall be, God declares, that I will pour out my Spirit upon all flesh, and your sons and your daughters shall prophesy, and your young men shall see visions, and your old men shall dream dreams; yea, and on my menservants and my maidservants in those days I will pour out my Spirit; and they shall prophesy" (Acts 2:17–18).

One of those eschatological days announced at the first Christian Pentecost is here today, dear brothers and sons, in this house full of charity and truth, built for the express purpose of preaching our faith to the whole world—a faith that in this festivity appears to us as more than ever actual and living, one and universal, dynamic and apostolic.

Let us bless the Lord!

NOTES—May 21, 1972 (I)

1. Cf. Jn 14:18, 16, 26; 16:7.
2. St. Peter's College, where this Mass was being celebrated is a residence for priests from mission countries.

# The Living Impulse of the Holy Spirit*

This is a great day for us. For the Church this is the feast of its inner animation through the infusion of the Holy Spirit with all his gifts. A sense of splendor, security, energy, youthfulness and joy should permeate the Church completely. A stream of good will and love; a living breath of religious poetry; a great desire to rush to the aid of the suffering and needy and to proclaim pardon, friendship and peace to our brothers; the overcoming of every baseness and evil; the need to communicate to others the secret of our happiness, which is Christ the Lord; and an original and sanctifying experience of being the Church, which is the organic communion of free souls in the breath of the one faith and of common charity—these and a hundred other joyous feelings and impulses in our minds and our hearts ought to form our spiritual experience today, an experience of holiness and of life. We had proof of this this morning while celebrating Mass in the college across from us on the Janiculum Hill, which is dedicated to St. Peter the Apostle. Bands of young men and women were there, who have vowed to take the Gospel to the so-called missionary countries, strengthened by nothing other than the formidable and imponderable impulse of the Holy Spirit.

This is also a great day for the world, for the torrent of the Holy Spirit must overflow on the world. Our prayer resounds today: "Send, O Lord, your Spirit and renew the face of the earth." The panorama of the world does not disappear from the Christian vision; rather it is illuminated in this ecstatic hour of Pentecost. Should we not look with trust on the events of our history—the meetings in Moscow,[1] the drawing together of countries kept at a distance from one another ever since the last appalling conflagration; Vietnam, Palestine and the neighboring countries which are still without peace; our most beloved Ireland which is rent with deep-seated conflict; the growth and spread of delinquency; the needs of the poor, which are still so immense; and the thousand other problems which afflict humanity?

Our joy is not without tears; but neither do we lack the comfort of a new hope. If the Holy Spirit were to come, would not everything be renewed?

Let us therefore invoke the consoling and vivifying Spirit, addressing ourselves to her who, through the work of the Holy Spirit, gave the world a Savior.

NOTE—May 21, 1972 (II)

1. President Nixon was at that time meeting with the heads of the Russian government in Moscow.

*Regina Coeli* message for Pentecost Sunday (*OR*, May 22–23, 1972; *ORe*, May 25, 1972).

# The Church's Greatest Need*

On several occasions we have asked about the greatest needs of the Church....[1] What do we feel is the first and last need of this blessed and beloved Church of ours?

We must say it, almost trembling and praying, because as you know well, this is the Church's mystery and life: the Spirit, the Holy Spirit. He it is who animates and sanctifies the Church. He is her divine breath, the wind in her sails, the principle of her unity, the inner source of her light and strength. He is her support and consoler, her source of charisms and songs, her peace and her joy, her pledge and prelude to blessed and eternal life.[2]

The Church needs her perennial Pentecost; she needs fire in her heart, words on her lips, prophecy in her outlook. She needs to be the temple of the Holy Spirit,[3] that is, of complete purity and interior life. In the empty silence of modern men, totally extroverted as we are under the spell of exterior life, so charming, fascinating and corrupting with its delusions of false happiness, the Church needs to feel rising from the depths of her inmost personality, almost a weeping, a poem, a prayer, a hymn—the praying voice of the Spirit, who, as St. Paul teaches us, takes our place praying in us and for us "with sighs too deep for words." He interprets the words that we would not be able to address to God by ourselves (Rom 8:26–27). The Church needs to rediscover the eagerness, the taste and the certainty of the truth that is hers.[4] She needs to listen with inviolate silence and in an attitude of total availability, to the voice, or rather the conversation, of the Spirit who speaking in the absorption of contemplation, teaches "every truth" (ib.). And then the Church needs to feel flowing through all her human faculties a wave of love, of that love which is called forth and poured into our hearts "by the Holy Spirit who has been given to us" (Rom 5:5). Finally, permeated with faith, the Church needs to experience a new stimulus to "activism"—an activism that will be the expression in works of this love[5] which creates the pressure, the zeal and the urging behind it.[6] This is apostolic witnessing.[7]

Living men, you young people, you consecrated souls, and you brothers in the priesthood—are you listening to us? This is what the Church needs, she needs the Holy Spirit! The Holy Spirit in us, in each of us and in all of us together, in us who are the Church.

### Pseudo-charismatics

Why has this inner fullness weakened in so many, though they say they belong to the Church? Why have the ranks of faithful, soldiering in the name of the Church and under its guidance, so often become lethargic or depleted? Why have so many become apostles of contention, laicization and secularization, as if thinking thereby to give freer course to the expression of the Spirit? Why do they sometimes trust more in the spirit of the world than in that of Christ? Again, why have some people loosened or

*From an address at a General Audience (*OR*, Nov. 30, 1972; *ORe*, Dec. 7, 1972).

183

even denounced as troublesome chains, the bonds of ecclesial obedience and of zealous, faithful communion with the Church ministry? This they do under pretext of
living according to the Spirit, freed from the forms and norms characteristic of canonical institutions; but the visible body of the pilgrim Church, being historical and human
as well as mystical, has to be composed of institutions. Is recourse to the Holy Spirit
and his charisms a pretext, not too sincere, perhaps, for living or thinking to live the
Christian religion authentically, whereas those who employ this pretext actually live
according to their own spirit, their own private judgment, and their own arbitrary and
often ephemeral interpretation?

### The Church's Attitude

Oh! If this were the true Spirit, we would not think of suppressing it![8] We are
well aware that "the Spirit breathes where he wills" (Jn 3:8). It is true that the Church
is very demanding toward the real faithful in regard to her established observances, and
is often cautious and diffident regarding the possible spiritual illusions of those who
claim extraordinary phenomena. Nevertheless she is and intends to be extremely
respectful of the supernatural experiences granted to some souls, and of the marvelous
facts that God sometimes deigns to weave miraculously into the pattern of natural
events.

But we wish once more to avail ourself of the authority of tradition, expressed,
as you know, by St. Augustine, who reminds us that "the Christian has nothing so
much to fear as separation from the Body of Christ. If in fact, he is separated from the
Body of Christ, he is no longer his member; and if no longer his member, he is not
nourished by his Spirit";[9] "only the Body of Christ lives by the Spirit of Christ."[10]
The reason is that humble and faithful adherence to the Church not only does not
deprive us of the Holy Spirit, but rather puts us in the best and, in a sense, indispensable, condition to profit personally and collectively from his life-giving bloodstream.

Each of us can put this into practice, first of all by invoking him. Our primary
devotion should be to the Holy Spirit (to which devotion to the Blessed Virgin leads us,
as it leads us to Christ!). Secondly, by cultivating the state of grace, as you know well.
Thirdly, by having one's whole life imbued with charity and in its service; for charity
is nothing but the outpouring of the Holy Spirit.

It is he, then, that the Church needs today above all! And so may all of you
always say to him: "Come!"

### NOTES—November 29, 1972

1. In several of his public audiences during 1972, Pope Paul dealt with the question,
   "What is the greatest need of the Church today?" On Sept. 27, he declared, "An
   increase of faith seems to us the first and great need of the Church today." He
   repeated this answer on Oct. 4 and 11. On Oct. 18, he said that the apostolate,
   which he described as the spreading of the faith, "is one of the essential and
   primary needs of the Church." On Oct. 25, he declared that "the needs of the
   Church are numberless and measureless." Then, after repeating that the first need
   is faith (entailing the need of the Church to define itself), he added that "Since the
   Council, the Church needs interior life. . ." and farther on, "This is what the
   Church needs: to understand more and more that she is loved, that an infinitely
   personal outpouring of Love is focused upon her." On Nov. 15, he said that one
   of the Church's greatest needs was to be defended against the devil (OR, Nov. 16,
   1972; ORe, Nov. 23, 1972). On Nov. 22, a week before the present talk, he said
   that "the Church needs holy people" (OR, Nov. 23, 1972; ORe, Dec. 7, 1972).
   He returns to the theme of the present talk on Oct. 16, 1974.

2. Vatican II, *The Church*, #5.

3. Cf. 1 Cor 3:16–17; 6:19; 2 Cor 6:16.

4. Cf. Jn 16:13: "When the Spirit of truth comes, he will guide you into all the truth; for he will not speak on his own authority, but whatever he hears he will speak, and he will declare to you the things that are to come."

5. Cf. Gal 5:6: "For in Christ Jesus neither circumcision nor uncircumcision is of any avail, but faith working through love."

6. Cf. 2 Cor 5:14: "The love of Christ impels us, for we are convinced that one has died for all; therefore all have died."

7. The last two sentences correspond to a clause in the Italian original which could not be translated except with considerable interpretation: *"la Chiesa ha bisogno di sperimentare un nuovo stimolo di attivismo, l'espressione nelle opere di questa carità, anzi la sua pressione, il suo zelo, la sua urgenza: la testimonianza, l' apostolato."*

8. Cf. 1 Thes 5:19: "Do not quench the Spirit."

9. Augustine, *Tracts on the Gospel According to John*, tr. 27, 6 (*PL* 35:1618; omitted from the *NPNF* translation).

10. *Ibid.* tr. 26, 13 (*NPNF*, first series, vol. 7, p. 172).

# Making Religion Flourish in Our Time *

When we look for traces of religion, and more specifically traces of the faith, our Catholic faith, in the modern world, we are often struck by the negative aspects that we find. We see man's religious sense diminishing and in certain sociological contexts dying out altogether. The fundamental notion of being and life as necessarily related to God is growing dim. Prayer is stilled. The worship and love of Christ and God is replaced by indifference, profanity, or even hostility to religion (sometimes official, active and fierce). Or it is replaced by that pseudo-security which sensible and material experience can offer us, or by those substitutes for real spirituality with which criticism, doubt and self-consciousness fill the mind of man, over-confident in his own culture.[1] Statistics speak clearly: religion is losing ground.

### God Has the Initiative

This may be true and, unfortunately, often is. But if we limit our observation to the purely sociological level, we commit an error of method; we forget to consider the objective reality of religion, authentic religion, at least. Religion is a composite, two-sided reality; it consists not only of man, but also and in the first place of God, who is not absent or inert in the realm of religion. In the plan of revelation and faith, God has the main part and the initiative, while man has a part which, while certainly necessary and not purely passive, is, when examined carefully, one of disposing himself and cooperating. The true religious relationship consists, on the one hand, in the gift that God makes of himself—a gift which is, of course, limited in form and extent, if only by God's own mystery and our corresponding need of faith.[2] This relationship consists on the other hand in man's acceptance. God seeks us, we can say, even more than we seek God; because God is love and it is he who has the first initiative; he loved us first.[3]

### The Spirit Breathes Where He Wills

This realistic vision of the world of religion is a source of gratitude and tenderness for the faithful who breathe the atmosphere of God's house. It can be a source of surprise for anyone who considers religion only from the human, historical and earthly standpoint. Let us recall the dialogue of Jesus with Nicodemus by night: "...You must be born anew. The Spirit blows where he wills" (Jn 3:7–8).

Hence, we have here a question which may be answered by facts that elude positivistic analysis. Religion may arise from spiritual processes that transcend purely scientific calculations. It is indeed a miracle; but it is, in a certain sense, normal, because it belongs to the economy of the Kingdom of God. The encounter with God may take place outside any calculation of ours. The lives of the saints offer us splendid examples, and the chronicles of our times record some that have made a great deal of

*Address to a General Audience (*OR*, Feb. 22, 1975; *ORe*, March 1, 1973).

186

noise,[4] and innumerable others that have taken place quietly. This is the charismatic sphere, about which there is so much talk today. The Spirit blows where he wills. We will certainly not suppress his breath, remembering the words of St. Paul: "Do not quench the Spirit" (1 Thes 5:19). However, we must at the same time recall the following words of the same Apostle, "but test everything; hold fast what is good" (*ib.* 21). The famous "discernment of spirits" is necessary in a field in which deception can be very easy.

But the fact remains that the marvelous meeting with God can take place in spite of the modern world's refractory attitude toward religion. We see strange and also consoling symptoms of this in various countries.

### The Ordinary Channel of the Spirit

Our thought returns to the crucial point: has our religion no longer a power of its own to witness on its own behalf, to preserve and renew itself in traditional and ordinary ways? Does the Spirit breathe only outside the usual framework of canonical structures? Has the "Church of the Spirit" left the institutional Church? Is it only in spontaneous groups, as they are called, that we will find the charisms of the real, original, Pentecostal Christian spirituality?[5]

We do not wish now to enter upon a discussion of this subject, although it merits respectful examination. We do, however, wish to say two things. The ordinary and institutional structure of the Church is always the great highway by which the Spirit comes to us.[6] Today too, and moreso than ever. Only our understanding of the Church, our *sensus Ecclesiae,* needs to be reestablished, rectified and deepened. Anyone who alters the conception of the Church as a way of renewing religion in modern society, thereby ruins the channel of the Spirit established by Christ and compromises the religion of the people.[7]

In this connection, our times have had the grace to see two elements of prime importance for making religion flourish again in our days, arise out of Church tradition by way of the Council: the Council doctrine on the Church, and the liturgical reform.

Let us remember this well; let us *all* remember it.

NOTES—February 21, 1973

1. Cf. J. Daniélou, *La culture trahie par les sens.* Epi, 1972.
2. Cf. 1 Cor 13:12: "For now we see in a mirror dimly. . . ."
3. Cf. 1 Jn 4:19; Rom 11:35–36.
4. See, for example, A. Frossard, *I Have Met Him; God Exists.* Herder & Herder, 1970.
5. ". . .soltanto nei cosi detti gruppi spontanei ritroveremo i carismi della spiritualità cristiana autentica, primitiva, pentecostale?"
6. Cf. 1 Cor 4:1: "This is how one should regard us, as servants of Christ and stewards of the mysteries of God." Cf. 2 Cor 6:4.
7. Cf. J. A. Jungmann, *Tradition liturgique et problèmes actuels de pastorale.* Mappus, 1962, pp. 271ff.

# The Sociology of Grace*

A difficult problem, one that is even insoluble in scientific terms, yet a real and extremely important problem, is what we may define as the sociology of grace. If a pastor of souls, for example, a parish priest, asks himself, how many of my faithful live in God's grace, he certainly will not be able to satisfy his pastoral curiosity. This curiosity is natural, but it goes beyond the limits of our possible experience. Nevertheless, the question persists, because the essential aim of his ministry is to put souls in the grace of God. Thus, anyone considering the religious condition of a people, a community, or even a single individual is tempted to ask himself whether, where and how God's grace arrives there, knowing how important grace is for man's inner life, for his morality, and finally for his relationship with God and his final destiny.

### Sociological Tokens of Grace

The problem is also interesting from the speculative point of view, because it is at once impenetrable and inexorable: are we or are we not in God's grace? We could be content with more superficial questions: how is religion practiced, in a given area? How widespread is religious observance? How deeply rooted and active in faith? How is God's word listened to and esteemed? How often are the sacraments received? How is the Church regarded? If we wish to take into account, at least empirically, the real conditions of Christianity in our times; if we wish also to foresee its fate on encountering new times; we must have recourse to these criteria of the normal observances of religious life. We must also look for expressions of its influence—whether positive or negative—in cultural, ethical and social manifestations.

### Modern Preference for the Charismatic

But this type of investigation, fashionable today, very useful and, it can even be said, necessary for those who observe the general phenomena of society, arrives only at the threshold of the intrinsic essence of the religious phenomenon. What is this essence? It is communication with God. And for us Catholics and believers, what does this communication consist of? To answer this last question, we must point out something new in contemporary spirituality, not just within our own fold, but also among those who are near to us, and sometimes even among those who are far off. It is esteem for the charismatic elements of religion over the so-called institutional ones. It is the seeking after spiritual facts into which there enters from without a certain indefinable energy which, to some extent, persuades the one who experiences it that he is in communication with God, or more generically with the Divine, with the Spirit in an indeterminate sense.[1]

What do we say about this? We say that this tendency is very risky, because it enters into a field in which autosuggestion, or the influence of imponderable psychic causes, can lead to spiritual error. But it can also sometimes lead to the great Christian

*Address at a General Audience (*OR,* March 1, 1973; *ORe,* March 8, 1973).

188

economy of supernatural contact with God, a contact which now, for the sake of brevity, we will call *grace,* and which contains a whole theological and mystical world.

It must be recalled that our real, vital and indispensable communication with God is not the merely natural one, achieved by the effort of our reason or sentiments; it is the one established by Jesus Christ, namely, that of the supernatural order, of grace.

## Grace

And what is grace? Oh! do not ask us that in this momentary conversation! In any case you know: it is a gift of God; an intervention of his Love, of the Spirit, in the free movement of our soul; in fact it mysteriously goes before and inspires our movement, yet without relieving it of its responsibility.[2] It is a quality of the soul, created grace instilled by God-Love, the Holy Spirit, uncreated Grace. It is the formal, immanent cause of our justification;[3] it is our elevation, while remaining men of this world, to the dignity of adopted sons of God, brothers of Christ and tabernacles of the Holy Spirit. It is God living in us; it is living contact with the divine Life; and therefore it is our link with salvation in this life and in the next.

To be or not to be in God's grace is a question of life or death. We can never overestimate God's grace; no effort of study, endeavor, hope or joy expended in order to keep grace in our souls will ever be in vain.[4] It is absolutely necessary to live in God's grace. Are we so living? How many of those who call themselves Christians, live in this state of grace? In the early years of Christianity, the name of saints was given to those who had entered the sphere of grace, that is of supernatural communion with God, by faith, Baptism, penitence and uprightness of life, and particularly with love for God-Love, and for their neighbor, who is the first practical term of our Christian love (cf. 1 Jn 4:20).

## Protecting the State of Grace

As Lent approaches, we will do well to fix our attention on this problem of grace. It may well be decisive for our destiny. We will not find it irksome to have recourse to some wise renunciation, to some spiritual "hygiene" in order to recover and defend the state of grace within us; and we will find it almost connatural to give a strong and straightforward moral style to our life. Can anyone living the mystery of divine presence, which is grace, be weak, ambiguous, two-faced, pleasure-seeking?

The invigoration of this authentic spirituality within us will give us the need and joy of the sacraments. Far from withdrawing us from the Church in separate groups, chosen arbitrarily, it will make us enjoy and live communion. In fact, "communion" is for us the "sociology of grace."

### NOTES—February 18, 1973

1. *"La novità è questa: la valutazione degli elementi carismatici della religione sopra quelli così detti istituzionali, la ricerca anzi di fatti spirituali nei quali gioca una indefinibile ed estranea energia che rende persuaso, in certa misura, chi la subisce d'essere in communicazione con Dio, o più genericamente con lo Divino, con to Spirito, indeterminatamente."*
2. Cf. Denziger-Schönmetzer, *Enchiridion symbolorum,* 1541.
3. Cf. St. Thomas Aquinas, *Summa Theologiae* I–II, 113, 8.
4. "In our souls:" *al vertice del nostro spirito,* literally, "at the summit of our spirits."

# Holy Spirit, Holy Year and Modern Reason*

Once again, Brothers, we beg you to regard the announcement we have made to the Church and the world of the coming celebration of the Holy Year, as a voice inspired by the Holy Spirit, according to Jesus Christ's promise to the Apostles in his prophecy after the Last Supper: "When the Spirit of truth comes, he will guide you into all the truth. . . . He will glorify me, for he will take what is mine and declare it to you" (Jn 16:13–14).

Consider it as the opening of a new period of religious and spiritual life in the world. Do not look upon it merely as one among the many events of our history, as a separate item, but as a principle, a genetic fact, as well as a consequence of the Council, destined to mark an interior and moral renewal of the human conscience. And consider it further as a great, propitious opportunity, "a favorable time, a day of salvation" (2 Cor 6:2), a blessed fortune, if we receive it as we should, or a grave responsibility if we neglect it out of foolish carelessness or malicious opposition.

### The Holy Year and the Holy Spirit

All of us need to place ourselves windward of the breath of the Holy Spirit. Although mysterious, it is now in a certain measure identifiable. The fact that the Holy Year unfurls its sails in the individual local churches precisely on the blessed day of Pentecost is not without significance. This date has been chosen in hopes that believing mankind may be carried in a single direction, and with harmonious emulation, toward the new goal of Christian history,[1] its eschatological "port," by a new current or movement that will be truly "pneumatic," that is, charismatic.

We are well aware that the present season of the world, psychologically and sociologically considered, is not the best one for this bold adventure. Storms, rocks and formidable opposition hinder us from sailing serenely and confidently. We hear the squalls of violent contrary winds whistling in our ears. We will not describe them now, for the irreligiosity which has taken possession of modern man in quite a few nations, schools of thought, and social phenomena, is now a common experience. God is out of fashion. Our view of reality is dazzled by the splendor and interests of science, which does, indeed, yield amazing results in its pragmatic application. However, the incalculable riches with which it floods human life drive and divide men in a continual struggle to possess them, and in an ambiguous craving for liberation.

We no longer have the tranquillity of spirit to relate our experience to stable, higher principles, *sub specie aeternitatis* (in the light of eternity). Everything is reduced to the dimensions of the temporal, of the contingent and changing relativity of history, which like the mythical Saturn begets and devours its sons. In this situation the cosmic conception of the earth and man as a "kingdom of God" in process (*adveniat regnum tuum*) meets with a hundred terrible difficulties. They are not experienced as stimuli to the ascent of religious man—which they truly are—but as insuperable obstacles.

*Address at a General Audience (*OR*, May 24, 1973; *ORe*, May 31, 1973).

### The Two Sources of Truth

To confront this agitated, hostile world, the man of the Church, the "faithful," would need at least to have ideas that are clear and certain, i.e., a natural reason that is genuine and operative, a mentality that is philosophical, and a common sense capable of grasping basic truths and of functioning in a really logical and normal way. But he no longer feels capable of this, drugged as he is by doubts of every kind, which are not calmed except by scientific studies on the one hand, and the instinctive reasoning of common sense, empirical and utilitarian, on the other. We wish that the power of reason would be reestablished in its integrity; this is one of the great and recurring needs of culture when it is really humanistic.

But for the present, let it suffice to express the wish. For the purpose we now have at heart, we will rather say that besides the purely rational source of knowledge, which is too weak and vulnerable to solve all the problems of human existence, there is another, which does not mortify, but fortifies rational thought. This source, extrinsic by its origin, but intrinsic in its operation, is the Holy Spirit; it is "faith working through love" (Gal 5:6).[2] We need this infusion of the capacity to understand Truth in its supernatural and vital expression which is characteristic of the Christian economy.[3] We need that inner illumination, which is the heritage of the humble and the simple,[4] this gift from the seven rays of the Holy Spirit. We need it to face the great experiment of the Holy Year, if we want it really to bring renewal and reconciliation. Let us not forget this.

### Example of the Council

It is well known to everyone how the Council filled the pages of its sublime but very topical teachings with frequent mention of the Holy Spirit. Two hundred and fifty-eight have been counted. Let us make our own the oft-repeated exhortation of the Council, and let us put as the preface to our Holy Year, the repeated and ever new invocation: "Come, Holy Spirit; come, Creator Spirit; come, Consoling Spirit!" We will not invoke him in vain![5]

### NOTES—May 23, 1973

1. The "new goal of Christian history" does not refer to something newly discovered in our time, but the supernatural goal which history has received from Christianity, namely the Kingdom of God. This is the "eschatological port" toward which all history is tending. (Editor's note.)
2. Cf. Phil 2:13: "God is at work in you, both to will and to work for his good pleasure." I Cor 12:11: "All these are inspired by one and the same Spirit, who apportions to each one individually as he wills."
3. Cf. Jn 1:4–5: "In him was life, and the life was the light of men. The light shines in the darkness, and the darkness has not overcome it."
4. Cf. Mt 11:25–26: "At that time Jesus declared, 'I thank you, Father, Lord of heaven and earth, that you have hidden these things from the wise and understanding and revealed them to little ones; yes, Father, such was your gracious will!'"
5. Cf. Lk 11:13: "If you then, who are evil, know how to give good gifts to your children, how much more will the heavenly Father give the Holy Spirit to those who ask him!"

# Availability to the Spirit*

...Why does the Holy Year start with Pentecost? Not only because this beautiful feast, which can be defined as the historical birth of the Church, offers a propitious and inspiring occasion, but above all because we hope and pray that the Holy Spirit, whose mysterious visible mission we celebrate at Pentecost, will be the principal source of the fruits desired from the Holy Year. This, too, will be one of the most important and fruitful themes of spirituality proper to the Holy Year: the Christology and particularly the ecclesiology of the Council must be followed by a new study of and devotion to the Holy Spirit, as precisely the indispensable complement of the Council teaching. Let us hope that the Lord will help us to be disciples and teachers in this successive school of his: On leaving the visible scene of this world, Jesus left two agents to carry out his work of salvation in the world: his Apostles and his Spirit.[1]

We do not wish to enter this magnificent theological field now. For the elementary purposes of this brief preparatory sermon it is enough for us to point out, in the first place, that the action of the Spirit, in the ordinary economy of the divine plan, is carried out in our spirits in respect for our freedom, in fact, with our very cooperation, if only as a condition of the divine action in us. We must at least open the window to let in the breath and light of the Spirit.

Let us say a word about this opening, this availability of ours, to the mysterious action of the Spirit. Let us ask ourselves what the psychological and moral states of our souls must be, in order to receive the *dulcis hospes animae* (''sweet guest of the soul''). This would be matter enough for endless treatises of spiritual, ascetical and mystical life. Let us now reduce these states to two only, so that at least they can be remembered easily, making them correspond to the preferred arenas of the action of the Paraclete, that is, the Holy Spirit who becomes our assistant, consoler and advocate.

### A Heart Prepared

The first arena is man's ''heart.'' It is true that the action of grace may prescind from the subjective correspondence of the one who receives it (in the case, for example, of an infant, a sick person, or a dying man); but normally man's conscience must be in a state of consent, at least immediately after the impulse of the supernatural action of grace. The Holy Spirit has his favorite cell in the human being, the heart.[2] It would take too long to explain what the word *heart* means in biblical language. Let us be content now to describe the heart as the intimate center, free, deep and personal, of our spiritual life. Anyone who does not have a spiritual life of his own lacks the ordinary capacity to receive the Holy Spirit, to listen to his soft, sweet voice, to experience his inspirations, to possess his charisms. A diagnosis of modern man leads us to see in him an extroverted being, who lives outside himself a great deal and in himself very little, like an instrument that is more receptive to the language of the senses, and less to that of thought and conscience.

*From an address at a General Audience (*OR*, June 7, 1973; *ORe*, June 14, 1973).

The practical conclusion at once exhorts us to the praise of silence—not of unconscious, idle and mute silence, but the silence that subdues noise and exterior clamor and is able to listen: to listen in depth to the sincere voices of conscience, and to the ineffable voices of contemplation, which arise out of the concentration of prayer. This is the first arena of the Holy Spirit's action; we will do well to remember it.

### Ecclesial Communion

And what is the other? It is *communio,* that is, the society of brothers united by faith and charity in one divine-human organism, the mystical Body of Christ. It is the Church. It means adherence to that mystical Body, animated by the Holy Spirit, who has his Pentecostal upper room in the community of the faithful, hierarchically united, authentically assembled in the name and the authority of the Apostles. So we might well consider whether certain ways of seeking the Spirit, which prefer to isolate themselves in order to escape both from the directive ministry of the Church and from the impersonal crowd of unknown brethren, are on the right path. What Spirit could be encountered in a selfish communion, that is, one arising out of flight from the true communion of ecclesial charity? What experiences or what charisms could make up for the lack of unity and of the supreme encounter with God?

And so the program of the Holy Year, inaugurated on the feast of the Holy Spirit, is at once placed on the right road; both the road of spiritual life, where he, the *Gift of Love,* inhabits, awakens, forms and sanctifies our individual personality; and the road of the company of the "saints," that is, the Church of the faithful, in which salvation is a continual rejoicing for everyone.

NOTES—June 6, 1973

1. Cf. Yves Congar, *The Mystery of the Church,* Baltimore, Helicon, 2nd ed. 1965, ch. 5.
2. Cf. Rom 5:5: "And hope does not disappoint us, because God's love has been poured into our hearts through the Holy Spirit who has been given to us."

# Spirit and Institution in the Church*

. . .

## II PERSON AND ORGANIZATION IN THE CHURCH

... the constitution of the Church is at once spiritual and institutional: the Church is a mystery of salvation made visible both by its constitution as a real human society and by its activity in the external sphere. Thus, in the Church, as a human social union, men unite with one another in Christ and, through him, with God, thus attaining salvation; and the Holy Spirit is present and working in the Church throughout the whole range of its life. This means that the Church as an institution is at the same time intrinsically spiritual and supernatural.

Consequently, rights and duties in the Church have a supernatural character. If the Church is a divine plan—*Ecclesia de Trinitate* ("The Church derived from the Trinity"), its institutions, although open to improvement, need to be made stable in order to communicate divine grace[1] and foster the good of the faithful according to the gifts and mission of each. This is the essential purpose of the Church. This social purpose, the salvation of souls, "*salus animarum,*" remains the supreme purpose of its institutions, law and statutes. The common good of the Church therefore coincides with a divine mystery, that of the life of grace, which all Christians, called to be sons of God, live by participating in the life of the Trinity: *Ecclesia in Trinitate* ("The Church in the Trinity"). In this sense the Second Vatican Council spoke of the Church also as a "communion,"[2] thus highlighting the spiritual foundation of law in the Church and its ordination to the salvation of man. Law thereby becomes the law of charity in this structure of communion and grace, throughout the whole ecclesial body.

### 3. The Human Person in the Church-communion

To be able to have a place in this communion, it is necessary first of all to possess the Spirit of Christ: "*si quis autem Spiritum Christi non habet, hic non est eius*" (Anyone who does not have the Spirit of Christ does not belong to him[3]). It is the sacramental life that confers the Holy Spirit on the faithful, particularly by means of the baptismal character. This unites the baptized person with Christ in a true, real way, in order that, by virtue of this union and configuration, he may be able to work not only for his own personal salvation, but also for that of others. Sacramental union with Christ, the Mediator and Head of the New Covenant, is the foundation of personality in the supernatural order. It is here, in the Church, then, that the human person attains his full dignity, because the baptized person is able to advance effectively toward the Triune God, his ultimate end, in whose life and infinite love he is ordained to share. This is the new freedom of the baptized person—"*libertas gloriae filiorum Dei*" (the glorious liberty of the children of God—Rom 8:21). It is the freedom characteristic of

*From an address to participants in the Second International Congress on Canon Law, Sept. 17, 1973 (*OR*, Sept. 17–18, 1973; *ORe*, Oct. 4, 1973).

the human person, but elevated in an exceptional way; for in exercising this freedom, not only is he no longer subject to the law of sin and of disorderly nature, but, illumined and strengthened by the Spirit, he is able to make progress in his way toward the divine Trinity.

This freedom is concretized in fundamental rights of a supernatural order with regard to supernatural goods. But since the baptized are united with Christ not only inwardly, but also socially, and form a single body in him, ecclesial charity, the union of men as brothers, takes on the value of a sign in the *communio* that exists in the Church. This means that Christian life should be carried on in this *communio*. The fundamental rights of the supernatural order are destined to be acquired and exercised in the Church. Corresponding to them are some precise duties, among which are the fundamental duties of professing the faith of the Church and acknowledging the sacraments and the hierarchical constitution. The realities conferred by the sacraments are intended to be actualized in the Church. The *communio* is the union of the baptized—a reality that is spiritual but is manifested socially. The baptized together form one single entity with Christ because they are united with him by the Holy Spirit who has been conferred on them through the sacraments. In this spiritual-social communication the source of activity is the Spirit, who does everything for the building up of the Body of Christ.

### 4. Hierarchical Communion

Ecclesial *communio,* furthermore, cannot exist socially, nor have an efficacious influence on Chirstian life, if it does not originate in a hierarchical ministry of the word, of grace and of pastoral direction, whereby order and peace are ensured. Hence it pertains to the hierarchical communion,[4] created and informed by the Spirit of Christ, to see to it that order and peace really reign, that the unity of the *communio* is preserved, and that the life of the latter evolves in such a way as to bear witness to Christ—a witness that has even a missionary value.

This same *communio* of the Church is ordered toward the building up of the social Body of Christ. Thus the task entrusted to Christ's Church requires the cooperation of all the faithful to carry it out. It devolves upon the hierarchical communion, however, to carry out its own proper tasks. These tasks to not devolve on the common priesthood of the faithful, because strictly speaking, the latter have not received either the mission, or the power, or the gift of the Spirit specially conferred on the former. The Supreme Pastor of the Church represents the universal Church, since he represents Christ to the whole *communio* of pastors and faithful; a bishop, for the same reason, represents the particular Church over which he presides as its head.

But the hierarchical communion, as we have said, is constituted by the gift of this same Spirit, and it is by this gift that it carries on its work, which is mainly to continue Christ's mission in all its fullness. It follows that everything that is imposed in order to guarantee order and peace in the community of Christians—here we have Canon Law on the external plane—proceeds in the last analysis from the Spirit. It does not, therefore, prejudice the freedom and dignity of the human person but on the contrary enhances and defends it.

### 5. Unity of the Objective and Charismatic Action of the Spirit

The gift of the Spirit, conferred on all the baptized, is the foundation both of the freedom of God's children in the exercise of their rights in the Church, and of the charismatic gifts which he confers directly on the faithful. By reason of his spiritual nature, man is always ordained in conscience directly to God, and does not find his own perfection except in God. The gift of the Spirit raises this fundamental, ontological relationship with God to the supernatural level. And because, in the Church, the faithful together with Christ form one single communion, which develops in an institutional and social form, it is likewise the gift of the Spirit that imparts a supernatural character to the personality, dignity, freedom, and rights of the baptized. This same gift unites the faithful in a mutual relationship of love, so that their place in the *communio* per se excludes any egocentricity and individualism. Hence too the value of the responsibility of individuals in the social organization of the Church. We will only touch briefly on this point. This responsibility certainly does not authorize a freedom understood as emancipation from authority and law, but commits individuals to the free gift of themselves, with a more demanding obligation vis a vis both themselves and others.

The guiding principles of the revision of the Code of Canon Law take these theological premises into account, and aim at the juridical protection of the rights of the individual faithful and also of every man as such. The new Code certainly corresponds to this intention. However, such a postulate must not be allowed to detract from the duty of pastors to provide effectively for the common good of their own community, and ultimately for the salvation of men.

### The Spirit Working Through the Hierarchy

The hierarchy of pastors, united in communion with the Supreme Pastor, is the Lord's instrument, in that the Lord himself works objectively in their ministry through his Spirit. It would be wrong, therefore, to consider as the activity of the Spirit only that of distributing his particular charisms to individuals. The Holy Spirit appointed the Apostles to govern the Church of God[5]; charism cannot be contrasted with *munus* (office) in the Church, because it is the same Spirit who works in the first place, in and by the *munus*. For this reason all members of the Church are bound to recognize in it the necessity of an order, without which *communio* in Christ could neither be realized socially nor operate effectively. St. Paul himself connects the exercise of charisms with the order existing in the Church.[6] And in fact the Holy Spirit cannot contradict himself; in so far as he confers the charisms, the latter are subordinate to what he does through the *munus*. As the Council put it so well, "There is only one Spirit who distributes his various gifts for the good of the Church."[7]

Therefore the institutional and juridical elements are all sacred and spiritual, because they are vivified by the Spirit. In reality, the "Spirit" and "Law," in their very source, form a union in which the spiritual element is determinant. The Church of "Law" and the Church of "charity" are one single reality in which the juridical form is the exterior sign of its interior life. It is evident, therefore, that this union must be preserved in the execution of every "office" and authority in the Church, because any activity of the Church must be such as to manifest and promote spiritual life. What is said of any other external activity of the Church applies also to Canon Law: while being a human activity, it must be informed by the Spirit. The polarity between the spiritual-supernatural aspect of the Church and the institution-juridical one, far from becoming a source of tension, is always oriented toward the good of the Church, which is both interiorly animated and exteriorly sealed by the Holy Spirit.

This is all the more true if we bear in mind that the prevalence of the institutional-juridical aspect of the Church in the external forum and in the hierarchical order does not hinder but on the contrary safeguards, promotes and exalts a prevalence of the spiritual-supernatural aspect in the souls of the faithful, to all of whom the higher degrees of the order of grace are open. In the scale of grace the little ones come first.[8] Hence the poor, the suffering, the pure in heart have the first places in the praise of holiness in the beatitudes. In fact, our Lord teaches us that "the tax collectors and the harlots go into the kingdom of God before you," if by their faith and penitence, they have responded better to his call (Mt 21:31). The hierarchical Church acknowledges this superiority of grace and holiness, for example, in the canonization of its best children, the elect, even if they are only humble faithful.

### III. TOWARD A THEOLOGY OF LAW

. . .

If Church law has its foundation in Jesus Christ, if it has the value of a sign of the interior action of the Spirit, it must accordingly express and foster the life of the Spirit, produce the fruits of the Spirit; it must be an instrument of grace and a bond of unity, in a line, however, that is distinct from and subordinate to that of the sacraments, which are of divine institution. Law defines institutions, provides for the necessities of life by its statutes and decrees, and fills out the essential features of the juridical relations between the faithful, pastors and laity by its rules. The latter are in turn counsels, exhortations, directives of perfection, and pastoral guidelines. To restrict Church law to a rigid order of injunctions would be to do violence to the Spirit who guides us toward perfect charity in the unity of the Church. Your primary concern, therefore, will not be to establish a juridical order modeled on civil law, but to deepen the work of the Spirit which must be expressed even in the law of the Church. . . .[9]

### NOTES—September 17, 1973

1. "*. . . le sue istituzioni, pur perfettibili, devono essere stabilite al fine di communicare la grazia divina . . .*"
2. Vatican II, *The Church,* #4, 9, 13, etc.
3. Rom 8:9; cf. Vatican II, *ibid.,* #14.
4. "*spetta alla comunione gerarchica.*"
5. Cf. Acts 20:28; Jn 16:13.
6. Cf. 1 Cor 14:37–40: "If anyone thinks that he is a prophet, or spiritual, he should acknowledge that what I am writing to you is a command of the Lord. If anyone does not recognize this, he is not recognized."
7. Vatican II, *The Church,* #7.
8. Cf. Mt 18:3–4; 19:14.
9. The numbered subtitles in this address all belong to the original text; the unnumbered one was supplied by the editor.

# The Hour of the Holy Spirit*
# (Holy Year a Prophetic Moment)

We have already spoken several times about the Holy Year, but a great deal still remains to be said. Today we will merely consider this forthcoming event in connection with time, history and the divine plan that is fulfilled at certain moments. Have you ever noticed how often Jesus speaks of the coming hour as of a very important circumstance? He says, for example, to the Samaritan woman: "The hour is coming, nay, has already come, when true worshipers will worship the Father in spirit and in truth. . . ."[1] That is, the succession of time sometimes has not only a chronological significance, but takes on a prophetic sense; it indicates the fulfillment of a divine plan. The clock of time marks the coincidence of a precious instant in which a transcendent Presence descends among men, or an invisible action of the Spirit occurs, taking on the shape of an observable fact.

It is not unusual to find the announcement of some surprising hour of this kind in Holy Scripture. Let us read again a well-known quotation of a similar oracle, familiar to everyone. Uttered by the prophet Joel in the Old Testament, it is echoed in Peter's inspired New Testament sermon to document the mystery of Pentecost: "I will pour out my Spirit upon all mankind, and your sons and daughters shall prophesy, and your young men shall see visions, and your old men shall dream dreams. . . ." (Jl 3:28; Acts 2:17–18).

Now it is our opinion that in God's plans, the Holy Year may be a time of grace for souls, for the Church, for the world. It *may* be; this is a hypothesis, a wish, a hope. Its fulfilment is beyond our power of achievement, precisely because of its supernatural character. The Lord must be its artisan; our inept, longing aspiration is not able. Perhaps the reality in which this new Pentecost takes its place in human affairs will remain hidden from our bodily eyes; but it is also possible, we repeat, that it may turn out to be a decisive event in our experience, human as well as divine in nature. Many reasons make this plausible.

*Signs of an Hour of the Spirit*

What are these reasons? We do not think we can apply ourself now to this extremely delicate and complex analysis. We will only point out the very conditions of our times, in which religious values seem to some people to be wiped out, to others, slumbering and dormant, and to others yet, in a state of vigilance, groaning under pressure, waiting to explode in a new liberation and splendor (cf. Rom 8:19 ff.). Such conditions would seem to be the prelude to a Christian epiphany of the Spirit.[2] We do not know whether this will be manifested in marvelous facts, or in the history of suffering witnesses, in which the tears and blood of "saints," that is of really faithful Christians, will be a more eloquent apologia than any human words. But we think it is

*Address at a General Audience (*OR*, Sept. 27, 1973; *ORe*, Oct. 4, 1973).

198

not an illusion when some very moving traces of such a manifestation seem to be glimpsed even in the chronicles of our own day. . . .[3]

NOTES—September 26, 1973

1. Jn 2:4; 17:1; Rom 13:11; etc.
2. *"Diremo soltanto che le condizioni stesse del nostro tempo . . . sembrano preludere ad una epifania cristiana dello Spirito."*
3. *". . .ma non ci sembra illusione intravvedere, anche nelle cronache contemporanee, alcune commoventi vestigia."* The address goes on to say that the ordinary economy of salvation requires that man do what he can to prepare for it by conversion, attention, etc. Nothing further is said about the traces of a manifestation of the Spirit.

OCTOBER 10, 1973

# The Grottaferrata Conference*

*We are very interested in what you are doing. We have heard so much about what is happening among you, and we are glad. We have many questions to ask you, but there is no time for them.*

And now a word to the members of the Grottaferrata congress.

We rejoice with you, dear friends, at the renewal of spiritual life that is being manifested in the Church today, under different forms and in various situations. Certain common notes appear in this renewal: the taste for deep prayer, personal and in groups; a return to contemplation; an emphasis on the praise of God; the desire to surrender oneself completely to Christ; a great availability to the calls of the Holy Spirit; more assiduous reading of scripture; generous concern for one's brothers; willingness to give active support to the works of the Church. In all this, we can recognize the mysterious, gentle work of the Spirit, who is the soul of the Church.

Spiritual life consists above all in the exercise of the virtues of faith, hope and charity, and is based on the profession of faith. The latter has been entrusted to the pastors of the Church, who must keep it intact and help it unfold in all the activities of the Christian community. The spiritual life of the faithful, therefore, comes under the active pastoral responsibility of the bishop of each diocese. It is particularly opportune to recall this in the face of these ferments of renewal which arouse so many hopes.

On the other hand, weeds can get mixed with the good seed, even in the finest examples of renewal. Hence we cannot do without the function of discernment, which devolves upon those who are in charge of the Church, to whose special competence it belongs, not indeed to extinguish the Spirit, but to test all things and hold fast to that which is good.[1] In this way, the common good of the Church, to which the gifts of the Spirit are ordained,[2] is promoted.

*We will pray for you that you may be filled with true fullness of the Spirit and live in his joy and holiness. We ask for your prayers and we will remember you at Mass.*

NOTES—October 10, 1973

1. Vatican II, *The Church,* #12. The text cited refers to 1 Thes 5:12 and 19–21.
2. Cf. 1 Cor 12:7: "To each is given the manifestation of the Spirit for the common good."

*Address to some representatives of the International Leaders Conference for the Charismatic Renewal in the Catholic Church which met at Grottaferrata, a suburb of Rome, Oct. 9–13, 1973 (*OR,* Oct. 11, 1973; *ORe,* Oct. 18, 1973). For more on this conference, see chapter 3 at notes 19 and 20.

At the beginning and end of his speech, the Pope made some impromptu remarks, which are given above in italics. They were not reprinted in the *Osservatore Romano,* but have been taken from *New Covenant,* December 1973, p. 5. Only that which is set in roman type belongs to the official text.

200

# The Spirit Acting in Our Time*

This is an opportune moment for an opening up of hearts. It suggests that our address should be a summary reflection, both confidential and substantial, on the life of the Church as it appears to us, so rich in events, so complex in the phenomena of its historical and spiritual development, and so afflicted interiorly by ever new anxieties, as well as animated by the impulses and consoled by the signs of the life-giving Spirit.

. . .

We are living in times that are difficult, unstable and characterized by great activity and great problems. The germ of protest seeks to enter also into the People of God under the overpowering title of "transformation" (which has become synonymous with progress and liberation) and by means of a violent break with tradition. For us tradition is an inalienable resource, not only of historical consistency and of victory over time (which "consumes its children") but also of the original, vital, immortal and divine content of Catholicism. At the same time, the breath-giving influence of the Spirit has come to awaken latent forces within the Church, to stir up forgotten charisms and to infuse that sense of vitality and joy which in every epoch of history marks the Church itself as youthful and up-to-date, ready and happy again to proclaim its eternal message to the modern age.

*From the closing address to the Consistorial Assembly, in response to the greetings of the College of Cardinals expressed by Cardinal Traglia (*OR,* Dec. 22, 1973; *ORe,* Dec. 27, 1973).

# Mary and the Holy Spirit*

. . . it seems useful to add a reminder that due weight should be given, in (Marian) devotion, to an essential article of the faith: the person and work of the Holy Spirit. Both theology and liturgy have made it clear that the intervention of the Spirit sanctifying the Virgin of Nazareth should be accounted as one of the high points of salvation history. Thus, for example, Fathers and writers of the Church attributed Mary's initial holiness to the Spirit's action, saying that she had been "molded and formed into a new creature" by the Holy Spirit.[74] Reflecting on the Gospel texts, "The Holy Spirit will come upon you and the power of the Most High will cover you with his shadow" (Lk 1:35) and "(Mary) was found to be with child through the Holy Spirit. . . She has conceived what is in her by the Holy Spirit" (Mt 1:18, 20), they saw in the Spirit's intervention an action consecrating Mary's virginity and making it fruitful.[75] It transformed her into the "Abode of the King" or "Bridal Chamber of the Word,"[76] the "temple or tabernacle of the Lord,"[77] the "Ark of the Covenant" or "of Holiness"[78]—titles that resound with biblical echoes.

As they probed more deeply into the mystery of the Incarnation, they perceived a nuptial aspect in the mysterious connection between the Spirit and Mary,[78b] which Prudentius expressed thus in poetic terms: "The unwed Virgin was wedded to the Spirit."[79] They also called Mary the "Sanctuary of the Holy Spirit,"[80] an expression that emphasized the sacredness of the Virgin who became the permanent dwelling of the Spirit of God. Moreover, in exploring the doctrine of the Paraclete, they recognized that he was the spring from which flowed the fullness of grace (cf. Lk 1:28) and abundance of gifts that adorned her. Hence they attributed to the Spirit the faith, hope and charity that animated the Virgin's heart, the strength that maintained her obedience to God's will, and the fortitude that upheld her as she suffered at the foot of the cross.[81] In Mary's prophetic canticle (cf. Lk 1:46–55) they saw a special working of that same Spirit who formerly had spoken through the mouths of the prophets.[82] In reflecting on the presence of the Mother of Jesus in the upper room, where the Spirit came down upon the nascent Church (cf. Acts 1:12–14; 2:1–4), they developed in a rich new way the ancient theme of Mary and the Church.[85] Above all, they earnestly besought the Virgin's intercession in order to obtain from the Spirit the power to engender Christ in their own souls, as witness a prayer of St. Ildephonsus that is striking both for the doctrine it contains and the vigor of its petition: "Holy Virgin, I beg and implore you that I may have Jesus from that same Spirit through whom your flesh conceived him. . . . May I love Jesus in the same Spirit in whom you adore him as your Lord and contemplate him as your son."[84]

27. It is sometimes said that many spiritual writings today fail to reflect sufficiently the full doctrine of the Holy Spirit. It is for scholars to verify this assertion and weigh its significance. Our concern is to exhort everyone, especially pastors and

---

*From the Apostolic Exhortation, *Marialis Cultus*, on the renewal and updating of devotion to Mary in the Church today. This document is by far the most elaborate and solemn teaching by Pope Paul on the significance of Mary for the Church (*AAS* 66 (1974), pp. 136–139; *OR*, March 23, 1974; *ORe*, April 4, 1974). The footnote numbers of the original have been retained in this excerpt (except of course for 78b, which is not in the original).

theologians, to deepen their appreciation of the Holy Spirit's work in salvation history and so ensure that Christian spiritual writings pay due attention to his life-giving action. Such a deepening will bring out in particular the mysterious connection between the Spirit of God and the Virgin of Nazareth, as well as their action on the Church. As the contents of the faith are more deeply meditated, they will give rise to a livelier piety. . . .

NOTES—February 2, 1974

74. Cf. Vatican II, *The Church, Lumen Gentium* #56 (*AAS* 57, 1965, 60) and the authors mentioned in note 176 of the document. (Editor's note: the note referred to has become n. 266 in the Abbott translation, and n. 5, p. 415, in the Flannery translation of *Lumen Gentium.*)

75. Cf. St. Ambrose, Cassian, and St. Bede. (Editor's note: in this and the following notes, the original footnotes give detailed references to the patristic sources of the statements in the text. Those wishing to consult these sources can have recourse to a complete edition of the document; we will retain here merely the names of the Fathers cited.)

76. Cf. St. Ambrose, St. Proclus of Constantinople, St. Basil of Seleucia, St. Andrew of Crete, St. Germanus of Constantinople.

77. Cf. St. Jerome, St. Ambrose, Sedulius, St. Proculus of Constantinople, St. Basil of Seleucia, St. John Damascene.

78. Cf. Severus of Antioch, Hesychius of Jerusalem, Chrysippus of Jerusalem, St. Andrew of Crete, St. John Damascene.

78b. *"in arcana illa necessitudine inter Spiritum Sanctum et Mariam . . ."* These same terms occur again below, in #27. (Editor's note.)

79. *Liber Apotheosis.*

80. Cf. St. Isidore, St. Ildephonsus, St. Bernard, St. Peter Damian, the Antiphon, *"Beata Dei Genetrix Maria."*

81. Paulus Diaconus, Paschasius Radbertus, Eadmer of Canterbury, St. Bernard.

82. Origen, St. Cyril of Alexandria, St. Ambrose, Severianus Gabalensis, Antipater of Bostra.

83. Eadmer of Canterbury, St. Amadeus of Lausanne.

84. *De Virginitate perpetua sanctae Mariae,* ch. XII (*PL* 96:106).

# Live the Faith with Enthusiasm*

...the authentic Christian faith which we profess has to be lived with enthusiasm. Enthusiasm is a flame which so many contrary winds today try to extinguish.[1] Where is the enthusiasm of our faith today? There are no doubt many living members of the Church—a great many—who feel and live this joyous and generous enthusiasm. To these brothers and sons, sincere Catholics, let us now give our greeting and blessing, like a breath of Pentecost! May the wisdom, fortitude, and joy of the Holy Spirit be with you!

But we would like Pentecost to bring its Spirit of truth, charity and unity also to the minds of so many people who still are and call themselves Christians but are listless and sad, vegetating in doubt and in foolish criticism. They acquire a bitter taste for contradicting Mother Church and delude themselves that they can live in her charisms, while isolating themselves from her hierarchical and community organism which cannot be renounced. They indulge in secularist and pagan concessions under the pretext of drawing closer to the world which then devours them. . . .

NOTE—June 2, 1974

1. Cf Eph 4:14: ". . .that we may no longer be children, tossed to and fro and carried about with every wind of doctrine, by the cunning of men, by their craftiness in deceitful wiles."

*Regina Coeli message on the feast of Pentecost (OR, June 3–4, 1974; ORe, June 13, 1974).

204

# Source of the Church's Perennial Youth*

While the light and joy of Pentecost, the feast of the animation of the Church by the work of the Holy Spirit, is still with us, an essential and vital aspect of this event comes to mind, namely its permanence. Pentecost is not a distant event, now part of history; it is a fact that remains, a perennial history. The Church still lives by virtue of this prodigious infusion of divine grace, this charity poured forth in our hearts (Rom 5:5).

. . .

### Perpetual Youth

Right now, however, our thought goes to another effect of Pentecost, which is, as we were saying, the mysterious and marvelous supernatural animation that comes from the infusion of the Holy Spirit into the visible, social and human body of Christ's followers. This effect is the perennial youth of the Church. "By the power of the Gospel," the Holy Spirit "makes the Church keep the freshness of youth and constantly renews it. . . ."[1] In a fountain, the jet of water remains high, lively and fresh as long as it is fed by the impetuous current of water, even though the water itself falls and is spread over the plain. So, too, the humanity that composes the Church is buried in temporal death undergoing the lot of time; but the Church's witness is not on that account suspended or interrupted with the passing of the centuries. Jesus prophesied and promised: "I am with you all days, even unto the end of the world" (Mt 28:20). He had also made this clear to Simon, when he conferred an immortal name on him: "You are Peter, and on this rock I will build my Church, and the gates of hell shall not prevail against it" (Mt 16:18).

It can at once be objected, as so many people do object nowadays: perhaps the Church is permanent, since it has lasted for nearly 20 centuries; but for this very reason it is old, it is ancient. Perennity is not youth. And the men of today like things that are modern, changeable and short-lived, not things that are old. They respect history, if you like, and admire archeology; but they opt for what is current. The Church may indeed be venerable because of its antiquity, because of a certain immobility it has retained while time passed. But, they say, it is not alive with that present-day breath that is always new. It is not young.

The objection is a strong one, and to answer it would demand a long treatise with many sections—cosmic, theological, philosophical, historical, anthropological, phenomenological, etc. However, perhaps the simple equation perennity = youth will suffice for minds open to truth. For it is really a fact, one that "is wonderful in our eyes" (Mt 21:42), that the Church is young. What is even more amazing is that the vigor of its youth stems from its unalterable permanence throughout the passage of time. Time does not make the Church grow old; it makes it develop and leads it to life and fullness. Let us be more exact. The human part of the Church may, and actually

*From an address at a General Audience (*OR*, June 13, 1974. *ORe*, June 20, 1974).

does, undergo the inexorable laws of history and time. Its human manifestation may decay, grow old and die; and in fact so many branches of the Church do die out. Whole nations have succeeded in suffocating the Church's temporal life and suppressing its historical presence. Further, it is clear that all those who compose the Church on the human plane die like all mortals (and perhaps even more readily and "aggressively" than others).[2] But the Church has within itself not only an invincible, supernatural, ultrahistorical principle of immortality, but also incalculable energies of renewal.

### NOTES—June 12, 1974

1. This citation from the Constitution on the Church, #4, does not appear in the Italian text of this address published by the *OR,* but is given in the English translation by *ORe*. It seems more plausible that it was omitted from the former by mistake than that it was inserted into the latter autonomously.
2. "*(e forse per più facili e aggressivi motivi)*."

# Suffering in the Christian Life*

Pentecost has offered several topics for our weekly talks at the Wednesday audiences, and it could offer many others. But let it be enough for us to dwell once more on a subject, which for now we regard as conclusive. It concerns a difficulty that confronts any optimistic affirmation about the conditions of human life imbued with the action of the Holy Spirit. As we know, Christ sent the Spirit after his Ascension in a sensational form and in a superabundant measure to animate the first core of his faithful followers with his grace, gifts and charisms. The Spirit was sent to give this core the being and the breadth of the mystical Body of Christ himself, his newborn Church.

## The First Pentecost

This privileged group appears to us so alive, so powerful, so happy, compact and holy. It consisted of about 120 persons (Acts 1:15), of homogeneous composition, including the Blessed Virgin and the pious women who were followers of the Lord. They persevered in a union of prayer, which was interspersed with some addresses by Peter and the Apostles. When the days of Pentecost were drawing to a close, the group suddenly became exultant and cried aloud because of a vehement irruption of the Spirit. He came with a wind, a roaring noise, a shaking of the house, and the hovering of tongues of fire over each of those present. A cosmopolitan crowd of different nations gathered. Everyone understood the various languages that most of those possessed by this lively, mysterious presence were speaking impromptu. Never was a religious feast or spiritual ceremony so exhilarating and exalting as that of the upper room. Then Peter spoke up and the Apostles along with him. People were stirred by what they said; about 3,000 were converted and baptized then and there. Thus the Church inaugurated its life and history triumphantly.

## Divine Indwelling and Charisms

This is a new expression of religion, elevated to the level of a communion of God with man, and to the indwelling of the Triune God, in the soul of Christ's follower.[1] Out of this incomparable intimacy will spring forth the mystical life of the Christian who has become the temple, the shrine of God,[2] with the famous "Seven Gifts" and abundant "Fruits of the Spirit," the list of which is long.[3]

All that is for the personal life of the Christian. But there is also the whole manifestation of charisms, that is, forces which the Holy Spirit arouses in members of the ecclesial body for the exercise of particular functions and ministries, for the benefit of the collectivity.[4] The Church is thereby seen to be alive, active, powerful, wise, incomparable (Rev 12:1). Remember Stephen, the first deacon, who was irresistible.[5] Remember Christ's promise to Peter: the enemies of the Church "will not prevail."

*Address given at a General Audience (*OR*, June 27, 1974; *ORe*, July 4, 1974).

207

The Church is, in a certain sense, invincible (Mt 16:18). And remember the promise to the Apostles: "I am with you even to the consummation of the world" (Mt 28:20): the Church is immortal.

### Suffering in the Christian Life

But we must at once complete this vision with another one, which is no less witnessed to by the words and example of the Lord, as well as the economy of salvation. This is the vision of the pain, persecution and death that turns the biography of each of Christ's followers, and the whole history of salvation, unfolding itself in time, into a drama. This second vision is dominated by the cross. The coming of the Holy Spirit does not take the cross away from human reality. It is not a charm, making human life immune to suffering and misfortune. It is not a preventive medicine, an insurance, a physical therapy against the ills of our present existence *"Non pacem sed gladium"* (I have not come to bring peace, but a sword—Mt 10:34).

In fact, there seems to be a secret sympathy between grace and human suffering. Why? The Lord taught us the reason with many weighty words that leave no doubt. With regard to himself, in the first place, he admonished the sorrowing travelers on the way to Emmaus: "Was it not necessary that the Christ should suffer these things and enter into his glory?" (Lk 24:26). What would be left of the Gospel without the Passion and death of Jesus? And is it possible to visualize the Church, which is his living continuation, without participation in the drama of his suffering? "I say to you," he declared at the Last Supper, "that you will weep and lament, but the world will rejoice" (Jn 16:20). He had said this several times in different words: "He who does not take up his cross and follow me, is not worthy of me" (Mt 10:38; 16:24). Indeed are not the Apostles of the same school? St. Paul's words are famous: "I rejoice now in the sufferings I bear for your sake; and what is lacking in the sufferings of Christ I fill up in my flesh for his body, which is the Church" (Col 1:24). There would be no end if we wished to make an anthology of the teachings of scripture on the necessity (Acts 5:41), the "normality," we could say, of suffering in the life Christ's follower.[6]

Now this easy documentation receives a repetition and painful verification in the history of the Church. It is before our very eyes. Who is not aware of the conditions of the Church, and of those who still adhere to it, in not a few countries in the world? We will say no more about this in order not to aggravate the oppressive situation of so many of our Catholic brothers and sons whose only fault is their faith. And what shall we say of the sad phenomenon of Catholics who are intent on afflicting the Church of God today? It is as if they adopted as their motto the prophetic and bitter words of our Lord: "a man's enemies will be those of his own household" (Mt 10:36).

### Sorrow and Joy Together

Thus, our problem becomes more difficult: Why are these things so? We always ask ourself this question in connection with the fact of Pentecost, which, as we said, dominates the whole life of the Church. Why these difficulties, these oppositions, these sufferings?

To answer such a question, we would have to be able to penetrate the secrets of divine Providence, that is, the plan of redemption. Let it be enough for us now to suggest a thought for the consolation of those who experience the ineffable fortune of grace and the often no less mysterious fortune of suffering. What we want to say is simply this, that the two experiences are not only possible together, but compatible.

They can be coordinated in a plan of goodness and salvation by the two principles of simultaneity and succession. (One day, we trust, the Lord will reveal to us the wisdom and harmony of this plan.)

The principle of simultaneity means that the Christian can at one same time have two different, opposite experiences, which become complementary: sorrow and joy. He can have two hearts: one natural, the other supernatural. Remember, for example, St. Paul's marvelous expression: "I abound with joy in the midst of all our tribulations."[7] There would be a great deal to say about this complex psychological and spiritual phenomenon.[8]

The other principle, we said, is that of succession. This is the principle which admits that there may be suffering even for the saints—especially for the saints—during this life but which is followed by happiness in the next life. As St. Francis said: "All pain is dear to me, so great is the joy that I await."

In conclusion let us invoke the Holy Spirit as the *"Consolator optime,"* the best consoler!

NOTES—June 26, 1974

1. Jn 14:17, 23.
2. 1 Cor 3:16–17; 6:19; 1 Cor 6:16; Phil 4:7; etc.
3. Gal 5:22; St. Thomas: *Summa Theologiae* I–II, 68; St. Teresa, *The Interior Castle,* etc.
4. 1 Cor 12:4–11; St. Thomas, *ibid.* Q. 111.
5. Acts 6:5, 8 and 12.
6. 1 Cor 4:12; 1 Cor 4:8; 2 Tim 3:12; 1 Pt 2:21; 5:9; etc.
7. 2 Cor 2:4; 2 Thes 1:4; Acts 5:41.
8. Cf. Simone Weil, *Gravity and Grace,* New York, Putnam, 1952; Edith Stein, *The Science of the Cross,* (tr. H. Graef), Chicago, Regnery, 1960; etc.

# The Church Lives by the Holy Spirit*

If we persist in posing again the question which we have already raised several times, about the primary needs of the Church,[1] we come to something very obvious. It almost seems a tautology, as if we should say that a living being needs above all to live. Well, we dare to refer this paradoxical question to the Church to discover the essential principle that confers its primary *raison d'etre,* the profound animation indispensable to its being. Here we reach an answer which gives us the key to this reality. The key is a mystery: The Church lives by the outpouring of the Holy Spirit, which we call grace, that is to say, a gift *par excellence,* charity, the Father's love, communicated to us in virtue of the redemption wrought by Christ in the Holy Spirit.[2]

. . .

This is a magnificent doctrine! Like a ladder coming down from the Trinity, the infinite and inaccessible mystery of divine life itself, it places at the center of the divine plans and human destinies Christ's work of redemption. From this it derives an extraordinary revelation that is somehow accessible to us: the communion of our human lives with an order of salvation and goodness, which is the order of grace. From this order emerges a plan of unity and supernatural charity. Likewise there develops a resplendent economy of holiness, in which human things, especially psychology but also moral and spiritual phenomenology, become a marvelous garden of superhuman beauty and variety.

### Know the Saints

These are well-known truths—or truths that should be better known (for in our ordinary acquaintance with them, the most important thing is lacking: the analysis of holiness as it springs forth from the vital breath of grace.) Here we have a first recommendation to make in this connection: knowledge of the lives of the saints. In the past they provided an agreeable nourishment for the people at large, and the matter of edifying reflection for the devout. For us today, trained in historical studies and psychological criticism, they could provide a museum of incomparable human experiences and exciting examples of how far moral and spiritual improvement can really go. Remember the saying: *"Si isti et istae, cur non ego"*? (If they could do it, why not I?)

But we must immediately recall that grace—a divine intervention, transcending the natural order—is necessary both for our personal salvation and to fulfill the plan of redemption for the Church and for all mankind, called to salvation by God's mercy (I Tm 2:4). Let us refer to the great chapter on the doctrine of grace and justification, about which the Council of Trent had so much to say,[3] and which modern theology still discusses as a subject of supreme interest. The necessity of grace presupposes an absolute need on the part of man; the need for the miracle of Pentecost to continue in the history of the Church and of the world. It must continue in the double form in which the Gift of the Holy Spirit is granted to human beings, first to sanctify them, and

*Address at a General Audience (*OR,* Oct. 17, 1974; *ORe,* Oct. 24, 1974).

this is the primary and indispensable form, by which man becomes the object of God's love, *gratum faciens*,[4] as the theologians say,[5]

| *Prepared text:* | *Actual Statement:* |
|---|---|
| and secondly to enrich them with special prerogatives, which we call charisms (*gratis data*), for the good of their neighbor, and especially of the community of the faithful.[6] | I would say that curiosity—but a very legitimate and very beautiful curiosity—pays close attention to another aspect. The Holy Spirit, when he comes, grants gifts. We are already familiar with the "Seven Gifts" of the Holy Spirit. But he also gives others that today are called . . . well, today . . . always are called . . . charisms. What does *charism* mean? It means gift. It means grace. These are special graces given to one person for another, for the common good. One receives the charism of wisdom so that he might be a teacher, and another the charism of miracles to do things that, through marvel and admiration, call people to faith, and so on. |
| | Now this charismatic form of gifts, which are no longer "*gratum faciens*" but "*gratis data,*" which are gratuitous gifts and, in themselves, not necessary but given by the Lord from his superabundant storehouse because he wants to make the Church richer, more lively, more capable of defining and proving herself, is called precisely "the outpouring of the charisms." |
| A great deal is said about charisms today; while taking into account the complexity and delicacy of such a subject, we cannot but hope that a new abundance, not only of grace, but also of charisms, will still be granted to the Church of God today.[7] | A great deal is said about this today. Taking into account the complexity and the delicacy of the subject, we cannot but hope that these gifts will come and with abundance; that in addition to grace there will also be charisms possessed and obtained by the Church today. |
| | The saints, especially the Fathers, St. Ambrose and St. John Chrysostom,[8] have said that the charisms were more abundant in ancient times. The Lord gave his outpouring of gifts in order to give life to the Church, to make it grow, to establish it, to sustain it. And since then the granting of these gifts has been, I would say, |

more discreet, more . . .economical. But there have always been saints who have done miraculous things—exceptional men have always existed in the Church. How wonderful it would be if the Lord would again pour out the charisms in increased abundance, in order to make the Church fruitful, beautiful and marvelous, and to enable it to win the attention and astonishment of the profane and secularized world.

We will mention a book which has just been written by Cardinal Suenens, called *Une Nouvelle Pentecôte?* In it he describes and justifies this new expectation of what may really be an historic and providential development in the Church, based on an outpouring of those supernatural graces which are called charisms.

### Work of the Spirit

For now, we will just recall the main conditions on the part of man to receive God's gift *par excellence,* which is the Holy Spirit, who, as we know, "breathes where he wills" (Jn 3:8), but does not refuse the longing of those who wait for him, call him and welcome him (even this longing itself comes from a profound inspiration of his). What are these conditions? Let us simplify the difficult answer by saying that the capacity to receive this *dulcis hospes animae* calls for faith, calls for humility and repentance, and normally calls for a sacramental act. Moreover, in the practice of our religious life it demands silence, meditation, listening, and above all invocation and prayer, like that of the Apostles with Mary in the upper room. It is necessary to be able to wait, to be able to call: Come, O Creater Spirit. . .; come, O Holy Spirit![9]

If the Church is able to enter a phase of similar preparation for the new and perennial coming of the Holy Spirit, he, the "light of hearts," will not hesitate to give himself, for the joy, the light, the fortitude, the apostolic virtue and unitive charity, which the Church needs today.

### NOTES—October 16, 1974

1. Cf. the address of Nov. 29, 1972, note 1. (Editor's note.)
2. In the portion of this allocution which we are omitting to save space, the Pope cites the same text of the Constitution on the Church, #4 which he has cited on many other occasions, e.g., May 18, 1966.
3. Council of Trent, Session VI: Decree on Justification. Cf. Denzinger-Schönmetzer, *Enchiridion Symbolorum,* 1520–1583.
4. All grace is ultimately an unmerited gift from God, and hence is called grace in the sense that it is given "gratis." But some grace can be said to be so called for a second reason, that it makes men "gracious," i.e., pleasing, in the eyes of God: whereas other graces do not have this effect *per se,* but are simply powers and helps given for some service. For example, the gifts of discernment or healing can

be possessed by a man who is himself a sinner. In scholastic theology, the former grace was called *gratum faciens* and the latter *gratis data*. (Editor's note.)

5. At this point, the Pope set aside his prepared text and spoke impromptu, as he often does in his allocutions. The prepared text, which is here given on the left hand side, was published in the *Osservatore Romano,* both Italian and English editions. The impromptu remarks, given here on the right hand side, were recorded on tape by someone in Rome. I have not been able to obtain a copy of this recording, but only a Spanish translation of it, made by the "Grupo de Oración de Lengua Espanola" in Rome. I am grateful to Bert Ghezzi, editor of *New Covenant,* for making it available to me. The above translation has been made from this Spanish translation.

6. Cf. Thomas Aquinas, *Summa Theologiae* I–II, 111, 4.

7. Cf. the recent study by Cardinal L. J. Suenens: *Une Nouvelle Pentecôte?* Desclée de Brouwer, 1974. (Editor's note: This reference is given in the Pope's published text. The English translation is: *A New Pentecost?* New York, Seabury, 1975.)

8. Pope Paul did not, of course, in this impromptu remark, give any specific references. St. John Chrysostom speaks of the decline of charisms in the Church in several places, e.g., in his *Homilies on St. John,* Hom. 24 (Jn 2:23–25; *Fathers of the Church,* vol. 33, pp. 232–241); *Homilies on St. Matthew,* Hom. 32:11 (*NPNF,* ser. 1, vol. 10, p. 218); *In principium Actorum,* (*PG* 51:81); *Homil. 36 in 1 Cor,* #4, 5. (*PG,* vol. 51, vol. 311–314).

I do not know of any texts of St. Ambrose on this subject. There are, however, texts of St. Augustine in this vein in *On Baptism,* bk. 3, ch. 16–23 (*NPNF* vol. 4, p. 442; *PL* vol. 43, col. 148); and in *The True Religion,* ch. 25/48 (*PL* vol. 34, col. 142). I suspect that the mention of Ambrose is a slip (by the Pope or by the transcriber) for Augustine. (Editor's note.)

9. Cf. *Les plus beaux textes sur le Saint-Esprit* by Mme. Arsène-Henry D'Ormesson, Paris, La Colombe, 1957.

# The Charisms of the Lay Apostle*

. . .

This mission of salvation is carried out by the Church through all its members: the recent Synod[1] reaffirmed, in fact, that the task of evangelization devolves on all the faithful. All without exception are impelled effectively by the Holy Spirit to bear witness to Christ and his Gospel, according to the Lord's exact promise: "When the Paraclete comes, whom I will send you from the Father, the Spirit of truth, who proceeds from the Father, he will bear witness to me; and you also are witnesses" (Jn 15:26-27).

### Communion with the Holy Spirit

We are sure that you realize the high priority of evangelization at the present time, and we exhort you to give it the valuable contribution of your lay apostolate. But this very realization calls for the prime duty of communion—communion first of all with the Holy Spirit, the source and inspirer of the witness which all the faithful are called to give to Christ, in the various epochs of history.

It is the Spirit who guides the Church in its fidelity to the work of evangelization. As we stressed in the recent Apostolic Exhortation on reconciliation within the Church for the worthy celebration of the Holy Year: "in order to cooperate with God's plans in the world, all the faithful must persevere in fidelity to the Holy Spirit, who unifies the Church 'in fellowship and ministry.' "[2] An intimate communion of life with the Spirit and dependence on him is, therefore, required particularly of members of Catholic Action, which has as its immediate purpose the evangelization of the contemporary world. This communion is very demanding and at the same time very fruitful. Nourished by the light of faith and meditation on the word of God, it is open to the signs of the times and the needs of the present, and is especially docile to divine calls. From its very beginnings, Catholic Action has prepared so many generous lay men and women who, despite the absorbing commitment of their profession and work, have hearkened to the voice calling them to holiness. This was the secret of its success and extraordinary growth.

. . .

### Communion with the Hierarchy

But you are members of the Church. You have voluntarily offered to collaborate in the lay apostolate to help the Church carry out her mission in the world with increasing pastoral effectiveness. Now, your apostolate is characterized as collaboration with that of the hierarchy and as active participation in the Church's mission.[3] Hence the necessity of a second vital communion, communion with the hierarchy, exercised in a spirit of brotherly and active service.

---

*Excerpt from an address to the General Council of Italian Catholic Action (*OR*, Jan. 12, 1975; *ORe*, Jan. 23, 1975).

214

Through her pastors, the Church trusts you particularly in the exercise of your apostolate, and you must respond with deep faithfulness. This is at bottom nothing but the reverse side of fidelity to the Spirit, by whom faith, hope and charity are diffused in the hearts of the members of the Church. Fidelity to the Holy Spirit calls for recognition of those whom he has made pastors of the Church of God,[4] and responsible for promoting the unity of the apostolate. This fidelity also requires that the lay apostolate should be exercised in perfect harmony of thought and operation, and in full conformity with the teaching office of the Church.

Now, Peter and the College of Bishops united with him have been given the charism of authentic teaching of the word of God, and of being the principle of unity. But the faithful in turn have received from the Holy Spirit particular gifts or charisms, ordained to the good of men and to the upbuilding of the Church. The Second Vatican Council made it quite clear that:

> . . .from the reception of these charisms or gifts, including those which are less dramatic, there arise for each believer the right and duty to use them . . . in communion with their brothers in Christ, especially with their pastors. The latter must make a judgment about the true nature and proper use of these gifts, not so as to extinguish the Spirit, but to test all things and hold fast to what is good.[5]

Along with the necessary adaptations to present cultural and sociological needs, what is asked of Catholic Action today is fidelity to essentials. This fidelity consists in recognizing sincerely:

a) the existence of the different charisms and functions, both of bishops and laity. The former have the essential responsibility to sanctify, teach and govern the pilgrim People of God. The latter have, in particular, the task of transmitting the divine message, received from God through the pastors, and embodying it at the heart of everyday realities, even temporal ones;

b) that these different charisms and functions must be united in the effort to bring the testimony of the Gospel to the world and effect the elevation of earthly reality to God in Christ.

This union should always respect the specific character of the above-mentioned charisms and functions, as well as their respective order. The secret of the fruitfulness of apostolic action lies solely in this harmony. During this Holy Year, can we not advance in a spirit of collaboration and ecclesial communion, humbly and in loyalty to the Gospel, recognizing the charisms of bishops and priests, on the one hand, and those of laymen, on the other, as complementary, harmonious and convergent in the work of the apostolate?

. . .

Press on, then, in the Lord's name! Do not be frightened, much less paralyzed, by the present difficulties. Look at the present with realism and at the future with hope! Indifference, inertia, fear and all kinds of obstacles can be overcome with the light of faith and the enthusiasm of love. We repeat to you with the Apostle Paul: "For God did not give us a spirit of timidity but a spirit of power and love and self-control" (2 Tm 1:7). And with you we pray to the Holy Spirit to assist you with his gifts and always to instill in you joy, courage and optimism.

NOTES—January 11, 1975

1. The Synod of Bishops held in Rome, Sept. 27–Oct. 26, 1974. (Editor's note.)
2. Apostolic Exhortation of Dec. 8, 1974, #2 (*OR,* Dec. 16–17, 1974; *ORe,* Dec. 26, 1974).

3. Catholic Action was for several decades defined as "the participation by the laity in the apostolate of the hierarchy," according to the classical definition formulated by Pope Pius XI (Letter to Cardinal Bertram, Nov. 13, 1928; *AAS* 20, 1928, 384–387. Cf. *Ubi Arcano Dei, AAS* 14, 1922, 673–700.) However, Vatican II, in its Decree on *The Apostolate of the Laity,* declared that every member of the Church has his own proper part in the apostolate (see especially #2, 3, 4, 7). This is what is referred to here.

In an earlier comment on the same text of Vatican II, Pope Paul said: "You know that the Christian vocation is of its very nature a call to the apostolate. This means that the apostolate is recognized as an activity inherent in the very fact of being a Christian; hence the promotion of the concept of Christian layman to that of collaborator with the hierarchical apostolate properly so-called." (Address at a General Audience May 24, 1972 [*OR*, May 25, 1972; *ORe,* June 1, 1972]).

4. Cf. Acts 20:18: "Take heed to yourselves and to all the flock, in which the Holy Spirit has made you guardians, to feed the Church of the Lord which he obtained with his own blood."

5. Vatican II, *The Apostolate of the Laity,* #3.

# Joy in the Holy Spirit*

At this time, when believers throughout the world are preparing to celebrate the coming of the Holy Spirit, we invite you to beg of him the gift of joy.

So far as we personally are concerned, we are carrying on the ministry of reconciliation amid many contradictions and difficulties,[2] but also with the joy of the Holy Spirit which arouses and accompanies it. Hence we can in all truth adopt the Apostle Paul's confidence regarding his community at Corinth for ourself, referring it to the universal Church: "...you are in our hearts, to die together and to live together. I have great confidence in you.... I am filled with comfort. With all our affliction, I am overjoyed."[3] Yes, for us too it is a demand of love to invite you to share this abounding joy which is a gift of the Holy Spirit.[4]

We have therefore felt as it were a happy interior need during this year of grace, and very fittingly on the occasion of Pentecost, to deliver to you an Apostolic Exhortation on this very theme of Christian joy—joy in the Holy Spirit. We would like to intone a kind of hymn to divine joy in hopes that it will arouse an echo throughout the world, above all in the Church. May joy be poured out in the hearts of men, along with the love of which it is the fruit, by the Holy Spirit that has been given to us.[5]

. . .

## *Pleasure or Joy?*

Technological society has succeeded in multiplying the opportunity for pleasure, but it has great difficulties in generating joy. Joy comes from elsewhere; it is spiritual. Money, comfort, hygiene and material security often are not lacking, and yet boredom, depression and sadness unhappily remain the lot of many.

. . .

## *Paschal Joy*[5b]

Paschal joy is not just joy over a possible transfiguration; it is joy at the new presence of the Risen Christ who imparts the Spirit to his disciples so that he, Christ, may dwell with them. Thus the Paraclete is given to the Church as the inexhaustible principle of the joy it has as bride of the glorified Christ.... And the Christian knows

---

*Excerpts from the Apostolic Exhortation, *On Christian Joy.* The official Latin text appears in *AAS* 67 (1975) 209–322, and also was published in *OR,* May 17, 1975. However, the Pope's original text appears to be the Italian, which was published in that same issue of *OR.* The Latin is obviously a translation (and a very awkward one) from it. The English translation published in *ORe* on May 29, 1975, seems to have been made from the Italian rather than from the Latin, and the revisions made in the present version follow that same policy.

This Exhortation had the form of a letter addressed to the entire Church. It appeared just a few days before Pentecost, which fell on May 19. The excerpts given here represent only a small fraction of this lengthy text, which has been published in a complete English translation by the USCC, Washington, D. C. The original numeration of the footnotes has been retained in these excerpts to make it easier for anyone to locate these passages in the full text; for the same reason, notes 5b and 42b have been added by the present editor.

that this Spirit will never be quenched in the course of history. The wellspring of hope revealed at Pentecost will never dry up.

...Together with him the Father and Son inhabit the human heart[41] where he stirs up a filial prayer that rises from the depth of the soul and expresses itself in praise, thanksgiving, reparation and petition. Then we can experience the properly spiritual joy, which is a fruit of the Holy Spirit.[42]

This comes from the fact that the human spirit finds rest and deep satisfaction in the possession of the Triune God, known by faith and loved with a charity that comes from him. This joy henceforth characterizes all the Christian virtues, and transfigures the humble human joys which are like seeds of higher reality in our lives.

### The Joy of the Pilgrim in the Holy Year[42b]

The Holy Year with its pilgrimage forms a natural part in this journey of the whole People of God. The grace of the Jubilee is in fact obtained only at the price of setting out and journeying toward God in faith, hope and love. We have altered the means and the times of this Jubilee in order to make it easier for everyone, but its essential element remains the inner decision to respond to the call of the Spirit in a personal manner, as a disciple of Jesus, as a child of the Catholic and Apostolic Church, and according to the intention of this Church. Everything else belongs to the order of signs and means. Yes, the desired pilgrimage is, both for the People of God as a whole, and for each individual within it, a change of place, a passover; it is a journey to that inner place where the Father, the Son and Holy Spirit welcome us into their own intimacy and divine unity: "If anyone loves me... my Father will love him and we shall come to him and make our home with him."[68] Reaching this presence always presupposes a deepening of true knowledge of oneself, as a creature and as a child of God.

Was not an inner renewal of this kind the fundamental desire of the recent Council?[69] This Council itself was a work of the Spirit and a Pentecostal gift. One must also recognize a prophetic intuition on the part of our predecessor John XXIII, who envisioned a kind of new Pentecost as a fruit of the Council.[70] We too have wished to place ourself in the same perspective and in the same attitude of expectation. Not that Pentecost has ever ceased to be an actuality throughout the whole history of the Church; however, the needs and perils of the present age are so great, and the horizons of mankind, drawn toward global coexistence but powerless to achieve it, so vast, that there is no salvation for humanity except in a new outpouring of the gift of God. May the Creating Spirit come, then, to renew the face of the earth!

### NOTES—May 9, 1975

2. Cf. Apostolic Exhortation, *Paterna cum Benevolentia, AAS* 67 (1975) p. 5–23.
3. 2 Cor 7:3–4.
4. Cf. Gal 5:22.
5. Cf. Rom 5:5.
5b. From Part III.
41. Cf. Jn 14:23.
42. Cf. Rom 14:17: Gal 5:22.
42b. From Part VII.
68. Jn 14:23.
69. Cf. Paul VI, Address for the opening of the Second Session of Vatican II, Sept. 29,

1963, part 1; *AAS* 55 (1963) 845 ff; Encyclical *Ecclesiam Suam*, *AAS* 56 (1964), 612, 614–618.
70. John XXIII, Address for the closing of the First Session, part 3, Dec. 8, 1962, part 3; *AAS* 55 (1963), 38 ff.

# Mary and the Spirit*

How could we fail to hope for very useful results from the careful study of the pure and sacred interior ties by which the Virgin Mary was (and is) bound up with the Holy Spirit in the work of human redemption?

. . .

We are well aware that Catholic theology in our times has given special emphasis to the study of the Marian truths contained in the Holy Scripture and in divine Tradition, in an effort to draw out their implications and shed light on their salutary effects. But this praiseworthy enterprise, which has in fact been very faithful, has not dimmed the primacy of faith and worship that the whole Church bestows on the Holy Spirit.

. . .

### Mary's Association with the Spirit

The Holy Spirit intervenes personally, while in indivisible communion with the other Persons of the Holy Trinity, in the work of human salvation![1] But the Catholic Church has always believed that he has associated the humble virgin of Nazareth with himself in this, and that he has done so in a way in keeping with his nature as Personal Love of the Father and the Son. That is to say, by an action at once very powerful and very sweet, he has adapted perfectly Mary's whole person, with all her faculties and energies, physical as well as spiritual, to the tasks assigned to her on the plane of redemption.[2] This belief springs from an understanding of the sacred texts that has grown deeper and clearer in the course of time. On this basis, Fathers and Doctors of the Church, in both East and West, have attributed Mary's fullness of grace and charity to the various missions of the Holy Spirit, who proceeds from the Father and the Son. This includes the gifts and fruits of every virtue, as well as the evangelical beatitudes and special charisms. Like a trousseau for a heavenly wedding, all of these adorned her who was predestined as the mystical Bride of the Divine Paraclete, and Mother of God's Word made flesh. Because of her privileges and exceptional gifts of grace, all of which come from the divine Spirit, Mary is greeted in the Sacred Liturgy as "*Templum Domini, sacrarium Spiritus Sancti*" ("Temple of the Lord, Sanctuary of the Holy Spirit").

### Action of the Spirit in Mary's Life

It will therefore be a source of great comfort for us to pause in joyful contemplation of the principal works of the Spirit of Christ in the chosen Mother of God. It was the Holy Spirit who filled Mary's person with grace at the first moment of her conception, and thus redeemed her in a more sublime way in view of the merits of

*Letter to Cardinal Léon-Jozef Suenens, President of the Permanent Committee for the Promotion of International Marian and Mariological Congresses. The occasion of this letter was the International Marian Conference, held at Rome May 18–21, 1975, and devoted to the theme, "The Holy Spirit and Mary."

Christ, the Savior of mankind, making her immaculate.[3] It was the Holy Spirit who came upon her, and inspired her to agree, on behalf of mankind, to the virginal conception of God's Son. He made her womb fruitful so that she might give birth to the Savior of her people, the sovereign of an everlasting kingdom (Lk 1:35–38). Again, it was the Holy Spirit that inflamed her spirit with joy and gratitude, impelling her to burst into the Magnificat praising God, her Savior (Lk 1:45–55). It was likewise the Holy Spirit that gave the Virgin the good counsel to keep faithfully in her heart all that was said and done about the birth and childhood of her only Son, in which she had taken so intimate and loving a part (Lk 2:19; 33:51).

Again, it was the Holy Spirit that led Mary to request from her Son the miracle of the transformation of water into wine at the wedding of Cana, by which Jesus began his work of miracles, and brought about the faith of his disciples (Jn 2:11). It was the Holy Spirit that sustained the Mother of Jesus at the foot of his cross, inspiring her, as he had already done at the Annunciation, with the *Fiat* directed to the will of the heavenly Father, who wished her to be associated maternally with the sacrifice of her Son for the redemption of mankind (cf. Jn 19:25). It was the Holy Spirit that made the heart of the grieving Mother swell with immense charity, so as to accept from the lips of her Son, as his last testament, the mission of being Mother to his beloved disciple John (Jn 19:26-7). "According to the perennial sense of the Church,"[4] this prefigured the spiritual motherhood she was to exercise in regard to all mankind. Again, it was the Holy Spirit that raised Mary, on the wings of fervent charity, to her role of prayer in the upper room, where Jesus' disciples "gave themselves up to prayer, together with Mary the Mother of Jesus, and the rest of the women" (Acts 1:14), in expectation of the promised Paraclete.

Finally, it was the Holy Spirit who, burning with supreme ardor in Mary's heart as she continued her earthly pilgrimage, made her eager to join her Son in glory. Thus he prepared her to attain worthily, as the crowning point of her privileges, her Assumption in soul and body into heaven. We are deeply moved in recalling that the 25th anniversary of the dogmatic definition of this mystery falls this year.[5]

### Mary's Action in the Church

But Mary's mission as partner of the Spirit of Christ in the mystery of salvation did not end with her glorious Assumption. While absorbed in joyful contemplation of the blessed Trinity, she continues to be present spiritually to all the redeemed. And it is Uncreated Love himself, the soul and supreme mover of the mystical Body, who impels her to carry on this noble task.

Mary's incessant presence within the pilgrim Church was confirmed by the Second Vatican Council when it declared: "This maternity of Mary in the order of grace... will last without interruption.... For, taken up to heaven, she did not lay aside this saving role, but by her manifold acts of intercession continues to win for us gifts of eternal salvation."[6]

It is, therefore, right and fitting that the Holy Mother of God, as she has been called since the early centuries of the Church,[7] should continue to be "called blessed by all generations" (Magnificat) and to be "invoked by the Church under the titles of Advocate, Auxiliatrix, Helper and Mediatrix."[8] But, as the Council wisely admonishes: "these, however, are to be so understood that they neither take away from nor add anything to the dignity and efficacy of Christ the one Mediator"[9]; and, we must add, in such a way that they do not take away anything from the dignity and efficacy of the Spirit, who sanctifies both the head and the individual members of the mystical Body.

We must consider, therefore, that the activity of the Mother of the Church for the benefit of the redeemed does not replace, or compete with, the almighty and universal action of the Holy Spirit. Rather, the former implores and prepares for the latter, not only by prayer of intercession, in harmony with the divine plans which Mary contemplates in the beatific vision, but also with the direct influence of her example, in particular the extremely important one of her supreme docility to the inspirations of the Divine Spirit.[10] It is, therefore, always in dependence on the Holy Spirit that Mary leads souls to Jesus, forms them in her image, inspires them with good advice and serves as a bond of love between Jesus and the faithful.

### Testimony of the Fathers

To confirm these reflections, we are happy to recall the testimony of the Fathers and Doctors of the Eastern Church. They are models of belief in and worship of the Holy Spirit; they have also witnessed to the Church's belief in and veneration of the Mother of Christ,[11] as the mediatrix of divine favors. Their affirmations may surprise us, but they should not disturb anyone, since they take it for granted, and sometimes expressly declare, that the Virgin's mediative activity depends upon and has its source in that of the Spirit of God. So, for example, St. Ephraem exalts Mary in these superlative tones: "Blessed is she who has been made the spring from which flow all good things for the whole world."[12] Elsewhere he says: "Most holy Lady . . . ; the sole abode of all the graces of the Holy Spirit."[13] St. John Chrysostom sums up Mary's salvific work in the following stupendous eulogy: "A virgin drove us out of paradise; thanks to the intervention of another virgin, we have found eternal life again. As we were condemned by the fault of a virgin, so we have been crowned by the merit of a virgin."[14] They are echoed, in the eighth century, by St. Germanus of Constantinople, who addresses the following moving invocations to Mary: "You, O pure, excellent and most merciful Lady, comfort of Christians . . . , protect us with the wings of your kindness; guard us with your intercession, giving us eternal life; you are the hope of Christians that never disappoint us. . . . Your gifts are innumerable. For no one attains salvation, O holy one, except through you. No one is delivered from evil except through you. Who is there that cares for mankind, as you do, in concord with your Son?"[15]

### Conclusion

This traditional faith, which is common to the Eastern and the Western Church alike, received authoritative confirmation in the teaching of our great predecessor, Leo XIII. He published numerous encyclical letters promoting the veneration of the Mother of God, especially under the title of Queen of the Holy Rosary; but he also devoted a long and documented encyclical to the much greater exaltation of the Holy Spirit and to the promotion of his worship.[16]

This is a very critical hour for the history of the Church and the fate of humanity. If the Church is to be "in Christ a kind of sacrament—i.e., sign and instrument—of intimate union with God, and of the unity of all mankind,"[17] the interior renewal of Christians and their reconciliation with God and with one another are absolutely necessary. These can occur only if the soul of the faithful is dominated by the worship of the Spirit, who is the supreme source of charity, unity and peace. But in harmony with this worship, kindled and enlivened by the fire of Divine love, there must also be the veneration of the great Mother of God and Mother of the Church, the incomparable model of love for God and for our brothers.

NOTES—May 13, 1975

1. Cf. G. Philips, *L'Union personelle avec le Dieu vivant. Essai sur l'Origine et le sens de la grâce créée.*

2. Cf. St. Thomas, *Summa Theologiae* III, q. 27.

3. Cf. Pius I, Bull *Ineffabilis Deus,* Dec. 8, 1854; *DS* 2803.

4. Leo XIII, Encyclical *Adiutricem populi,* Sept. 5, 1895 (*Acta Leonis XIII,* vol. XV, p. 390.

5. Cf. Pius XII, Apostolic Constitution *Munificentissimus Deus,* Nov. 1, 1950; *AAS* 42 (1950), p. 768.

6. Vatican II, *The Church,* #62.

7. Cf. the antiphon, *Sub tuum praesidium* ("We fly to thy patronage...").

8. Vatican II, *The Church,* #62.

9. *Ibid.*

10. *Ibid.* #63–65.

11. The Italian text uses the same term, *culto,* in reference to both the Blessed Virgin and the Holy Spirit. In English, however, it seems more appropriate to speak of *veneration* in the one case and *worship* in the other.

12. *S. Ephraem Syri hymni et sermones,* ed. Th. Lamy, Malines, 1882–1902, II, p. 548.

13. *Assem. graec.* III, 542.

14. *Expositio in Psalmum* 44, 7; *PG* 55:193.

15. *Concio in sanctam Mariam; PG* 98:327.

16. Encyclical *Divinum illud munus,* May 9, 1897; *Acta Leonis XIII,* vol. XVIII, pp. 126–184.

17. Vatican II, *The Church,* #1.

# Preparing to Experience the Spirit*

...The subject set before us today is that of Pentecost, that is, the doctrine, theology and science of the supreme religious Reality, the very mystery of God's infinitely transcendent Life. We can never forget this even though it inundates our minds and overwhelms their incapacity. Yes, it is difficult, or rather impossible, for our eyes to gaze at the sun; they are dazzled and blinded by it. But the fact remains that we will never be able to see anything with these same eyes unless the object of our gaze is illumined by the sun.

### Union with God

God is our sun. His dazzling splendor has revealed to us that the interior relationships of his sovereign existence are Persons, the three divine Persons. The Father, the eternal first principle, engenders his own thought, the Word, the eternal Son, whom he sent into our world, so that, clad in our humanity and called Jesus, he might live out the drama of salvation. Then the Spirit, also a divine Person, proceeding as Love from the infinite satisfaction and bliss of the Father and Son, was also sent into the world to carry out and extend the work of the Son, that is of Christ. That is Pentecost—a moment of fullness, and a wellspring for the institutional form of this deifying and salvific work. This is the Church, "a sacrament or sign of intimate union with God," as the recent Council affirms,[1] thus designating the first transcendent effect, the first supernatural aspect, of the new, direct relationship which God has willed to establish with his humble and sublime creature, man, that is with us. The text of the Council goes on to amplify its definition of the Church, which it calls a "sacrament or sign of the unity of all mankind."

Our reason for focusing on this pivotal point of the whole religious and theological system, which defines the true, authentic and necessary relations of mankind with the divinity, is that these relationships are now realized in the Holy Spirit. "Truly, I say to you," Jesus teaches Nicodemus, "unless one is born of water and the Spirit, he cannot enter the kingdom of God" (Jn 3:5).

### Preparation for This Experience

After such a pronouncement, we today would like not only to possess the Holy Spirit at once, but to experience the tangible and wonderful effects of his marvelous presence within us;[2] for we know that the Spirit is light, strength, charism, infusion of spiritual vitality, the capacity of going beyond the limits of our natural activity. His riches comprise the supernatural virtues, the gifts (those seven famous gifts which make the workings of the Holy Spirit prompt and agile in us, and coordinate them with

*Homily at the Mass of Pentecost (*OR*, May 19–20, 1975; *ORe*, May 29, 1975). It is worthy of note that a large part of the Congregation at the Mass at which this homily was delivered consisted of participants in the International Conference on the Charismatic Renewal in the Catholic Church, which was held at Rome May 16–19.

224

the complex system of human psychology) and finally the spiritual fruits which beautify the fruitful garden of Christian experience (Gal 5:22–23).

But now, in the act of proclaiming the mystery of Pentecost, we pause at its threshold: How, oh how can we obtain it for ourselves? This phase of the Pentecost event also desires reflection and gives plenty of matter for it. Preparation is not superfluous, even though the great Gift of the Spirit is gratuitous, and can be instilled in us with the rush of his mighty wind and with the sudden kindling of his fire, as happened on that unique and historic day of the first Pentecost.

### Inner Silence

For that matter even that miraculous day had its preparation. It was the preparation of interior silence, in which the conversion, purification and *metanoia* of conscience gradually ripened. We moderns are too extroverted: we live outside our own homes. Perhaps, as a well-known philosopher has said, in going out we lost the key which we need in order to return. No doubt, traces of the Spirit are scattered everywhere on the stage of exterior things (for "nothing is without a language" [1 Cor 14:10] for those who know how to listen). Nevertheless, our encounter with the holy and sanctifying Spirit takes place in the depths of the heart, the place where the Lord's word is kept (Jn 14:23), and where man is himself, in the solitude of his personality. For this reason the Apostles, before the great day, "devoted themselves to prayer . . . with Mary the Mother of Jesus." This was the first spiritual retreat, and the most blessed of all.

### Prayer and Confession

To silence, therefore, is joined prayer, which in the tradition of the Church is uttered in that well-known expression of invitation and yearning, "Come, Creator Spirit, Come!" "Come, Holy Spirit!" This miracle takes place for us at the sacramental moment of justification, when our sins are forgiven. And this comes about as we know, through confession, which brings life back to the soul raising it to the state of sharing in the divine life (2 Pt 1:4). We call this "the state of grace." Yes, of ineffable grace. The saints teach us that this state ought to be dearer to us than natural life itself, because it is of higher worth. It is in fact a state of supernatural life, and it has, so far as its own nature is concerned, the assurance of the fullness and bliss of eternal life.

### Effects of the Spirit

At this point, preparation is already leading into the completion of the Pentecostal mystery: the Holy Spirit, that is, God-Love, lives in the soul, which feels overcome at once by a sudden need to surrender itself to Love, a super-Love. At the same time it is taken by surprise, so to speak, by an unusual courage—the courage of those who are happy and assured, the courage to speak, sing and proclaim "the wonderful works of God" (Acts 2:11) to others, in fact to everyone. Here erupts the miracle of tongues. For us remote but not inert heirs of this marvel, this gift is expressed in the form of a certain ease and aptness in bearing witness to all and for all, in an apostolate that knows no bounds. Not just in ministry, but in apostolate: that is the positive, voluntary, courageous activity of pouring forth Christ's message and spreading it abroad.

Let our proclamation of Pentecost today stop here: it is the proclamation of the gift of a new interior life, animated by the presence and energy of God, and communicated in Love. It is the sublimation of natural life into supernatural life, the life of grace. It is the conscious, personal enkindling of our twofold vocation: poor, short-lived, timid and foolish as we are, we have been qualified for both interior contemplation and exterior action. It is the birthday of the Church, one, holy, catholic and apostolic, our Church, the Church of Christ! Let us rejoice!

## NOTES—May 18, 1975

1. Vatican II, *The Church, #1.*
2. *"...ma sperimentare gli effetti sensibili e prodigiosi di questa meravigliosa presenza dello Spirito Santo dentro di noi."*

# Addresses to the International Conference on the Charismatic Renewal in the Catholic Church

*The 1975 International Conference on the Charismatic Renewal in the Catholic Church was held in Rome May 16–19, with an estimated 10,000 people taking part. On the closing day, Monday, May 19, a Mass was concelebrated in St. Peter's Basilica by Cardinal Suenens, several bishops and several hundred priests. Afterwards the Pope came and gave a lengthy address in French. Then he made a series of briefer remarks, first in Spanish, then in English, and finally in Italian. These remarks were not mere summaries of the main address, and they did not duplicate one another; each ·has a different point to make. Hence they are all reproduced here in full.*

## Main Address in French
## The Signs of Authentic Renewal*

Dear sons and daughters:

In this Holy Year you have chosen the city of Rome for your third international Congress.[1] You have asked us to meet with you today and speak to you: in so doing you wished to show your attachment to the Church instituted by Jesus Christ and to everything that this See of Peter represents for you. This concern to situate yourselves firmly in the Church is a genuine sign of the action of the Holy Spirit. For God became man in Jesus Christ, whose mystical Body the Church is. Likewise it is in the Church that the Spirit of Christ was communicated on the day of Pentecost, when he descended on the Apostles gathered in the "upper room," "devoted to prayer," "with Mary, the mother of Jesus" (Acts 1:13–14).

### Signs of Spiritual Renewal Today

As we said in the presence of some of you last October, the Church and the world need more than ever that "the miracle of Pentecost should be continued in history."[2] In fact, modern man, intoxicated by his conquests, has ended up by imagining that, according to the expressions of the last Council, he is "an end unto himself, the sole artisan and creator of his own history."[3] Alas! God has become a stranger in the lives of how many people, even of those who continue to profess his existence by tradition, and to pay him worship out of duty!

For such a world, more and more secularized, nothing is more necessary than the witness of this "spiritual renewal," which we see the Holy Spirit stirring today, in such diverse regions and circles. Its manifestations are varied: deep communion of hearts and close contact with God in faithfulness to the commitments undertaken at Baptism, and in prayer that is often in groups, in which each one expresses himself freely, thus helping, supporting and nourishing the prayer of others. At the basis of everything, there is a personal conviction which has its source not only in instruction received by faith but also in a kind of personal experience of the fact that, without God, man can do nothing, whereas with him, everything becomes possible. Hence this need to praise him, thank him, celebrate the marvels that he works around us and in us everywhere. Human existence finds again its relationship with God, its so-called "vertical dimension," without which man is irremediably mutilated.

Not, of course, that his quest for God appears as a desire for conquest or possession; it seeks to be a pure welcome of him who loves us and gives himself freely to us, who, because he loves us, wishes to communicate to us a life that we receive from him gratuitously, but not without humble fidelity on our part. And this fidelity

*OR, May 19–20, 1975; ORe, May 29, 1975.

must be able to unite action and faith according to the teaching of St. James: "For as the body apart from the spirit is dead, so faith apart from works is dead" (Jas 2:26).

How then could this "spiritual renewal" be anything but beneficial for the Church and for the world? And, if this is the case, how could we fail to take all means in order that it may remain so?

### Discernment of Genuine Renewal

The Holy Spirit, dear sons and daughters, will in his graciousness show you these means, according to the wisdom of those whom he himself made "guardians to feed the church of God" (Acts 20:28). For it was the Holy Spirit that inspired St. Paul with certain very precise directives, which we will merely recall for you. Fidelity to them will be your best possible guarantee for the future.

You know how highly the Apostle esteemed "spiritual gifts": "Do not quench the Spirit," he wrote to the Thessalonians (1, 5:19), adding immediately: "Test everything; hold fast what is good" (5:21). He deemed, therefore, that discernment was always necessary, and he entrusted responsibility for it to those he had put at the head of the community (5:12). With the Corinthians, some years later, he went into greater detail. In particular, he pointed out three principles, in the light of which they could more easily carry out this indispensable discernment.

### St. Paul's Three Principles

The first one, with which he began his exposition, is fidelity to the authentic teaching of the faith (1 Cor 12:1–3). Nothing that contradicts it could come from the Holy Spirit. The one who distributes his gifts is the same one who inspired the scriptures·and who assists the living Magisterium of the Church, to which Christ entrusted the authentic interpretation of scripture, as Catholic faith holds.[4] That is why you feel the need of a deeper and deeper doctrinal formation in scripture, spirituality and theology. Only such a formation, the authenticity of which must be assured by the hierarchy, will preserve you from deviations, which are always possible, and will give you the certainty and the joy of having served the cause of the Gospel "without beating the air" (1 Cor 9:26).

The second principle. All the spiritual gifts are to be received gratefully; and you know that the list given[5] is a long one, and does not claim to be complete.[6] But while the gifts are accorded "for the common good", (1 Cor 12:7) they do not all procure it to the same degree. Hence the Corinthians must "earnestly desire the higher gifts" (1 Cor 12:31), those most useful to the community (14:1–5).

The third principle is, in St. Paul's mind, the most important. It has inspired what is surely one of the most beautiful pages in all literature, which a recent translator has piquantly entitled, "Love soars over everything."[7]

However desirable the spiritual gifts may be and really are, only the love of charity, *agape,* makes a perfect Christian. It alone makes man "pleasing to God"— *gratia gratum faciens,* as the theologians say. For this love presupposes not merely a gift from the Spirit; it implies the active presence of his Person in the heart of the Christian. In commenting on these verses, the Fathers of the Church vie with one another in explaining this point. According to St. Fulgentius, to quote only one example, "the Holy Spirit can confer all kinds of gifts without being present himself; it is when he grants love that he shows himself present through grace" (*"se ipsum demonstrat per gratiam praesentem, quando tribuit caritatem"*).[8] When he is present in the soul, he communicates, along with grace, the very life of the Blessed Trinity, the same love with which the Father loves the Son in the Spirit (Jn 17:26), the love with which Christ loves us and with which we, in turn, can and must love our brothers (Jn 13:34), "not in word or speech but in deed and in truth" (1 Jn 3:18).

Yes, the tree is judged by its fruits, and St. Paul tells us that "the fruit of the Spirit is love" (Gal 5:22), which he has depicted in his hymn to love. All the gifts which the Holy Spirit distributes to whom he pleases are ordained to love, for it is love that "builds up" (1 Cor 8:1). Thus it was love that, after Pentecost, made the first Christians a community "devoted to the teaching of the apostles and fellowship" (Acts 2:42), "all having one heart and soul" (Acts 4:32).

### Further Counsels

Be faithful to these directives of the great Apostle. And likewise be faithful in celebrating the Eucharist frequently and worthily, according to the teaching of the same Apostle (1 Cor 11:26–29). This is the way chosen by the Lord whereby we may have his life in us (Jn 6:53). Likewise, go with confidence to the sacrament of reconciliation. These sacraments express the fact that grace comes to us from God, through the necessary mediation of the Church.

My dear sons and daughters, with the help of the Lord, fortified by the intercession of Mary, mother of the Church, and in a communion of faith, charity and apostolate with your pastors, you will be sure not to be mistaken. And thus you will make your contribution to the renewal of the Church.

Jesus is the Lord! Alleluia!

### NOTES—May 19, 1975 (I)

1. There are different ways of numbering the international charismatic conferences, which developed gradually out of meetings held annually at the University of Notre Dame since 1967. Only Americans were present at the first two meetings. The participation of other nationalities began in 1969, when some Canadians took part. The 1971 meeting was the first to be announced as international; but by ellipsis was usually referred to as the *fifth* international conference. The 1975 conference was the ninth in the entire series, the seventh or fifth international according to whether the count begins with 1969 or 1971. Why Pope Paul calls it the third is not clear; it was, however, the third of which the Holy See had taken official notice, and the third at which Cardinal Suenens participated.

   A brief survey of the conferences from 1967–1973 will be found in my book, *The Pentecostal Movement in the Catholic Church,* Ave Maria Press, 2nd ed. 1974. (Editor's note.)

2. Oct. 16, 1974. The text is given above.

3. Cf. Vatican II, *The Church in the Modern World,* #20.

4. Cf. Vatican II, *Divine Revelation,* #10.

5. 1 Cor 12:4–10, 29–30.

6. Cf. Rom 12:6–8; Eph 6:11.

7. E. Osty.

8. *Contra Fabianum,* Fragment 28; *PL* 65, 791.

9. "*...de ne pas vous tromper.*" The meaning is not that "you will never make any mistakes," but that, if you follow the principles and counsels here given, you will not be deceived about what is authentic renewal. (Editor's note.)

# Remarks in Spanish
# The Basis of Renewal*

Beloved sons and daughters:

You have wanted to come here for your Third International Conference in order to demonstrate your adherence to the Church and to the See of Peter. This desire to insert yourselves in the Church is an authentic sign of the action of the Spirit, who is working in the Church, the mystical Body of Christ.

Ecclesial communion is the solid foundation with which the whole spiritual renewal needed by the Church and the world today must start. This means a communion of minds and hearts in absolute fidelity to the teachings of Faith. It is from this that the search for means to make God present to human minds ought to proceed. This presence must be supported by a more intense cultivation of supernatural values, contact with God and prayer. These will make man transcend the human; they will situate him in the true perspective in regard to God and his fellows.

This is how you must collaborate in building up the Church.

*OR, May 19–20, 1975. Translation by Thomas Bonaiuto.

# Remarks in English
# Renewal in Christian Living*

Dear sons and daughters,

We are happy to greet you in the affection of Christ Jesus, and in his name to offer you a word of encouragement and exhortation for your Christian lives.

You have gathered here in Rome under the sign of the Holy Year: you are striving in union with the whole Church for renewal—spiritual renewal, authentic renewal, Catholic renewal, renewal in the Holy Spirit. We are pleased to see signs of this renewal: a taste for prayer, contemplation, praising God, attentiveness to the grace of the Holy Spirit, and more assiduous reading of the Sacred Scriptures. We know likewise that you wish to open your hearts to reconciliation with God and your fellow-men.[1]

### Sacramental Life

For all of us this renewal and reconciliation is a further development of the grace of divine adoption, the grace of our sacramental Baptism "into Christ Jesus" and "into his death" (Rom 6:3), in order that we "might walk in the newness of life" (v. 4). Always give great importance to the sacrament of Baptism and to the demands it imposes. St. Paul is quite clear: "You must consider yourselves dead to sin but alive to God in Christ Jesus" (v. 11).

### The Sacraments and Brotherly Love

This is the immense challenge of genuine sacramental Christian living, in which we must be nourished by the Body and Blood of Christ, renewed by the sacrament of Penance, sustained by the grace of Confirmation and refreshed by humble and persevering prayer. This is (likewise) the challenge of opening your hearts to your brethren in need. There are no limits to the challenge of love: the poor and needy and afflicted and suffering across the world and near at hand all cry out to you, as brothers and sisters of Christ, asking for the proof of your love, asking for the word of God, asking for bread, asking for life. They ask to see a reflection of Christ's own sacrificial self-giving—love for his Father and love for his brethren.

Yes, dear sons and daughters, this is the will of Jesus: that the world should see your good works, the goodness of your acts, the proof of your Christian lives, and glorify the Father who is in heaven (Mt 5:16). This indeed is spiritual renewal and only through the Holy Spirit can it be accomplished. And this is why we do not cease to

---

*OR, May 19–20, 1975; ORe, May 29, 1975. There are slight differences between the texts published in the OR and the ORe. It appears as though the latter edited the text before publishing it. I have followed the OR text, except for the very important second sentence of paragraph 2, "We are pleased to see... ," which is missing from the OR (due to a typesetter's mistake?), and for the word likewise, which the ORe added in paragraph 4.

exhort you earnestly to ''desire the higher gifts'' (1 Cor 12:31). This was our thought yesterday, when on the Solemnity of Pentecost we said: ''Yes, this is a day of joy, but also a day of resolve and determination: to open ourselves to the Holy Spirit, to remove what is opposed to his action, and to proclaim, in the Christian authenticity of our daily lives, that Jesus is Lord.''

NOTE—May 19, 1975 (III)

1. Renewal and reconciliation were the two aims proposed by Pope Paul for the Holy Year. The reason he introduces this otherwise gratuitous allusion to reconciliation is obviously to relate the aims of the Charismatic Renewal to the aims of the Holy Year that was then being observed.

# Remarks in Italian*

Dearly beloved,

Allow me to add a word in Italian also—or rather two words, one for those of you who are here with the charismatic pilgrimage, and another for those pilgrims who just happen to be present at this huge assembly.

The first is for you: ponder the twofold name which defines what you are: spiritual renewal. When the Spirit comes into the picture, we[1] are immediately alert, happy to welcome his arrival. Even more, we invite him and pray to him. There is nothing we desire more than that the Christian people, the people of faith, should have an awareness of the presence of the Spirit of God among us, should reverence it, and find a higher joy in it. Have we forgotten the Holy Spirit? Certainly not! We want him, we esteem him, we love him, and we call upon him. And you, with your devotion and fervor, you wish to live by the Spirit.

This should be a renewal. Here is where your second name comes in. This renewal should rejuvenate the world and put back into it a spirituality, a soul, a religious way of thinking. It should reopen the closed lips of the world to prayer, to song, to joy, to hymns and to witness. And it will be a great good fortune for our times and for our brothers, if[2] there should be a whole generation of young people—your generation—who, on the occasion of Pentecost, cry out to the world the glory and greatness of God.

In the hymn which we read in the breviary this morning, one which dates back as far as St. Ambrose around the third or fourth century, there is this exclamation, which is hard to translate but should be very simple: *Laeti,* that means "joyously," *bibamus,* "let us drink,"[3] "*sobriam,*" that means "well-defined and well-moderated," *profusionem spiritus* ("libation of the spirit"[4]). *Laeti bibamus sobriam profusionem spiritus.* This could be a motto imparting both a plan and an approval to your movement.

The second message is for those pilgrims present here but who do not belong to your movement, that they too should join with you in celebrating the feast of Pentecost—the spiritual renewal of the world, of our society, and of our souls—that they too, as devout pilgrims to this center of the Catholic faith, might nourish themselves on the enthusiasm and spiritual energy with which we should live our religion. We would say only this: today either you live your faith with devotion, depth, vigor and joy, or that faith dies out.[5]

---

*As these remarks were made impromptu, there is no official text published in the *Osservatore Romano*. The present text is a revision of that which was published in *New Covenant* 5/1 (July, 1975), p. 25, which had been translated from the transcript of a tape recording of the Pope's actual words.

## NOTES—May 19, 1975 (IV)

1. The term *we* in this sentence is ambiguous. When first introduced, it sounds as though Pope Paul is simply declaring the openness of all true Christians to the Spirit. When he asks, "Have we forgotten the Holy Spirit?" he is apparently adverting to an accusation often made against the Church, or at least against the Latin Church. But when he goes on to say, "there is nothing we desire more than that the Christian people . . . should be aware of the presence of the Spirit of God among us . . . ," he seems to be speaking in his own name, according to the Vatican protocol whereby the Pope designates himself in the plural, when speaking formally. Thus he is indicating to the assembled charismatics his own devotedness to the Holy Spirit, which accords with their fervor. But it is his own, not just as an individual, but as the supreme shepherd of the Church.

2. Instead of "if there should be," the transcript reads literally, "that there should be" (*che i sia*), which is not quite as hypothetical as the *if* suggests, but would make intolerable English.

3. The transcript here gives *assolviamo*, "let us absolve." In all likelihood the transcriber mistook some other word. At any rate, the meaning of the Latin is undoubtedly, "let us drink." The whole passage means, "Let us drink joyously the sober libation of the Spirit."

4. In these impromptu remarks, the Pope forgot to translate the part given in brackets.

5. The transcription from which this translation was made reads *si spegna*, literally, "let it die out." Pope Paul would hardly have expressed this as a wish. As there are several other obvious spelling errors in the transcription, I am supposing that the actual word was *spegne*, "dies out."

## The Spirit Prompts Our Witness*

A follower of Christ must not be afraid. He feels wrapped in an atmosphere of divine Providence, which profits even from hostile things, which can cooperate for our good if we love God (Rom 8:28). He has a duty of bearing witness, which frees him from timidity and opportunism, and at the right moment prompts him with behavior and words which come from an inner source, of which he was previously unaware. Even if you are overwhelmed by adversaries stronger than yourselves, the Lord teaches us in the Gospel, "do not be anxious how you are to speak or what you are to say; for what you are to say will be given to you in that hour; for it is not you who speak, but the Spirit of your Father speaking through you" (Mt 10:19–20).

*From an address to a General Audience (*OR*, May 30–31, 1975. *ORe*, June 5, 1975).

# Action of the Spirit in Today's World*

A current of intense spirituality pervades the world and one would have to be blind not to recognize it.

. . .

We see every day now and we hear from our window, which opens onto the world, how our sons and daughters of all peoples, all languages, and all cultures have understood this invitation[1] and put it into practice. It is the Holy Spirit who is making his voice heard strongly, today as always, and who is calling to interior life, to peace and to new life. Everyday, "groanings that cannot be uttered in words" (Rom 8:26), but which have been inspired by him, go up from the hearts of thousands and thousands of the faithful who come here to pause in prayer and meditation.

. . .

The Church is holy because the Holy Spirit animates it, urging it to imitate the humble, poor and crucified Christ, and stirring up in it the gift of repentance. As we wrote in our Apostolic Exhortation on Reconciliation, he is "already present and working in the inmost heart of each member of the faithful, and he will lead all, in humility and peace, along the paths of truth and love."[2]

. . .

It is truly consoling that the Holy Year should have exerted a powerful attraction on [non-Catholic Christians], and especially on the youth—an attraction in which it is impossible not to see an inspiration of the Holy Spirit.

. . .

A new era is unfolding, of faithfulness to the Holy Spirit, of love of the Crucified Christ, of dedication to the brethren, of the building up of a more humane and just society.

NOTES—June 23, 1975

1. The Pope is referring here to his invitation in calling for a Holy Year devoted to renewal and reconciliation, above all in the interior life.
2. Apostolic Exhortation, *Reconciliation. AAS* 67 (1975), p. 22. English tr.: *ORe*, Dec. 26, 1974.

*From an address to the College of Cardinals (*OR*, June 23–24, 1975; *ORe*, July 3, 1975).

# Priests and the Charism of the Laity*

...the laity, which is now conscious of its life[1] in the Church and wishes to make its own contribution, must be encouraged and directed along the great river-bed of Catholic faithfulness, because it has its own peculiar charism for giving a Christian inspiration to temporal realities in a loyal and frank dependency on the hierarchy. In this generous lay charism, there is heard the voice of the Holy Spirit, who guides to the knowledge of the truth (Jn 16:13) and makes all virtues germinate (Gal 5:22). This having been duly said, it must be recalled at once, however, that this charism reaches its fulness when, alongside the children, youths, students, graduates, workers, and so on, there are the right kind of priests: humble and generous priests, able to cause the gifts of the Spirit to mature with their watchful presence, their prayer, sacrifice and enthusiasm; priests ready to bear the burden of their grave responsibilities: "You are the salt of the earth.... You are the light of the world" (Mt 5:13–14).

NOTE—July 3, 1975

1.  ... *il lacicato, che si sente vivo nella Chiesa* ...Lit.: "the laity, which feels itself alive in the Church."

*From an address at a reception for the "ecclesiastical Assistants" of Italian Catholic Action. In a paragraph not reproduced here they are described as "the priests, the spiritual leaders, the supernatural animators of the various branches of Catholic Action at all levels" (*OR*, July 5, 1975; *ORe*, July 24, 1975).

# The Holy Spirit and Evangelization*

Evangelization will never be possible without the action of the Holy Spirit. He descended on Jesus of Nazareth at the moment of his baptism, when his election and mission were manifested externally by the voice of the Father, "This is my beloved Son in whom I am well pleased." Before beginning this mission, Jesus, led by the Spirit, underwent the decisive combat and supreme test in the desert. "In the power of the Spirit," he returned to Galilee and began his preaching at Nazareth, applying to himself the passage of Isaiah: "The Spirit of the Lord is upon me." And he proclaimed, "Today this scripture has been fulfilled."[110] As he was about to send the disciples forth, he breathed on them and said, "Receive the Holy Spirit."[111]

In fact, it was only after the descent of the Holy Spirit on the day of Pentecost that the Apostles went out to all the ends of the earth and began the great work of the Church's evangelization. Peter explained this event as the fulfillment of the prophecy of Joel. "I will pour out my Spirit."[112] Peter himself was filled with the Holy Spirit so that he could speak to the people about Jesus, the Son of God.[113] Paul too was filled with the Holy Spirit[114] before dedicating himself to his apostolic ministry, as was Stephen when he was chosen for the ministry of service, and later on for the witness of blood.[115] The same Spirit who caused Peter, Paul and the Twelve to speak, and inspired them with the words they were to utter, also descended "on those who heard the word."[116]

It is in the "consolation of the Holy Spirit" that the Church grows.[117] He is the soul of the Church. He enables the faithful to grasp the deep meaning of Jesus' teaching and of the mystery of Jesus himself. Today just as at the beginning of the Church, the Holy Spirit acts in every evangelist who lets himself be possessed and led by him. The Holy Spirit prompts the evangelist with words which the latter could not find by himself, at the same time predisposing the soul of the hearer to be open to receive the Good News and the Kingdom being proclaimed.

Techniques of evangelization are good, but not even the most perfect of them could replace the gentle action of the Spirit. Without the Holy Spirit, the finest preparation of the evangelist has no effect. Without him, the most convincing dialectic is powerless over the mind of man, and the most elaborate projects based on sociological or psychological data prove vain and worthless.

We are living a privileged moment of the Spirit in the Church. People everywhere are trying to know him better as he is revealed in scripture. They are happy to place themselves under his inspiration. They gather together around him; they want to be guided by him. But while the Spirit of God has a preeminent place in the entire life of the Church, he is active above all in the mission of evangelization. It is no accident that evangelization had its great beginning on the morning of Pentecost, under the breath of the Holy Spirit.

*From the Apostolic Exhortation, *Evangelii nuntiandi* (on evangelization in the modern world), #75 (*OR*, Dec. 19, 1975; *OR*, Dec. 25, 1975). For the convenience of anyone who wants to consult the context of this brief excerpt from a long document, the footnote numbers of the original have been kept unchanged.

The Holy Spirit can be called the principal agent of evangelization, since it is he who impels each individual to proclaim the Gospel, and he who, in the depths of consciences, causes the word of salvation to be accepted and understood.[118] But he can equally well be called the goal of evangelization. He alone brings into being the new creation, the new humanity at which evangelization must aim. He is the one who produces that new unity in variety which evangelization tends to evoke in the Christian community. Through the Holy Spirit the Gospel penetrates to the heart of the world, since it is he who guides to the discernment of the signs of the times—God's signs—which evangelization uncovers in historical reality and puts to profit.

The Bishops' Synod of 1974 insisted strongly on the place of the Holy Spirit in evangelization. It likewise expressed the desire that pastors and theologians—and we will add also the faithful, marked as they are with the seal of the Spirit in Baptism—would study more intently the nature and manner of the Holy Spirit's action in modern evangelization. We make this wish our own as we urge evangelists, whoever they may be, to pray incessantly to the Holy Spirit with faith and fervor. Let them be prudent; but let them surrender themselves to his guidance, for he is the one who gives the decisive inspiration to their evangelical program, initiatives and activities.

NOTES—December 8, 1975

110. Lk 4:18–21; cf. Is 61:1.
111. Jn 20:22.
112. Acts 2:17.
113. Acts 4:8.
114. Acts 9:17.
115. Acts 6:5, 10; 7:55.
116. Acts 10:44.
117. Acts 9:31.
118. Cf. Vatican II, *The Missionary Activity of the Church*, #4. *AAS* 58 (1966), pp. 950–951.

# The Mystery of Pentecost*

Sons and brothers! Let us not fail to grasp the beauty, the power, and the joy of this feast.

Yes, it is a mystery, and what a mystery! It introduces the timid thought of man to the discovery (insofar as this is accessible to us) of the ocean of divine, triune life; and at the same time of its historical and, to a certain extent, experiential, but always supernatural outpouring in human life. God is everywhere, but not in the same way, or with the same measure of his presence and his goodness. Today's feast is, more than ever, that of God-Love, communicated to us.

In two directions, we can say, by way of simplification. There is a personal, interior direction, in every single soul that accepts this privilege of an indwelling which makes us adopted sons of God and brothers of Christ; makes us sanctuaries of a divine presence; makes us participants in the very nature of divinity; makes us saints. Today is the feast of holiness offered to every living person. It is a feast in which everyone must feel called to an inspiring conversation that is deep and ineffable.

The second direction consists in this, that Pentecost, the feast of souls invited to the consolation of the Spirit, becomes the feast of the People of God, the feast of the Church, of humanity made brothers in the one faith, animated by the one love.

This is not an ideological dream, nor a mere theological question. It is not just a memory of the first, apostolic Pentecost. It is not a mere charismatic nostalgia. It is a perennial and present fact; it is the plan of redemption, which by virtue of the Holy Spirit spreads among the peoples, and in time. It reaches us and arouses in us the new and true vision of the world and its history. It gives us breadth of spirit to know everything and to hope for everything. It gives us new strength to act, suffer and love. It opens our heart and lips to the humble and simple prayer of which everyone is capable, and associates us with the choral song of the pilgrim Church, already mother of the saints.

Be of good cheer, sons and brothers! Hear again, spoken for you, the words of the prophecy of Joel, recalled by the Apostle Peter at Pentecost: "I will pour out my Spirit, the Lord says, upon all mankind, and your sons and daughters will be prophets" (Acts 2:17). Mary was there: let us invoke her!

---

*Angelus* message on Pentecost (*OR*, June 7-8, 1976. *ORe*, June 17, 1976).

# The Two Aspects of Pentecost*

Today is Pentecost. It is one of the greatest feasts in the history of the world. It celebrates the mission of the Holy Spirit. It is an event in which we see God himself operating in humanity. It is a revelation of the ineffable life of God, one in essence, three in persons, who enters into a new and superlative communion with this puny creature, man, and instils in him a new presence of his, a new capacity of action, a new perennial destiny. We can never meditate sufficiently on this extraordinary fact, but we can admire two extremely interesting aspects of it, both coming from the depths of God himself.

The first aspect is *personal*. It is grace, the sanctifying indwelling of the Holy Spirit, which comes into the individual human soul and brings it new life for a higher degree of existence and activity.[1] It is the personal sanctity, sometimes even charismatic, of the humble and frail virtue of man raised to the divine level (Rom 8:16).

The other aspect, which is particularly celebrated today, is the *social* one. It is the one that constitutes the soul of the Church; it structures her unity, kindles her charity, and then characterizes her different operations. All of us, by the one Spirit, are one body, but with different functions.[2] From this divine gift of unity in charity are excluded, St. Augustine comments, those who oppose the grace of peace.[3]

Therefore opening our spirits to the wind and fire of Pentecost, we must cultivate brotherly peace and the taste for true Christian and ecclesical community, without which the mystery of the Holy Spirit would become for us a "motive of responsibility, not of fortune."[4]

May the Blessed Virgin, the mystical mother of the Church, educate us to such a great mystery.

NOTES—May 29, 1977

1. Cf. Jn 14:23; 1 Cor 3:16: Rom 8:11, 26.
2. Cf. Rom 12:4; 1 Cor 10:17; 12:4–31.
3. St. Augustine, Sermon 271 (fifth homily for the feast of Pentecost); *PL* 28:1246).
4. *Ibid.*

*Regina Coeli* message for Pentecost Sunday (*OR,* May 30–31, 1977; *ORe,* June 9, 1977).

# Appendices

# The Meaning of the Term *Charism*

We must attempt to fix the meaning of the term *charism* as Pope Paul uses it. This is not easy, for he uses it with great flexibility. Even St. Paul, who introduced the term *charisma* into the Christian vocabulary, employed it in such a wide range of meanings that scholars have tried in vain to reduce them to unity. Scholastic theology never made enough use of this Greek term to give it a determinate sense. It has come into the idiom of modern theology in a variety of streams, each of which colored it with certain associations not always compatible with the others. The documents of Vatican II reflected this variety, and Pope Paul, rather than attempt to restrict the usage in any way, has on the contrary used it with all the variety of denotations and connotations which contemporary practice allows.

It may help to form a schematic plan of derivation of the chief meanings of *charism*. The text which has had the greatest influence on the use of this word is I Corinthians 12:4–31, in which St. Paul enumerates a variety charisms: wisdom and knowledge in speech, faith, "charisms of healing," the working of miracles, prophecy, discernment of spirits, various kinds of tongues, and the interpretation of tongues. A few verses farther on, he associates apostles, teachers and administrators with the recipients of the aforementioned charisms. Some of the items in these lists are marvelous and preternatural, some are ordinary offices or functions in the Church, but all of them are said to be workings of the Spirit and, by the very name *charism,* all are in some way associated with grace (*charis*).

Emphasis on diverse aspects of this text has led to the development of four diverse meanings of *charism* in modern literature. The first puts the emphasis on the miraculous and extraordinary; in this sense, the gifts of *miracles* and of *healings* are the typical charisms. The second sense, without stressing the miraculous, insists that the charisms are free, unpredictable workings of the Spirit, not conferred by any sacrament or associated with any office. In this sense, *prophecy* is the typical charism, and is often contrasted with priesthood, taken as the typical office (both in Israel and in the Church). Here the prophet is seen, not as one who predicts future events, but as one who speaks out of a personal inspiration rather than in the exercise of a public office. The third sense focuses on St. Paul's insistence (verse 7) that the manifestations of the Spirit are given for the common good. In this sense, any "ministry gift," i.e., any grace given to a person primarily for the benefit of others rather than for himself, is a charism. The mediaeval scholastics called such graces gratuitous (*gratiae gratis datae*) as opposed to sanctifying graces, and modern scholastics often replace the old Latin term and its fatuous-sounding English translation with the term *charism*. In St. Paul's list, apostles, administrators and teachers represent this meaning of charism. In today's Church, the ordained priesthood is a more familiar example. Hence, the paradox that in the second sense of the term *charism,* priesthood is not a charism but its opposite; whereas in the third sense, priesthood is one of the most prominent instances of charism. Finally, a fourth usage that is appearing more and more today focuses on the element of grace which underlies every charism. In this sense, the term is applied to any grace, regardless of whether it is sanctifying or ministerial. Usually, however, this usage is restricted to graces that are somehow outstanding, or to a deep personal experience of grace. In the latter case, since the grace in question will ordinarily be for the benefit of the one who experiences it, the meaning is almost the direct opposite of the third meaning (ministry grace) given above.

In sum, the four chief senses of charism in contemporary usage are: 1) miraculous power, 2) inspiration not associated with office, 3) ministry gift and 4) any grace, especially if it is somewhat remarkable. These four meanings are typified respectively by the healer, the prophet, the priest and the mystic. Each of these four basic meanings is susceptible of further subdivisions, or of being blended with one or another of the other meanings; but we need not pursue these ramifications further.

Pope Paul seldom speaks of *charism* in the first sense, i.e., for gifts that are miraculous and extraordinary. When he does, it is in reaction to reports that have been made to him. Thus, in reference to Cardinal Suenens' book, he observes, "how wonderful it would be if the Lord would again pour out the charisms in increased abundance, in order . . . to enable (the Church) to win the attention and astonishment of the profane and secularized world" (Oct. 16, 1974). But he also stressed the principle that the charisms are for the service of the

Church, thus turning the third meaning of the term into an affirmation about the first.

The second sense of *charism* occurs in a famous text of Vatican II that distinguishes between "hierarchical and charismatic gifts," and another which declares that the Spirit made charismatics subject to the Apostles.[1] Pope Paul frequently cites these two texts, but seldom uses this language on his own. However, in discussing the tensions between public office and private inspiration, he declares that the Holy Spirit brings about accord "between the charismatic inspiration and juridical structure of the Church" (May 25, 1973). Similarily, a conversion worked by the Holy Spirit without human mediation is called charismatic (Feb. 21, 1973).[2]

There is, however, a modification of this second sense that is fairly frequent in the language of Paul VI. He speaks of the distinctive grace or calling of a person as a charism. Thus he says that the "spiritual experience of the saints illustrates the mystery of Christian joy according to the diversity of charisms and particular vocations."[3] He speaks similarly of the charisms of particular religious communities. Thus, to the Sisters of Charity, he said, "Charity! This is your charism."[4] Here, there is no connotation of extraordinary powers, nor any vestige of opposition to what is official or institutional, but merely the designation of a salient and characteristic grace. But when St. Joseph is said to have had "the charism of revelation in dreams,"[5] not only his peculiar grace, but also the fact that it was preternatural, is apparently intended, in what is, therefore, a blend of the first two senses of the term.

The third sense, which interprets the charisms as ministry gifts, is the one preferred by Pope Paul. He says that the term refers to "forces which the Holy Spirit arouses in members of the ecclesial body for the exercise of particular functions and ministries, to the advantage of the collectivity."[6] He generally observes the scholastic tradition which distinguishes the charisms from the seven 'Gifts of the Holy Spirit,' which make a person amenable to the promptings of the Spirit, but are not necessarily ordained to ministry.[7] Thus the Pope often speaks of "the gifts and charisms of the Spirit" as two distinct types of grace (May 26, 1971; June 26, 1974; etc.)

In this sense, he speaks of the charisms of the laity (Jan. 11, 1975), of the Christian family,[8] of office (March 26, 1969), of priests (Jan. 11, 1975), of bishops (Feb. 13, 1972; cf. Oct. 10, 1973), and of Pope and bishops together as exercising the pastorate collegially (Jan. 11, 1975). In reply to those who think that charisms are the prerogative of exceptional personalities, he implies that charisms are given by preference to those who hold directive functions in the Church (March

26, 1969). He says that the ecclesiastical magisterium is a charism of determining what belongs authentically to Christian tradition.[9] The Pope in particular has a "charism of certainty."[10] The Church teaches not only by a divine mandate, but by a charism,[11] and it exercises its "charism of truth" in the canonization of the saints.[12]

In the fourth and broadest sense, charism embraces everything of the order of grace. In this sense, Pope Paul contrasts "supernatural charisms" with "natural gifts,"[13] and understands the former to include both graces of holiness and graces of ministry (just the opposite of what is said when *charism* is used in the third sense). In fact, grace (understood as "sanctifying grace") is said to be the first charism (May 25, 1969); equivalently, charity is called the first charism.[14] The purpose of using the term in this broad sense seems to be to stress that even these very "ordinary" graces are due to the breath of the Spirit. Hence there is mention of "charismatic inspiration" (May 25, 1969). And joy, which traditionally is classified as a "fruit of the Spirit,"[15] is called a charism (April 25, 1970), as indeed are all gifts and fruits that attract us to God (Sept. 9, 1970). "Those who, with simple and generous hearts, put themselves in the service of evangelization, undergo— certainly because of a secret but unfailing charism of the Holy Spirit—a characteristic psychological and moral metamorphosis."[16] *Charismatic* in this perspective is equivalent to *pneumatic,* i.e., "inspired by the Spirit"; and so, in announcing the Holy Year, Paul calls for a "new movement, really 'pneumatic,' that is, charismatic" (May 23, 1973). Elsewhere, he says that priestly vocations are inspired by "the superlative charism of wisdom and love."[17]

Sometimes he uses *charismatic* in this broad sense in order to contrast inner grace with the external functions of the Church, or personal experience of grace with rational theology. Thus, he speaks of "intimate and 'charismatic' relationships with the Holy Spirit" as contrasted with relationship to the visible Church (May 18, 1967). Similarly, "charismatic spirituality" is said to be experiential, in contrast with "rational dogmatism."[18] In both of these texts, however, he is citing the views of others.

Finally, it may be noted that these various usages are not always rigorously distinguished from one another. Some texts could be understood in more than one sense or, while bearing mainly one sense, may carry connotations of another. In the frequent phrase, "gifts and charisms," the latter could be understood in the first, third or fourth of the senses we have distinguished. Accordingly, the phrase would designate either (1) ordinary and extraordinary gifts, (2) sanctifying and ministry graces, (3) natural and supernatural endowments, or simply

(4) graces in an all-embracing sense. And it could well be argued that this flexible usage returns very closely to the style of St. Paul.

## NOTES

1. Constitution on the Church, #4 and 7.
2. Note also the last two texts cited in note 2 to chapter 3, from the period while he was still Cardinal.
3. Apostolic Exhortation, *Christian Joy* (May 9, 1975), part iv (*OR,* May 17, 1975; *ORe,* May 29, 1975).
4. Address of April 7, 1975, to the General Chapter of the Sisters of Charity of Saints Bartolomea Capitanio and Vincenza Gerosa (*ORe,* April 24, 1975).
5. March 19, 1975 (*ORe,* March 27, 1975).
6. June 26, 1974, with express citation of 1 Cor 12:4–11 and of St. Thomas' *Summa Theologiae* I–II, Qu. 111.
7. Cf. chapter 6.
8. March 19, 1975 (*ORe,* March 27, 1975).
9. Aug. 7, 1974 (*ORe,* Aug. 15, 1974).
10. Feb. 25, 1974 (*ORe,* March 7, 1974).
11. Address to the Third Symposium of European Bishops, Oct. 18, 1975 (*ORe,* Oct. 30, 1975).
12. Homily at the Mass for the canonization of Elizabeth Seton, Sept. 14, 1975 (*ORe,* Sept. 18, 1975).
13. At the canonization of St. Teresa of Jesus Jornet Ibars, Jan. 27, 1974 (*ORe,* Feb. 7, 1974).
14. Frequently, e.g., June 7, 1972; Aug. 29, 1973; Sept. 12, 1973; etc.
15. Cf. chapter 6.
16. General Audience of Jan. 12, 1977 (*ORe,* Jan. 20, 1977).
17. Homily at an ordination, June 29, 1975 (*OR,* June 30–July 1, 1975; *ORe,* July 10, 1975).
18. Nov. 20, 1974 (this text is cited in chapter 3 at note 25).

# A Note on the Preparation of This Book

This book originated in a few texts of Pope Paul which I mimeographed in 1967 and 1968 for the benefit of people who were wondering how the Charismatic Renewal fitted in with the teaching of the Church. The first of these was the address to Patriarch Athenagoras (Oct. 26, 1967), followed by the General Audience of Oct. 12, 1966, and the address of Sept. 14, 1964, opening the Third Session of Vatican II.

In 1969, I tried in vain to persuade someone to bring out a pamphlet on the Pope's teaching on the Holy Spirit. In 1973, still thinking in terms of a booklet, I enlisted my nephew, David Foster, and after him Thomas Bonaiuto, to search out the Pope's more important statements on this subject. The materials gathered by them form the nucleus of the present collection. When I got seriously to work on it myself in the fall of 1974, I had no inkling of the vast amount of labor that would be involved. I expected to have a work of some 150 pages ready for the Rome Conference of 1975.

Besides going back into the early statements of the Pope for documents which, in the course of my study, took on new significance, I have continued to scrutinize the later statements right to the end of 1977, when this work was substantially completed. That there are so few texts from 1976 or 1977 cited here is due both to the fact that the Pope seems to have spoken less about the Holy Spirit during these years than before; and to the fact that his later statements have tended to repeat earlier ones. The Charismatic Conference of 1975 seems to have been a culminating point in this teaching. To avoid making this book too long, I have not reproduced texts that added little to their predecessors.

It also took a long while to discover the drama and the dynamic developments hidden under the calm and objective tones of Paul VI.

Not until late in my work with these documents did I begin to perceive that his preoccupation with the charismatic began to grow from about 1969 onwards, or that under his bland statements of universal truth, there may often have been a deliberate intention of speaking to the Renewal.

Most of the texts reproduced here are from what may be called the Pope's popular talks. Every Wednesday (except the first week in Lent, when he is on retreat), Paul holds a General Audience for whatever pilgrims who may be there. (Cf. what is said of these audiences above, in chapter 5, p. 59–60.) Some are taken from the shorter talks he gives each Sunday at noon, from his balcony in St. Peter's, when he recites the *Angelus* or the *Regina Coeli* (depending on the season of the year) with the pilgrims gathered in the piazza of St. Peter's. The rest are taken from various sources indicated in each case.

Ordinarily the Pope speaks in his native Italian. When addressing people of a particular nationality, he sometimes speaks in their language. He often uses French, as accessible to a wider audience than Italian. His talks are all printed in the *Osservatore Romano*. Encyclical letters and documents that have an official character or special solemnity are always published in Latin. However, the *Osservatore Romano* usually publishes an "Italian translation" along with the Latin, and after frequent comparisons of the two, I am convinced that the Italian usually represents the Pope's own original document, the Latin being a translation made from it, presumably by someone else. In any case, the Latin usually gives a cumbersome, obscure and sometimes puzzling expression to thoughts that are much clearer in Italian. Hence, I have treated the latter as the standard for these translations (and it is my distinct impression that those who translate for the English edition of the *Osservatore Romano* have done the same).

The translations used here have been basically those of the English *Osservatore Romano* for the period it covers. Earlier ones are taken from *Papal Addresses* or *The Pope Speaks* (with permission of the respective editors). A few have been made from the originals by Thomas Bonaiuto. Rendering Pope Paul's Victorian periodicity, scholastic vocabulary, intense reflectiveness and careful qualifications into readable English is difficult, and must have been especially so for those who had to do it rapidly to meet newspaper deadlines. Hence I have revised the translations wherever this seemed called for, with the help of Thomas Bonaiuto, who has been my Italian expert, and with the occasional consultation of Dr. Paul Bosco, associate professor of Italian at the University of Notre Dame.

My aim in this work has been to make the teaching of a great pastor accessible to his people, not to produce a critical edition. Hence some of the paraphernalia and procedures called for by scholarship have been neglected where they would have made the work more cumbersome, or would have added a considerable burden to a task that has already been very time-consuming.

I am grateful to Cardinal Suenens for taking time from a busy schedule to write the Foreword. Others who have helped in various ways are Cardinal John Wright, Bishop Carlo Colombo, Msgr. Richard Malone, Rev. Wilfred Brievens, Rev. Francis Sullivan, S.J., Mrs. Bert Kovacsics, Mary Byrne, Bert Ghezzi, Ralph Martin and Frank Clark.

The ladies of Carmela Rulli's steno pool have been especially patient and faithful in typing the manuscript: Bobbi Thompson, Shirley Schneck, Anita Sanna, Janet Wright and Amy Kizer.

To all the above mentioned, I express my thanks.

# Sources and Abbreviations

Wherever a text of Pope Paul is referred to simply by date, the text is reproduced in Part II of this book under that date, and further bibliographical data will be found there. In references to texts of his not reproduced there, complete bibliographical information is given at once in a footnote.

## A. ORIGINAL TEXTS OF POPE PAUL

AAS. *Acta Apostolicae Sedis, Commentarium Officiale,* Typis Polyglottis Vaticanis, Vatican City. This is the official organ for documents. It publishes (mostly in Latin) the official text of encyclical letters, apostolic constitutions and exhortations, and some of the more solemn allocutions of the Holy Father. It does not, however, reproduce the weekly audiences or *Angelus* (or *Regina Coeli*) messages.

OR. *L'Osservatore Romano, Giornale quotidiano politico religioso,* Vatican City. This semi-official daily newspaper reproduces all of the Pope's public talks, and is the original source of most of the material collected here. It also publishes official documents, both in the official Latin text and in an Italian translation. I have given references to it for all of the texts of Pope Paul that have been reproduced here at length, as well as to the more important ones cited in my own text. For lesser references, and also in some cases where lacunae at the library made it difficult to find the needed issue, I have been content to cite the *ORe.*

For anyone who wishes to locate the original text when I have not cited it, an easy rule to follow is that the papal addresses are almost invariably published the day after they have been given. That is, an address delivered on Jan. 1 will normally appear in the *OR* of Jan. 2. It should be noted, however, that the *OR* publishes simply the written text used by the Pope, and takes no account of the impromptu remarks with which he frequently supplements or even supplants his prepared text.

*Discorsi al Populo di Dio.* Editrice Studium, Rome. A yearly edition of the addresses at General Audiences and other selected popular addresses of the Pope, beginning with the first year of his pontificate.

## B. ENGLISH TRANSLATIONS OF POPE PAUL

ORe. *L'Osservatore Romano,* weekly edition in English, Vatican City. This journal, which began on April 4, 1968, publishes an English translation of those addresses and documents of the Pope which the editors judge to be of interest to the English-speaking world. In fact, nearly all statements of any significance appear in it, and it is the most convenient source for English translations for the period which it covers. I have ordinarily used these translations in the present collection, but have corrected them where this seemed necessary, and have tried to improve their English style. In such cases, with the help of Mr. Thomas Bonaiuto, I have carefully compared them with the Italian (or other) original, and scrupulously tried to remain faithful to the sense of the Holy Father. Italics are not used in the original texts; I have introduced them occasionally to aid readability.

TPS. *The Pope Speaks, The American Quarterly of Papal Documents,* Washington, D.C. This journal publishes a selection of papal addresses and documents in English translation. It is the most convenient source for the addresses of Pope Paul prior to the publication of the *ORe,* i.e., for the period June, 1963, to March, 1968. Because it is very selective, however, many documents cannot be found in it.

*The Teachings of Pope Paul VI,* Libreria editrice Vaticana, Vatican City. Reprinted by the United States Catholic Conference, Washington, D.C. A yearbook, publishing the texts of the public audiences and a selection of other discourses and documents of the preceding year. It did not begin to appear, however, until 1968 (i.e., in 1969, giving documents from 1968). I have not made much use of it, because it does not become available until well after the year which it covers, and because it is not so complete as the *ORe*; but for the material which it has given, it is now the most convenient source available in English.

*Papal Addresses.* Scepter Publishers Chicago. A loose-leaf series published at first weekly, giving English translations of papal addresses. It began publication on Oct. 2, 1965, with an address of Sept. 10, 1965. Copies of this series are very difficult to find. In 1968, the name of the series was changed to the following.

*Talks of Pope Paul VI.* Scepter Press, Chicago. Beginning with no. 130, Sept. 18, 1968. "Weekly addresses and other important talks." Each address appears as a separate leaflet. Beginning with issue no. 226 (June 17, 1970) publication was carried on by the Franciscan Marytown Press, Kenosha, Wisconsin. Now published by the *Pro Ecclesia* Foundation, 663 Fifth Ave., N.Y., 10022.

Giovanni Battista Cardinal Montini, *The Church.* Helicon Press, Baltimore and Dublin, 1964. English translation of *La Chiesa (1957–1962),* Milan, 1962. A set of addresses on the Church given by the Archbishop of Milan during the period when Vatican II was in preparation.

## C. SOURCES USED BY POPE PAUL

Whereas the more solemn acts of Pope Paul, such an encyclical letters and apostolic exhortations, are published with footnotes, the popular talks, as printed in the *Osservatore Romano,* usually give their references in parentheses, within the text itself. For the sake of uniformity, and for a cleaner text, I have put them all into footnotes, except for very short scriptual references. Occasionally, for the convenience of the reader, I have given the entire scriptural text in the footnote, instead of the mere reference which appears in the *OR.*

When the Pope cites scripture in Latin, it is, of course, from the Vulgate. Church Fathers are usually cited from the patrologies of Migne in the case of the popular talks; in the more solemn acts, critical editions are often cited. I have let all these references stand as they are, but have given the titles in English when they appear in the *NPNF* edition, along with references to it. For works not given in that edition, I have cited other translations where they were easy to locate, but I have not undertaken systematically to search out all of them, or to determine the best. (The new revision of the Vulgate, recently published at Pope Paul's behest, is intended to replace that of Jerome in official Church documents; but it appeared too late to be reflected in the texts reproduced here.)

Texts from Vatican II I have translated directly from the original; the English version cited below is given merely for the convenience of those who wish to check the context or compare a different translation.

Pope Paul often cites a phrase from scripture or the Fathers in Latin, and follows it with a translation. Occasionally, however, he neglects to give a translation. In such cases, I have added one, putting it in parentheses just as I do with his own. It would have been more correct to use brackets to indicate my own additions, but as the typographical practices of the original editors and translators was inconsistent in this regard, it would have occasioned a great deal of trouble for very little purpose to observe such a fine distinction. For similar reasons, I have not maintained the distinction in scripture references between mere allusions (indicated by *cf.*) and actual citations (referred to without *cf.*). The reader can easily tell which is which.

PL *Patrologiae Cursus Completus. Series Latina.* ed. J.-P. Migne, Paris, 1879 ff.

PG *Patrologiae Cursus Completus. Patrologiae Graecae.* ed. J.-P. Migne, Paris 1886 ff.

CSEL *Corpus Scriptorum Ecclesiasticorum Latinorum.* Vienna, 1866 ff.

Denziger-Schönmetzer. *Enchiridion Symbolorum Definitionum Declarationum,* ed. 32. Herder, Freiburg etc. 1963.

NPNF *The Nicene and Post-Nicene Fathers,* edited by Philip Schaff, Buffalo (later New York) 1886 ff. (Reprinted by Eerdmans, Grand Rapids, 1956).

ACW *Ancient Christian Writers.* Edited by J. Quasten and J. Plumpe, Newman, Westminister, Md., 1946 ff.

*The Fathers of the Church.* Edited by Ludwig Schopf, New York, 1946 ff.

ASS *Acta Sanctae Sedis.* Rome, 1865–1908.

Flannery, Austin. *Vatican Council II; the Conciliar and Post-conciliar Documents.* Liturgical Press, Collegeville, MN, 1975.

# Other Texts of Pope Paul

A number of texts which I originally intended to include in the present collection have been omitted in order not to lengthen this book unduly. I list them here for the convenience of anyone wishing to pursue this topic further. The titles are mine and refer only to that part of the address relevant to the subject of this book.

May 14, 1964, "The Living Water and the Fountain" (General Audience; *OR,* May 14, 1964)

May 17, 1964, "The Meaning of 'Catholic' " (Sermon for the Feast of Pentecost; *OR,* May 18–19, 1964; *TPS* 10 (1964–1965)

June 9, 1965, "The Dove and the Pulpit" (General Audience; *OR,* June 10, 1965)

Nov. 4, 1965, "Prayer for a New Pentecost" (Excerpt from a letter of Pope Paul to the Bishops of the Church, Adhortatio Apostolica, *"Postrema Sessio,"* AAS LVII, 1965, pp. 865–871; *OR,* Nov. 7, 1965)

Dec. 29, 1965, "The Spirit of the Council" (*OR,* Dec. 30, 1965)

Nov. 12, 1969, "The Church as Communion" (General Audience; *OR,* Nov. 13, 1969; *ORe,* Nov. 20, 1969

May 24, 1972, "The Spirit and Witness" (General Audience; *OR,* May 25, 1972; *ORe,* June 1, 1972)

June 7, 1972, "The Church Beautified and Sanctified by the Spirit" (General Audience; *OR,* June 8, 1972; *ORe,* June 15, 1972)

Oct. 25, 1972, "The Church Must Believe in Love" (General Audience; *OR,* Oct. 26, 1972; *ORe,* Nov. 5, 1972)

Aug. 29, 1973, "Contentiousness and Its Cure" (General Audience; *OR,* Aug. 30, 1973; *ORe,* Sept. 6, 1973)

May 5, 1974, "Discerning the Call of the Spirit" (Message for "Vocations Day" [May 5], but dated Feb. 15, 1974, and released April 27, 1974; *OR,* April 28, 1974; *ORe,* May 9, 1974)

June 5, 1974, "The Beauty of the Church Through the Spirit" (General Audience; *OR,* June 6, 1974; *ORe,* June 13, 1974)

Dec. 8, 1974, "Destroyers of Church Unity" (From the Apostolic Exhortation, *Reconciliation Within the Church,* published at the opening of the Holy Year of 1975; *OR,* Dec. 16–17, 1974; *ORe,* Dec. 26, 1974)

Jan. 15, 1975, "Exigencies of Christian Renewal" (General Audience; *OR,* Jan. 16, 1975; *ORe,* Jan. 23, 1975)

April 2, 1975, "Inner Silence and Joyous Allelujas" (General Audience; *OR,* April 2, 1975; *ORe,* April 10, 1975)

April 16, 1975, "Baptismal Renewal" (General Audience; *ORe,* April 24, 1975)

May 18, 1975, "Come to Meet the Living God!" (*Regina Coeli* message; *OR,* May 19–20, 1975; *ORe,* May 29, 1975)

May 26, 1976, "Experience of the Spirit and Visible Communion," (Address to participants in a dialogue between some Pentecostal leaders and the Secretariat for Promoting Christian Unity; *ORe,* June 3, 1976)